DMU 0592014 01 0
DE MONTFORT UNIVER
LIBRARY

D1521068

Reason's Grief

An Essay on Tragedy and Value

GEORGE W. HARRIS

College of William and Mary

CAMBRIDGE UNIVERSITY PRESS

CAMBRIDGE UNIVERSITY PRESS
Cambridge, New York, Melbourne, Madrid, Cape Town, Singapore, São Paulo

Cambridge University Press
40 West 20th Street, New York, NY 10011-4211, USA

www.cambridge.org
Information on this title: www.cambridge.org/9780521863285

© George W. Harris 2006

This publication is in copyright. Subject to statutory exception
and to the provisions of relevant collective licensing agreements,
no reproduction of any part may take place without
the written permission of Cambridge University Press.

First published 2006

Printed in the United States of America

A catalog record for this publication is available from the British Library.

Library of Congress Cataloging in Publication Data

Harris, George W.
Reason's grief : an essay on tragedy and value / George W. Harris.
p. cm.
Includes bibliographical references and index.
ISBN 0-521-86328-7 (hardback)
1. Tragic, The. 2. Values. 3. Ethics. I. Title.
BH301.T7H37 2006
128 – dc22 2005026789

ISBN-13 978-0-521-86328-5 hardback
ISBN-10 0-521-86328-7 hardback

Cambridge University Press has no responsibility for
the persistence or accuracy of URLs for external or
third-party Internet Web sites referred to in this publication
and does not guarantee that any content on such
Web sites is, or will remain, accurate or appropriate.

DE MONTFORT UNIVERSITY LIBRARY

Fund: 60 Date: 11/07/08

Sequence:

Class: 128

Suffix: HAR

Barcode:

To the memory of my parents, Mary O. and Theron J. Harris,
and to Patty, Rachel, and Jenny

Reason's Grief

An Essay on Tragedy and Value

In *Reason's Grief,* George Harris takes W. B. Yeats's comment that we begin to live only when we have conceived life as tragedy as a call for a tragic ethics, something the modern West has yet to produce. He argues that we must turn away from religious understandings of tragedy and the human condition and realize that our species will occupy a very brief period of history, at some point to disappear without a trace. We must accept an ethical perspective that avoids pernicious fantasies about ultimate redemption, one that sees tragic loss as a permanent and pervasive aspect of our daily lives yet finds a way to think, feel, and act with both passion and hope. *Reason's Grief* takes us back through the history of our thinking about value to find our way. The call is for nothing less than a paradigm shift for understanding both tragedy and ethics.

George W. Harris is Chancellor Professor of Philosophy at the College of William and Mary. He is the author of *Dignity and Vulnerability* and *Agent-Centered Morality,* and he has contributed to *The Journal of Philosophy, Nous, The Monist, American Philosophical Quarterly, Public Affairs Quarterly,* and other journals. He is a Distinguished Member of the National Society of Collegiate Scholars and a receipient of a fellowship from the National Endowment of the Humanities.

Contents

Acknowledgments

For constributions to *Reason's Grief*, I am grateful to many. Tony Cunningham, Paul Davies, Robert Fudge, Danny Statman, and anonymous referees for Cambridge University Press read different versions of the manuscript at different stages of its development, providing invaluable feedback. Others provided responses to parts of the manuscript from which I was able to clarify and sharpen my understanding. Discussion with Lanny Goldman on the topic of the incomparability of values was especially helpful in this regard. Laurence Thomas and Henry Richardson were helpful in gaining research support for the project, and Noah Lemos was helpful in recommending the manuscript to Cambridge. Feedback from audiences at the Royal Institute of Philosophy Conference on Emotions at the University of Manchester, England, in 2001; at the British Society for Ethical Theory meeting in Glasgow, Scotland, in 2001; at the Virtue Ethics: Old and New Conference at the University of Canterbury, Christchurch, New Zealand, in 2002; at the Perspectives on Evil and Human Wickedness Conference in Prague, Czech Republic, in 2003; and at the Beijing International Conference on Democracy in Beijing, China, in 2004 was exceedingly helpful. So too has been the response of my students in several seminars I have taught here at William and Mary over recent years. Research leave was made possible by a Faculty Research Assignment granted by the College of William and Mary for the 2000–01 academic year and by a National Endowment for the Humanities Fellowship for the year 2001–02. For this assistance, I am most grateful.

For permission to include revised material from articles published in *American Philosophical Quarterly* and *Ethical Theory and Moral Practice*, I thank these journals. For bringing the manuscript to print at Cambridge University Press, I am indebted to three people: Beatrice Rehl, for her editorial guidance through the review process; Sarah McColl, for her management of the production process; and Russell Hahn, for his excellent copyediting. Of course, I am deeply indebted to many others whom I cannot acknowledge here. I hope that they will rest assured that their contributions are not less cherished for their anonymity. I cannot, however, leave implicit my undying gratitude to my wife, Patty, and my wonderful daughters, Rachel and Jenny, for the support and love they provide for an incurably pensive husband and father.

An Aesthetic Prelude

The great Shakespearean scholar A. C. Bradley once said that "tragedy would not be tragedy if it were not a painful mystery."[1] Yet through the ages we have studied that mystery with great and serious purpose from a variety of perspectives to significant cultural benefit with little threat of exhausting the subject. So why do I return to it here: to make the bold offer of the final word or to add a modest footnote or two to a body of learned literature? Neither of these, really. Less modest than the latter and differently ambitious than the former, my aim is to bring the subject to bear on how we are to think fundamentally about our cultural, political, moral, and religious horizons in the twenty-first century. We get our bearings best, I will argue, by framing our most central issues in terms of what I will call the problem of tragedy. In Chapter 1, I will characterize that problem as I see it more precisely, but here I want to try to convey what I mean for tragedy to be central to how we frame the issues we face. I will do so by providing my own interpretation of developments in views about tragedy that run in one direction in the world of ancient Greece and in just the opposite direction in nineteenth-century Germany. The point of the exercise is not to settle a scholar's quarrel about whether my interpretation is the correct one, though I believe that it is. Rather, the point is to illustrate how I want to bring thinking about tragedy and the tragic aspects of life to the

[1] See A. C. Bradley, *Shakespearean Tragedy: Lectures on Hamlet, Othello, King Lear and Macbeth* (New York: Penguin, 1961), 51.

center of our ethical thought. I defer the scholarly disputes to another occasion. The interpretive exercise will provide a setting in which I can locate my own discussion of tragedy within my interpretation of what several "canonical" philosophers, Aristotle, Hegel, Schopenhauer, and Nietzsche, have said about tragedy. It will also allow me to place my project within the context of recent thought on the subject.

I begin with a question: which is the greater work of Homer, the *Iliad* or the *Odyssey*? The answer, I believe, is the *Iliad*, and there are two reasons why. First, the *Iliad* did more to make Greek readers of the time keenly aware of their highest values than did the *Odyssey*. It did so by unrelentingly subjecting them to the tragic costs of human excellence and guiding them almost effortlessly to the thought that Achilles was the greater hero than Odysseus, that despite their different fates it was more noble to be Achilles than Odysseus.[2] The second reason is parasitic on the first: by means of the same tragic device, the *Iliad* is superior to the *Odyssey* in revealing to us the values and the mind of Greece in the late eighth century B.C.

Both the *Iliad* and the *Odyssey* characterize the human condition as radically vulnerable to the vicissitudes of fortune and the whims of the gods. The universe is composed in part of forces that are indifferent to human excellence and well-being. In this sense, a good human life must be lived in light of the fact that the world is an unfriendly place. There are no promises that things will turn out well. In fact, they are likely to turn out very badly, the more so the more noble you are. The questions of how to live and what kind of person to be are questions about how to live in this unfriendly world and what kind of person it is best to be in such a world. In the face of this, there are at least two honorable ways of proceeding. On the one hand, we can follow Achilles and confront the vagaries of fortune with uncompromising resolve and

[2] After commenting on what he sees as the best tragedies (like the *Iliad*) that end in the death of the hero, Aristotle comments on those critics who favor the happy outcome of the *Odyssey* and consequently rank it as the first kind of poetry. He says, "It is ranked first only through the weakness of the audiences; the poets merely follow their public, writing as its wishes dictate. But the pleasure here is not that of tragedy." Of lesser exemplifications of this form, he says that they "belong rather to comedy, where the bitterest enemies in the piece (e.g. Orestes and Aegisthus) walk off good friends at the end, with no slaying of any one by any one." See Aristotle, *The Complete Works of Aristotle*, ed. Jonathan Barnes, vol. II, *The Poetics*, translated by Ingram Bywater (Princeton, New Jersey: Princeton University Press, 1984), 2325–6.

accept the consequences. We may even instigate the confrontation. If we do, we express to the unfriendly world just what we are made of and who we are, but we virtually ensure our own demise. On the other hand, we can follow Odysseus and try to manipulate the unfriendly forces of the universe through cunning, resourcefulness, and perseverance. If we do, we express less clearly to the unfriendly world just what we are made of and who we are, but we increase our chances of avoiding the worst outcomes. Life will test us and be filled with many hardships. It will require a noble character to survive, but it will not demand the best and most noble in us. Either way, the choice of how to live is predicated on a view of the human condition as one in which the human good is a project pursued in a hostile or indifferent universe. That its prospects cannot be guaranteed by the best in human effort and by a modicum of good luck is central to the tragic view that Homer and the later Greek tragedians of the fifth-century B.C. were concerned to convey.

Here we have a body of literature that reflects a culture in which the problem of how to live, act, feel, and think about life is centered in framing life's issues in terms of a tragic view of the human condition. Here we have a culture guided in thought, action, and feeling by its tragic sense. That is what it is for the issue of tragedy to be brought to the center of how a culture frames its values and the major issues it faces. What brings tragedy to center stage are two variables: a sense of high value and a belief that high value is pervasively and perpetually vulnerable to destructive forces. It is the sense of what high value is and what has high value that determines the substance of a tragic sense, and it is the degree of vulnerability to destructive forces that brings a tragic sense to the center of ethical thought. The more vulnerable high value is to destructive forces, the more central a tragic sense is to the ethical thought of a culture. Most importantly, we have in Homeric culture a culture with a tragic ethics, one that recognizes that life is pervasively and perpetually tragic, that this will always be so, and that the ethical task is to construct a life that is on balance good, despite the tragedy involved.

We find a contrast in Aristotle and the Greeks of the Late Classical period. The Late Classical Greeks of the fourth century B.C. were not guided by a tragic sense in the way that the Archaic or even the Early and High Classical Greeks were. That the later Greeks had a tragic sense and that it was important to them it would be foolish to deny. But it was not the same tragic sense as that of Homer and the tragedians, nor did it play the same central role in ethical thought that it had in the previous culture. By the time we get to Aristotle, the Greeks have come to think of the universe as being morally friendly. There was on Aristotle's view a harmony between nature and human goodness and excellence.[3] In fact, the universe is a whole in which all the parts are harmoniously related. The goodness of any natural kind, including human kind, is in the realization of its nature, and the environment is such that with a modicum of good luck we can realize that nature. Thus the Late Classical Greek view of the human condition was an extremely optimistic one. Though these Greeks interpreted the world as having its unfriendly dimensions, on the whole they saw it as favorable toward human excellence and well-being. Tragedy is found in the various ways in which we can fail to have the modicum of good luck that protects us against the vicissitudes of the unfriendly, destructive elements.

All this is important to understanding how Aristotle viewed tragic literature and his account of its aesthetic dimensions in his work *The Poetics.* There is a difference, however, between his aesthetic account of tragedy and the role that tragic concepts played in his ethical thought. The aesthetic account attempts to explicate the general form of tragic genre in the Greek tradition from Homer through the tragedians, Aeschylus, Sophocles, and Euripides.

For our purposes, the essential features of the account are these. Tragic literature aims at a certain tragic effect through the employment of a regular set of literary devices. The effect is the evocation of tragic emotions in such a way as to achieve catharsis, a kind of purging or purification of the emotions. The tragic emotions attach to a person of high worth: fear and pity for his plight and, as Aristotle should have said, awe for his noble character. Included in the devices employed to achieve the tragic effect are a hero and a plot. The plot includes an action on the part of the hero that plays a significant role, along with forces over which the hero has no control, in a reversal of his fortune from happiness to misery. It is the awareness of the interplay between the hero's actions, his character, and the external forces of chance that produce the tragic effect. What emerges from this account is the fact

[3] See Aristotle, *Nicomachean Ethics*, translated by Martin Ostwald (Indianapolis: Bobbs–Merrill, 1962).

that Aristotle saw tragic literature, in Martha Nussbaum's memorable phrase, as a study in the fragility of human goodness.[4]

Yet the relevance of that study for ethics was different for Homer and the tragedians than it was for Aristotle. Within the period ranging from the Archaic through the High Classical, there were changes in the tragic sense due to changes in perceptions of what is noble. Odysseus is held in high regard by Homer but subject to ridicule by Euripides, and women are more the subject of tragic treatment later in the period than earlier. These are cases of a change in the tragic sense because of a change in what is seen to be of high and noble value. Yet, these differences aside, what remains from the beginning of the period to the end is that what is most noble about the noble is that they are people of action. The tragic sense finds its response in an encounter with the fragility of *actors*. Hence, the warrior ethic.

Aristotle's ethic is not a warrior ethic (although it includes an ethic for warriors). What is most noble about us, according to Aristotle, is that we are *thinkers*. To be sure, we are actors as well, but the best part of us is found in our thinking capacities. The life that is predominantly contemplative is better than the life that is predominantly active. It is the realization of the higher part of our nature. Yet if tragedy flows from action rather than thought, then tragic concepts are less central to ethical thinking than other concepts, which is why conditions of flourishing are for Aristotle more central to his ethical thought than conditions of conflict and calamity. Moreover, even as actors we are primarily social animals whose most noble actions are expressed in cooperation and harmony with others rather than in conflict with them. In either case, whether it be our contemplative nature or our nature as actors in the social arena, our most noble side is expressed and realized under the most favorable conditions rather than under conditions of conflict.

The sum of these observations goes a long way in demonstrating that Aristotle has retained tragic concepts but has moved them off center stage in his ethical thought. His tragic sense is different than that of his Greek ancestors, and it plays a different role in his ethical thought. When we add to this that Aristotle thought that human goodness is

4 See Martha Nussbaum, *The Fragility of Goodness* (Cambridge: Cambridge University Press, 1986).

considerably less vulnerable to unfriendly or indifferent forces than the pre–Late Classical dramatists believed, we can see that though he was interested in the study of the fragility of human goodness, it was not central to his ethical conceptual scheme in the way that it was for Homer or Sophocles or even Euripides. That bad things sometimes happen and that it takes noble character to deal with them is a far different set of thoughts than the thought that destructive forces lurk all around us and are highly likely to thwart our actions with calamity unforseen.

This direction away from tragic concepts continued through the Hellenistic thinkers to the very end of the ancient Greek period. The more human goodness and nobility were attached to our being thinking things, the less human goodness was vulnerable to unfriendly or indifferent forces of chance. The more the Epicureans and the Stoics emphasized these themes, the more they removed a tragic sense from the center of ethical thought. Christianity, of course, was to take this even further. If this is correct, then the direction of movement within the ancient Greek world was from a tragic to a nontragic ethics, from an ethical conceptual scheme in which a tragic sense was central to framing the ethical life to one in which it was moved more and more to the margins.

When we come to nineteenth-century Germany, we find a movement in just the opposite direction. A brief examination of Hegel, Schopenhauer, and Nietzsche and their thoughts on tragedy will illustrate the point.

Nineteenth-century Germany, especially early to mid-century, was alive with thoughts of progress. This is why the philosophy of history played such a prominent role in the intellectual climate of the period. But prior to Immanuel Kant, Germany was largely an ahistorical culture, a culture without a sense of historical direction. I say this in part because of the dominance of the intellectualized Christianity of Leibniz.[5] In the seventeenth century, Leibniz had argued that a series of necessary truths should lead us to the conclusion that this is the best of all possible worlds.[6] Whatever evil it contains is necessary to the

5 No doubt the Thirty Years' War played a significant role as well.

6 See G. W. Leibniz, *Theodicy: Essays on the Goodness of God, the Freedom of Man, and the Origin of Evil* (New York: Open Court, 1985).

overall goodness of the created universe, and we can know this because we can know a priori that there is an all-powerful, all-knowing, wholly good God who could and would create only the best possible universe. Such a view dulls the historical sense because it renders a sense of direction both impossible and unnecessary. Whatever the direction of history and whatever the events of history, it is all for the best. Moreover, we needn't worry about its course. God, who is the only one who knows or who can know the ultimate historical destination, is fully in charge. We are not. The upshot is that we can be consoled by the thought that no matter how tragic events might appear, the appearances are deceiving.

Here the tragic sense is as distant from ethical thought as it can get. During the period from the late seventeenth to the late eighteenth century, Leibnizian thought rendered Germany virtually immune to the enthusiasm for the idea of progress found in England and France. John Locke's Christianity, a version contemporary with Leibniz's, was immersed in the humanism sweeping the rest of Europe and brought with it a sense of historical direction, a movement toward social improvement through hard work, market mechanisms, and religious tolerance. Though Locke's Christianity differed from Leibniz's in its enthusiasm for progress, it also made little use of tragic concepts. Indeed, the British Enlightenment was infused with the thought that tragedy was virtually eliminable through human effort. That is what distinguished French and English thought from German thought through most of the seventeenth and eighteenth centuries.

The intellectual event that changed the German climate was the Kantian Copernican revolution, and with this revolution came a sense of direction, a sense that history can and should be put on a course intelligible to human reason and put in effect by the human will. Immanuel Kant interpreted the forces of history as guided by the logic of the categorical imperative. He saw historical currents converging on social arrangements within nations that removed obstacles to individual freedom and autonomy, and he saw the same currents converging on arrangements among nations that would lead to international peace.[7] Such optimism had little patience with talk about tragedy.

7 See Immanuel Kant, "Perpetual Peace," in *Perpetual Peace, and Other Essays on Politics, History, and Morals* (New York: Hackett, 1983).

In fact, it is one of the most revealing observations on Kant's thought that he never wrote a significant essay on the concept of tragedy. To my knowledge, he never wrote anything at all on the subject. He seemed interested in it neither morally nor aesthetically. His understanding of Greek ethics makes no connection with the topic, which suggests just how superficial his understanding of Greek ethics was. Indeed, the brilliance of Kant is found in the purity of his ethical theory, and one central feature of that theory is that it is purely nontragic. The most fundamental good is that we have wills that stand above the laws of nature, and the highest good, a combination of good will and happiness, is secured in the hereafter. Taken literally, nothing ultimately tragic can happen on this view. Of course, if evil were ultimately to triumph over goodness, that would be a great tragedy, but, according to Kant, it is an a priori postulate of practical reason that such a tragedy will not occur. Moreover, *The Critique of Judgment*, Kant's major work on aesthetics, makes no reference to tragic literature and its worth.[8] Given the dominance of Aristotle in the history of aesthetics, this omission is startling until reflection on the structure and content of Kant's view of the human condition and the human good reveals that there is nothing essentially tragic in Kant's understanding of these matters. We know that he had a dim view of the Romantic literature of his times. He thought it was sentimentalist fluff, with little moral value. About much of this, he was surely right. Whether he thought the same of all tragic literature, including that of Homer and the Greek tragedians, is something about which we can only speculate. If he did, he was just as surely wrong.

With Hegel, however, we do not have to speculate. He was explicitly enamored both with the Greeks and with Greek tragedy. Moreover, his entire philosophical "system" was focused on the essential role of conflict and resolution in aesthetics, in ethics, and in history. In many ways, his aesthetics can be used as a guide to understanding the rest of his thought.

Most revealing in this regard is Hegel's aesthetic theory of tragedy. As on the Aristotelian theory, the tragic artist aims at producing a tragic effect on the audience by employing a variety of literary devices: a plot

[8] See Immanuel Kant, *The Critique of Judgment*, edited by J. H. Bernard (New York: Prometheus, 2000).

that involves a hero who suffers a calamity that results in a reversal of fortune from happiness to misery through a combination of his own actions and unforseen events over which he has no control. The major difference between Hegel's theory and Aristotle's lies in their accounts of tragic effect.[9]

Like Aristotle, Hegel thought of fear and pity and awe for the plight of the hero as essential tragic emotions and central to achieving tragic effect. But where Aristotle believed that the evocation of these emotions must culminate in catharsis, Hegel believed that they must culminate in reconciliation. It is this latter requirement that is at the heart of Hegel's theory. The tragic hero experiences a divided spirit, and it is witnessing the struggle with this division within the hero that evokes fear and pity and awe in the audience. In part, what makes the hero a hero is that he is capable of such a divided spirit and such a struggle. But the greatest of the heroes are those who can reconcile themselves to their struggle and its devastating effects. They do so by coming to understand the conflict within them in a way that moves them beyond where they were before the reversal of fortune. Their spirits are changed in regard to the polarized values that caused the conflict in the first place. They see the validity of the conflicting claims, yet are reconciled to their choice between them and the loss that is involved in it. The aesthetic tragic effect is experiencing this resolution with aesthetic distance.

Hegel's theory is also enriched by a broader understanding of the kinds of "spiritual" conflicts we can experience and identify with. This paves the way for understanding modern as well as ancient tragedy. But what must be understood is that on Hegel's view spiritual conflict is a conflict among the hero's highest values. The conflict between family and state was his major conflict of emphasis. The tragic sense is a kind of response to witnessing the struggle to find reconciliation between the things we value most when the realization of some of those values precludes the realization of others. That is what tragedy is about for him. In this sense, then, the Hegelian study of tragedy is not as much the study of human fragility (as it was for Aristotle) as it is the study of the conflicting structure of human values.

9 See G. W. F. Hegel, *Aesthetics: Lectures on Fine Art* (New York: Oxford University Press, 1998).

The ethical significance of tragedy finds a related expression in Hegel's philosophy of history.[10] History is the story of our struggle to reconcile the conflicts between the things we value most highly. History moves by the dialectic of ethical conflict in which the resolution of conflicting particulars resolves in an ever-ascending movement toward ethical universalism. The most humanistic interpretation of this is that we can learn from the conflicts among our values as history proceeds in such a way that we can hope that ultimately we will have a set of values that are harmoniously reconciled. We do not have such an understanding now, but we are headed in that direction. In this sense, we still live in a tragic age. The end of politics and the end of tragic art will converge. What is envisioned is an ethic that no longer depends on tragic conflict.

The direction of movement from Kant to Hegel is thus a development away from a nontragic ethic toward an ethic that makes tragic concepts more central. Hegel's ethics, however, falls short of a truly tragic ethics because it becomes decreasingly tragic in its framework as historical progress is made. By contrast, a truly tragic ethics does not have the Hegelian hope of transcending tragic conflict. It accepts tragic conflict as a permanent feature of the ethical life.

We get something closer to an ethic of this sort in Schopenhauer, which his aesthetic theory of tragedy helps us to see.[11] He begins by rejecting the idea that all the Aristotelian elements of tragedy are necessary. For example, the tragic artist does not need a hero in the narrative in order to achieve the tragic effect, though the incorporation of a hero often heightens that effect. Still, on Schopenhauer's view tragedy can even happen to a villain who inspires no awe. Here I am thinking of someone who is unlike even Macbeth, who has flaws but inspires awe nonetheless. For Schopenhauer, we can experience the tragic emotions of fear and pity even for those who suffer justly. What this reveals is that Schopenhauer sees tragedy as essentially caught up with suffering itself, and it is this fact that loosens artists from the chains of Aristotelian principles in pursuing tragic art. Not only

[10] See G. W. F. Hegel, *The Philosophy of History* (New York: Dover, 1956).
[11] See Arthur Schopenhauer, *The World as Will and Representation*, translated by E. F. G. Payne (Indian Hills, Colorado: Falcon's Wing Press, 1958).

are heroes not essential, but a plot that requires a reversal of fortune is not essential either, though it is effective. In fact, the greatest tragedy might be a story in which the protagonist lives an entire life of suffering, never achieving happiness or heights of value from which there is a reversal of fortune. In these cases, it is good fortune denied that is the tragedy, not good fortune reversed. It is no wonder, then, that Schopenhauer preferred modern to ancient tragedy and did much to open up the genre in terms of the possibilities of its forms.

But it is the tragic effect itself that is the most essential difference between Schopenhauer and Aristotle, and even Hegel. For Schopenhauer, tragedy is most centrally about the failure to avoid extreme suffering, whereas for Aristotle and Hegel the suffering is less central to what is tragic. The protagonist is caught in an extremely unfriendly world in which the avoidance of suffering is difficult and where the positive values that might make the suffering bearable are either scarce or insufficiently robust to allow him to endure it. The tragic struggle is the struggle with the will to live in a world in which pessimism seems a reasonable attitude to take toward life's prospects. The aesthetic resolution to this struggle is not to be found in catharsis or in reconciliation but in what Schopenhauer calls resignation.

A well-crafted tragedy, on Schopenhauer's view, enables the audience to give up the struggle, to give up the will to live, but it does this without leading to thoughts of despair or suicide. That is what resignation is for Schopenhauer. What the tragic artist does is to take the suffering out of the struggle by providing a kind of aesthetic distance that leads to an experience of sublimity. To experience the world aesthetically, even the suffering of the world, is to be taken out of a world of willing and action into a world of aesthetic enjoyment, including the enjoyment of the sublime. The tragic artist does not so much take the suffering out of tragedy as he takes the struggle out of the suffering; what remains is aesthetic joy or pleasure. That is the tragic effect.

For Schopenhauer, the human condition as constructed by the tragic artist is true to actual human life, and this fact draws together Schopenhauer's aesthetics and ethics. For him, the ethical problem just is the problem of suffering. There are two great evils, pain and boredom; both are forms of suffering; and the ethical life is centered on the struggle to avoid these evils. Moreover, the problem is exacerbated by the fact that the world is very unfriendly in providing goods that can counterbalance the evils of suffering. Schopenhauer scoffed at the thought that our best days are comparable in their goodness to how our worst days are comparable in their badness. Nature prepared us to suffer far more than it prepared us to flourish. Contrary to what Aristotle thought, nature seems to be more an enemy to human well-being and excellence than an ally. And contrary to Hegel, neither our nature nor the conditions of life are going to change in fundamental ways. Dealing with the tragedy of suffering, then, is the fundamental task of ethics, for which the solution, ironically, is to live as much as possible the life of aesthetic observation. The only kind of joy that can relieve us of the struggle with suffering is the kind made available through withdrawal from action and will. It is that that is provided by the aesthetic turn toward life.

By the time we get to Schopenhauer, there is almost a complete reversal from a nontragic ethic found in Leibniz and Kant to a fully tragic one found in his own thought. Despite his dislike for Greek drama, he endorsed a central feature of the Homeric outlook: the issue of how to live, act, feel, and think about life is an issue about how to live, act, feel, and think in a very unfriendly world. The tragic sense is brought to the very center of his ethical conceptual scheme by the high degree to which he thinks human well-being and excellence are vulnerable to destructive forces. What, then, is lacking to make Schopenhauer's a fully tragic ethic?

The answer is to be found in Nietzsche, who brazenly claimed to be the world's first tragic philosopher.[12] Was he merely taunting his intellectual competitors, or was he making a claim that properly interpreted is true? If it is the latter, then what makes him fit such a grand description?

Nietzsche believed that all the philosophers who had written on tragedy from Aristotle to Schopenhauer had failed to penetrate the mind of Homer and of Archaic Greece. He literally thought that he had unearthed the Homeric age after it had been buried by the Western philosophical tradition under a series of fundamentally

[12] See Friedrich Nietzsche, *On the Genealogy of Morals and Ecce Homo*, edited and translated by Walter Kaufman (New York: Vintage, 1989), 273.

mistaken interpretations.[13] Nietzsche thought that Western culture is fundamentally blind to Homer, to tragedy, and to the realities of the human condition, and that the blindness is most fundamentally about tragic effect.

For Nietzsche, Homeric study of tragedy was not a study in human fragility but a study in human strength. To see the best in tragedy as a study in human fragility is to miss its most central point. And it is this point that Nietzsche claims to have rediscovered in a way that had been lost since the Early Classical period of ancient Greece.

The point is best seen in Nietzsche's view of what the tragic artist aims to accomplish. The tragic artist aims to effect in the audience an "orgiastic" experience of joy that is the subjective correlate of a willful act, namely, an act of self-overcoming of fear and pity and saying yes to life. This is not a purging of emotions in Aristotle's sense nor a reconciliation of conflicting values in Hegel's sense. And above all it is not joyful resignation in Schopenhauer's sense. Nietzsche believed that on one level, tragic effect is just a physiological reaction of the human organism to certain events. People see or read tragedies and have a reaction to them. What is that reaction? According to Schopenhauer, it is how the physiological response of a certain cessation of struggling feels. This is what resignation is, the joyful emotional feeling of the will being relieved of its struggle through the distance of aesthetic observation. For Nietzsche, tragic effect is anything but this. Rather, it is the emotional feel of what happens in our nervous systems when we affirm the struggle involved in the will to live in the face of suffering and a hostile world. Affirmation is something we do, rather than observe. The tragic artist aims at provoking the audience into becoming actors not observers, joyful affirmers of life rather than joyful observers, whom Nietzsche identified as despairers of life. Those who do not see this in Homer, according to Nietzsche, simply do not understand *anything* of the Archaic Greek mind and culture. For Nietzsche, this included everyone from Socrates to Schopenhauer.

What Nietzsche saw himself as restoring to the tragic sense that Schopenhauer and others had removed is its central focus. For

[13] See Friedrich Nietzsche, "The Birth of Tragedy," in *The Birth of Tragedy and Other Writings*, edited by Ramond, Geuss, Spiers Ronald, and Karl Ameriks (Cambridge: Cambridge University Press, 1999).

Schopenhauer, the tragic sense is a response to us as sufferers, as victims of the unfriendly circumstances of life. But for Nietzsche, the tragic sense is a response to the fact that we are actors who endorse the struggle with suffering as a joyous opportunity to express the strength of our will to live. Those who retreat from this struggle have both a philistine's view of art and a slave's view of ethics. Just as they are mistaken in their stance toward art, they are mistaken in their stance toward life and what its issues are. From this all the notorious claims about master and slave morality follow, culminating in an ethic of the artist, the creator of a meaningful and beautiful life where suffering is an essential medium out of which meaning and beauty are constructed.

There is, then, a very real sense in which Nietzsche could truly claim to be the world's first tragic philosopher: he was the first (and perhaps last) philosopher to see both aesthetics and ethics in just this way. The move away from the nontragic ethic with which nineteenth-century Germany began is in Nietzsche complete.

Now to the way in which this understanding of developments from Homer to Nietzsche facilitates an understanding of my project here. It is this. To understand the human condition and the issues about how to live, act, and feel about life in the twenty-first century requires us to recapture central elements of the Homeric tragic outlook on life. It requires us to see our place in nature and the social world in many fundamental ways as occupying a hostile environment. It requires us to see the hostility as a permanent feature of the human condition, emanating both from the conditions under which we live and from the things we value most highly. Finally, the ethical task it poses is how, as actors, to affirm life, given these tragic facts. Our tragic sense must become an ethical sense, not just an aesthetic one. So it is the study of our encounter with tragedy in real life that will be the central focus.

Contrary to Nietzsche, however, I will be defending basic elements in Western culture that he thought were doomed. But I will not be defending them in the ways that others have, nor will they come out to be just what they have been to us in the past. When we see the tragic structure of our values, they take on a different meaning and give birth to a tragic ethics. To recommend such a change is to recommend a fundamental change in cultural perspective, and to this extent, Nietzsche was right. I add only one last requirement for a truly tragic ethic, that it accepts the result that in the end the story of humanity ends in tragedy. I require this not for aesthetic reasons or because of some misguided romanticism but because I believe that it is true. Yet I will argue for an ethic that includes a place for hope, even recognizing the tragic ending.

Before I can proceed, however, I would be remiss if I did not say something about the relationship between the project here and recent works on tragedy by Bernard Williams and Martha Nussbaum, both of whom have made important and original contributions to philosophical ethics. I begin with Williams.

In *Shame and Necessity*, Williams says, "Tragedy is formed around ideas it does not expound."[14] He then writes a book that expounds ideas he takes to be central to the Greeks, especially the Archaic Greeks, and argues against what he calls "progressivism," the view that modern ethical concepts are related to ancient ethical concepts in the way that advanced development is related to primitive development. He is especially interested in establishing that Homer had a sophisticated notion of agency, that shame is a more sophisticated ethical concept than guilt, and that we identify with our actions in ways that are subject to the forces of chance more than advocates of modern, allegedly more advanced, ethical concepts would admit. We learn all these things by studying Archaic Greek tragedy, and all are themes that Williams has developed and expounded over the course of his career. What makes *Shame and Necessity* a distinct contribution to that development as a whole is its greater emphasis on the particular contribution of the Archaic rather than the Classical Greeks, especially Aristotle.

I agree with Williams about many of these claims, but they will play virtually no role in what I do here. In fact, the study of Greek tragedy is not central to my project, though it will play some role. I am concerned to articulate a tragic ethic for our time by focusing on our ethical sense of tragic loss. By focusing on the tragic effect of perceived loss on our ethical sensibilities, I hope to establish that when we understand the kinds of loss that can occur regarding the things we value most, including love, equality, freedom and autonomy, prosperity, cultural excellence, happiness, and the relief of suffering, we see that our values are pursued in a world that is very unfriendly and hostile to our efforts

14 See Bernard Williams, *Shame and Necessity* (Berkeley: University of California Press, 1994), 15.

and that our own deepest values themselves war against each other to tragic results. This requires that we see our primary ethical task as dealing with tragic conflict in a way that accepts tragic outcome. I want to examine what our experience of regret,[15] grief, horror, despair, and hope reveals to us about our values, not those of the Archaic or even the Classical or Hellenistic Greeks. I also want to see what it reveals to us about the human condition in the twenty-first century, not in the eighth century B.C. Had he lived, Williams may well have approved of my project, but be that as it may, it is not a project that he pursued in any detail.

There is a different distinction to be made between my project and Martha Nussbaum's. Since the publication of *The Fragility of Goodness*, Nussbaum has been trying to find in Aristotle, suitably adjusted to take on what she sees as the insights of the Stoics, an ethical conceptual scheme applicable to our own troubles. Sometimes with Amartya Sen, she has addressed a wide variety of contemporary issues, ranging from the condition of women in third world countries to the state of education and the rule of law in the United States. What is clear in the direction of her thought is that the concepts she seeks in the ancient period to bring to bear on contemporary ethics are thought by her to lie with developments either in the Late Classical or the Hellenistic period. If I am right, this is a mistake, a mistake because it is a fundamental flaw of those conceptual schemes that they did not fully appreciate the significance of tragic concepts for an adequate ethical conceptual scheme. Specifically, in later chapters when I discuss the contributions of the Classical tradition I will argue that any "Aristotelean ethics" for our time, whether it is Nussbaum's or anyone else's, must accommodate four tragic dimensions to human experience that are hard to square with Classical optimism: facts about the tragic impurity and corruptibility of even the best human character; facts about the tragic dimensions of even the best lives available to us; facts about the sometimes tragic unintelligibility of conflicts between things of high value; and finally the fact that these tragic dimensions of

[15] Williams made significant contributions to our notion of what he called agent regret, which is related to shame rather than guilt. The idea is that some forms of regret attach to our evaluation of ourselves even where we think we had no control over our actions. The notion of regret that I will pursue in the pages that follow is another concept, one that I will explain later that is more related to work by Michael Stocker.

life, especially the latter two, are pervasive and perpetual, rather than merely peripheral and temporary. It is not enough, then, to reject Plato, the Epicureans, and the Stoics and their view that goodness is not fragile. Nor is it enough to recognize that good character is corruptible, that there are tragic losses in good lives, and that momentous choices between things of high value are sometimes unintelligible. It is the recognition that these tragic dimensions are pervasive and perpetual that motivates the move to a tragic ethics, an ethics of high value under constant and pervasive threat where the task is to live a life in which the good outweighs the bad.

1

The Problem of Tragedy

We begin to live when we have conceived life as tragedy.
W. B. Yeats, *Autobiography*

Despite its neglect by most contemporary moral philosophers, the problem of tragedy is the most important philosophical problem facing the twenty-first century. More important than the problem of consciousness, more important than the problem of relativism, and even more important than the problem of justice. I say this despite the fact that the problem of justice has dominated the thought of moral and political philosophers since John Rawls published *A Theory of Justice* in 1971.[1] That these problems, including the problem of justice and several others, are both pressing and challenging is clear. But we stand at a pivotal point in history in which our values and the conditions under which we try to guide our lives by them have pressed us to limits previously only dimly understood and now frightening to behold.

Soldiers witnessing nuclear tests in the desert of the American Southwest during World War II were warned against looking into the explosion. The results, they were advised, could be devastating. Staring into the sun is something not long endured, but even a glimpse at close range of the explosion at Hiroshima would have meant instant blindness. Consider in this regard what it would have been like to have

[1] John Rawls, *A Theory of Justice* (Cambridge, Massachusetts: Harvard University Press, 1971).

been among the first liberators to arrive at Auschwitz. The emotional impact could have been well-nigh nuclear in magnitude. But consider what it would be like emotionally to have even a glimpse of the total suffering in the world at this particular moment. What would that be like emotionally? And what would it be like emotionally to have a brief but vivid experience of the total amount of suffering, both human and animal, in the history of the world? I suspect that getting over witnessing Auschwitz would be easy by comparison. Indeed, it would no doubt be both unbearable and permanently devastating. It would probably destroy even the most calloused among us. What it would do to a reasonably decent person is unfathomable.

The truth, then, will not always set you free, regardless of what Jesus said. Nevertheless, we have an obligation to ourselves and others to get a better understanding of suffering and other, distinct forms of tragedy than we currently have. We need it in order to come to grips with the horrors of the century just passed and to prepare ourselves and our progeny for the horrors that might come. Perhaps by understanding how our values generate tragic conflicts we can manage to avoid some of those horrors, and those we cannot, perhaps we can better endure in ways that leave some room for joy. It is in this sense that the problem of tragedy is the most important philosophical problem of the twenty first century. A look into the abyss can no longer be avoided without risk to everything we hold dear.

More generally, then, what is the problem of tragedy?

Put most generally, it is the problem of coping with loss, both personally and culturally, where the losses are very deep and when it is no longer possible to ignore them or to be consoled by pernicious fantasies. Making sense of the bad, even horrible, things in life and resolving how to feel, to think, and to act in the clear knowledge of good and evil is the task.

For much, though certainly not all, of civilized history, religion has been the primary source of how we understand the nature of tragedy as well as how we should cope with it. The religion of the Homeric Greeks reflected a tragic view of human existence that offered none of the consolations for loss that later religions were to make so central to their appeal. Indeed, the Homeric gods were irrational, often arbitrary forces in the world that were indifferent to the fate of mortals. The losses, great and small, suffered by mortals were as inconsequential to those Greek gods as the effects of natural calamity on human affairs are to the blind forces of modern physics. For the Homeric Greeks, then, the gods were more a cause of human tragedy than a solution to the problem of its losses, which goes a long way in explaining why Greek religion does not have a doctrine of salvation. But all the major religions that were to follow the Homeric Greeks in the West– Judaism, Christianity, and Islam – were to see (and continue to see, in their most influential forms) tragedy as a problem involving God's creation, the solution to which is religious salvation in one form or another.

According to all three of these religious traditions, the earthly world is an extremely unfriendly place: it is a place of the fallen. Though interpretations of the doctrine of the Fall vary within these traditions, all assert that there was a great reversal of fortune, from bliss in the company of God to suffering and alienation from Him, brought about by human sin, that transformed a friendly paradise into an extremely unfriendly world. This is clearly part of a doctrine asserting the tragic nature of the human condition. An additional feature of that condition, especially on Islamic and Christian interpretations, is that it is the ultimate fate of all who have come after the Fall to join either the saved or the damned. The suffering of the saved here on Earth may be tragic in the short term, but in the end their suffering will all be redeemed. That is what heaven is for, and it is by faith that they will be fully restored to God's presence that the saved, the faithful, find consolation in their earthly sufferings. For the saved, then, the message is clear that there will be a day in which there is no pointless suffering, and this is a message of great consolation. Though the Earth is now an unfriendly place, for the faithful the wider universe is not. For the damned, opinions vary, from the view that it is no tragedy at all that they are damned (because they brought their suffering on themselves or because, as in Calvinism, it is simply God's will) to more gentle interpretations to the effect that ultimately all will join the saved in paradise restored. Though there are great variations in how to interpret all the components of this theology, from very literal, crass interpretations to very metaphorical interpretations of great theological complexity, the intellectual history of Western civilization regarding views of the human condition have largely been conditioned by this framework. The tragedy is paradise lost, and the solution is paradise restored.

Speaking of this religious tradition, Marx, whose perspective was much different than the one I will defend here, said:

Religion is the general theory of this world, its encyclopedia, its logic in popular form, its spiritualistic *point d'honneur*, its enthusiasm, its moral sanction, its solemn complement, and the general ground for the consummation and justification for this world.... Religious suffering is at once the expression of real suffering and the protest against real suffering. Religion is the sign of the oppressed creature, the heart of a heartless world, just as it is the spirit of spiritless conditions. It is the opium of the people.[2]

Many read this passage as aimed at insult, but this is not Marx's intent. At its worst, religion is a form of manipulation for more or less crass ends: money, class privilege, certain forms of morality. At its best (and this is Marx's point), religion is the attempt, a very understandable and human attempt, to cope with tragedy and loss. It does so by trying to make all suffering and tragedy intelligible. But if our values are anything like what I will argue that they are, religion is, even at its best, a deception.

In contrast with the religious view, the problem of tragedy as it is conceived in this book starts with the thought that the cost of deception has become too high, that neither the problem of tragedy nor the solution for dealing with it is a religious matter. This is a godless, completely secular book. It calls for a paradigm shift away from our religious past and all hope of any kind of religious redemption, no matter how such redemption is understood. Similarly, it calls for a shift away from many secular views that are the legacy of our religious traditions, some of which grew out of the Enlightenment of the seventeenth and eighteenth centuries, some out of the Classical Greek and Hellenistic tradition, and some out of nineteenth-century Romanticism. Starkly put, what must be accepted is a form of hopelessness: the conscious recognition that the value of life, both personal and political, does not turn on even the possibility of things turning out well in the end, that some forms of significant loss are both ineradicable and unintelligible, and that ultimately all that we cherish will be lost. Like the best of Shakespearean and Greek tragedy: in the end, the hero – humanity at its best – dies. Any new hope that emerges must be sustained in

[2] Karl Marx, *The Portable Marx*, edited by Eugene Kamenka (New York: Viking Penguin, 1983).

the conscious recognition that the old hopefulness is dead, personally, religiously, and politically. The new hopefulness that I will advocate is hopefulness without God and grand political narratives of a secular sort, a hope that can be sustained in the recognition that ultimately things will not turn out well. Positively, then, I will be advocating the secularization of hope and its limitations. It is this form of hopefulness that is the new paradigm, and it is every bit as important that humanity make this shift as it was that astronomy make the shift from Ptolemy to Copernicus and biology from Aristotelian teleology to Darwinian natural selection.

Given the current religious revival, ranging from the rise of Islamic fundamentalism to the wedding of religion and politics in the recent U. S. presidential election, all this may seem to be swimming against the current of history. The message seems to be that we have tried godlessness in twentieth-century political experiments and found it hopeless. It is time, on one interpretation or another, to return to God. American religionists interpret the return to God as one that weds market economics with a return to Christian morals, a restoration of the traditional family, and faith-based initiatives that blur the boundaries between church and state. On this interpretation, the godlessness of both the communist regimes and the secular democracies of the twentieth century has been repudiated. We must, on this view, bring democracy closer to God. Religionists of the Islamic fundamentalist sort want us even closer to God. What we learned from the political experiments of the twentieth century, on their interpretation, is that the defeat of godless communism was half a victory. What remains is the defeat of any democracy that allows any significant cultural secularity, any society in which women depart from traditional roles, homosexuality is accepted, and atheists are allowed to speak and are honored as citizens. Only theocracy can save us. If I am right, all this is desperation, hopefully temporary, but desperation nonetheless. It all rides on the hope that we have a clear view of who the hero is and that he doesn't die but is saved. It rides on the hope that the tragedy of the human condition can ultimately be made intelligible with a happy ending. I will argue that this is a false hope and that a true hope must be found in a form of godlessness, a form freely chosen and uncoerced.

For many, this godlessness and hopelessness will be sufficient reason to read no further. There is not much I can do about that.

Unlike entertainers and others who must write to feed themselves or to advance their careers, philosophers cannot be guided in what they write by the necessity of making themselves popular with their audience. That said, I am confident that there are many who fall into one of the following categories: (i) those who do not believe in God but nevertheless experience loss and need to cope with it; (ii) those who have doubts about God but no doubt whatsoever that they experience loss and need to cope with it; and (iii) those who want to understand what it is like for those who have to cope with loss who cannot believe in God. That there are many who fall into these categories I am fairly confident, because I am fairly confident that the world must increasingly accommodate people who simply cannot believe in God anymore, not because of obstinance, as many would understand the lack of religious belief, but because of the simple inability to make sense of the world any longer from the theistic perspective. This book is written primarily but not exclusively for those in the secular world in the first category, those who have to make sense of life and its losses and how to live emotionally, culturally, politically, and morally in the face of those losses. In another sense, it is written for those who recognize and are proud of the fact that Western culture is, as many have accused it of being, essentially a secular culture.

So how is the problem of tragedy framed from that secular perspective? It starts with thoughts of the beginning, the middle, and the end. As to the beginning, it starts with the realization that it is a matter of cosmic accident that there is a problem of tragedy at all. That there is life and value is not a product of design but of the blind forces of natural evolution. Life and what we value in it, including ourselves, emerged through the blind forces of nature out of a primordial soup. As to the end, it starts with the realization that some day everything that has and will transpire here on Earth, including all that we cherish, will perish without a trace, leaving behind a universe indifferent to our history, to our values, and to our sorrows. As to the middle, it starts with the realization that human civilization with all its joys and sorrows is located somewhere between the primordial soup and the end of our natural history.

Within this framework comes the realization that each person gets one and only one life, and that humanity gets one and only one history. Moreover, whatever redeems the losses of history must be found in a history that is bound to end badly. That it will end badly is virtually certain. On the best-case scenario, we will avoid self-destruction and live for a time of virtual peace and prosperity for all, something that has thus far eluded us. But even on the best-case scenario, at some point nature will decide that our time has passed. Perhaps the end will be quick, painless, and unanticipated, leaving little room for reflection on what will be lost. Perhaps it will be slow and painful and greeted with relief after a long struggle. But given the human capacity for knowledge, it is more likely that we will have some idea of the end in a way that will leave us with some time to be puzzled and horrified about how to live in the face of finality. Imagine the confusion that would result from suddenly discovering that you have only a week to live. Now imagine a point in history where it becomes clear to everyone regardless of culture that in ten years hence an unavoidable natural catastrophe will instantly end all life, human and nonhuman, here on Earth. The cultural confusion of such knowledge about how to feel, to think, and to act would be devastating.

Of course, this is not something we know, but we do know that the end will come and that it is possible that it will come sooner rather than later. With the Cold War behind us, we do not worry as much as we did about global nuclear destruction, though there are reemerging reasons for that fear. On the other hand, we are acutely aware that the world's natural resources can be depleted through burgeoning population growth and industrial pollution, something that has not been a pervasive part of our cultural awareness until very recently. These and other concerns make it true that at no other point in human history have we lived in the shadow of our finitude and the awareness that human history does in fact have limited horizons in the way that we do now. This should affect how we think of what is important in life, how to cope with the losses that will come along the way, and which losses are worth enduring and which are not. Most generally, this is the secular problem of tragedy.

Increasingly, we are showing signs of realizing that things might not turn out well. In the meantime, we are left with the problem of how to cope with the conflict between good and evil and between good and good, when more and more we have difficulties grasping what these conflicts are really like. The age of secularization that began with the Protestant Reformation has pretty much run its course in the developed nations of the world, and the rest may follow suit in due time. One of the things we secularists believe is that God is not going to save us from whatever mess we make of things. He is neither here nor there; we are, and always have been, alone. To be sure, in times of crisis, people are called upon to pray, and some claim that the remedy is to return to God. But soon we prepare for war, as we sometimes should, not to defend our God against theirs but to defend our secular democratic values against a way of life that puts its trust in the divine in a way in which we neither can nor should. Only one of countless species, on a planet in only one of innumerable galaxies, in a universe with unfathomable dimensions, we stand divided. Like all other animals, we gape into eternity with either the naivete of ignorance or the stress of fear. What divides us is our values. Yet the space in which it is possible for us to see our conflicts as the conflict between good and evil is increasingly small. The Holocaust convinced us of evil but left us unsure of the good. We keep trying to recoup a faith irredeemably lost: that there is an ultimate good, that it is pure, and that it will prevail. Ultimate good is whatever would make heaven heaven, a place where there is no loss, no grounds for conflict, and no occasion for sorrow.

But it is not to be. As Nietzsche suggested over a hundred years ago, Christian theocracy is (hopefully) dead in the West, and Islamic alternatives find themselves either taking the same road to secularization that began for Christianity with Locke's *Letter Concerning Toleration* or striking out in terror against forms of freedom they cannot assimilate and declaring war on historical forces they cannot contain. As for secularism: our attempts to replace heaven with utopia have all failed, leaving us drained of faith and suspicious of grand reform. The evidence for this is that those who now preach salvation by socialism or salvation by the market speak in the same shrill voice as those who preached the hell fire and brimstone of the past. The moral law has revealed itself no more clearly than has God and has left us in just the same predicament regarding the ultimate good. To be sure, there are those in the classrooms of the finest universities in the world who lecture as passionately as the religious zealots on the airwaves that our salvation is to know the moral law and to live by it. But they are no more convincing and no less desperate. There is no ultimate good.

But the fact that there is no ultimate good is not the ultimate tragedy. Rather, the ultimate tragedy is believing that there is an ultimate good. This is the pernicious fantasy, the deadly opium. It is fantasy because it is false, and pernicious because belief in it leads us to live in ways that are even more tragic than they need to be. The problem of tragedy is coming to see in a very clear analytical way why we should quit thinking that there even could be something called the ultimate good that would make heaven heaven, a place with no occasion for sorrow, or, at the very least, would reconcile all our values. When we do come to see that there is no ultimate good, no ultimate reconciliation, we can begin to accept the fact that we are rather marvelous animals that emerged out of the soup of the universe, that the accident of life will someday vanish, but that the brief history that is ours is worth the ride, and hopefully for a while longer.

Darwin's arrival on the Galapagos Islands found him astonished at the teeming variety of life. He then spent the remainder of his days trying to explain both the variety and the genealogy of species. He left God behind, went out on his own, and forever changed the way we see nature and our place within it. He taught us to see ourselves naturalistically, as a part of nature. He was able to do this because he dared to ask the question, How can nature produce life and its variety? Similarly, we need to ask a new question about our values. Not the question of what God commands us to do, or what the moral law commands that we ought to do. Rather, we need to ask, What do we as natural organisms, as a matter of fact, value, and what is the structure of our deepest values? We need to naturalize our values in the way that Darwin naturalized the study of species. When we muster the courage to look into nature in our own persons in relationship to our environment as the source of value, we will find nature as teeming with value as with life. What we will discover is that though there is no ultimate good, there are many extremely good things. We will also discover that our values are in competition in the same way that species and individual organisms are. Good opposes good in tragic ways. It is this discovery in its depth that the pernicious fantasy conceals from view. A recurring theme in the pages that follow is the way in which pernicious fantasy relentlessly generates conceptual strategies for rendering invisible what is often unbearable to see. By doing so, it refuses to look into the abyss of tragedy, but it compounds the tragedy by concealing the source of joy that must be tempered by sorrow. What follows is an attempt to advance our knowledge of our values when we get beyond the fantasies of philosophical opiates and their diverse strategies for rendering tragedy invisible and understand the facts about our own multiple forms of caring.

So what do we see when we leave otherworldly fantasies behind and approach our values naturalistically?

We discover that our emotional capacities are at least as basic to our values and the sorts of animals we are as our cognitive capacities. When we come to know much more about the experience of the so-called lower animals, a far different understanding of what life is like for them than the one that has dominated much of the Christian era may well emerge. Instead of being dumb brutes, some may speak a language previously unknown to us; instead of being locked into an eternal present, some may have a developed sense of their own future; and instead of being limited to the demands of their appetites, some may have a sophisticated repertoire of emotions, including joy, sorrow, grief, even dread. But as far as we know, there are some things no other animals besides ourselves can do or experience. No other animals to our knowledge can do higher mathematics or keep an extended history. Nor are their powers of induction sufficient to support anything like a science. Music may exist among them, but there is no three-part harmony, chord progression, or counterpoint. These things are not part of their experience because they lack nervous systems that support higher-level cognitive capacities, the capacities of sophisticated reason. Much has been made of this, so much that many philosophers have claimed that the distinctive feature of being human is our higher-order capacity for reason.

Perhaps so, but it strikes me that we have a capacity for loss that stakes as much claim to being a distinctive quality as any, including our capacity for reason. It is not that no other animal has a sense of loss; some certainly do. But no other animal has a sense of tragedy as developed and as sophisticated as ours. Though a baby ape may grieve the loss of its mother even to the point of starving itself to death, there is no evidence that any other species lives in the shadow of loss the way we do. When we appreciate the achievements of Galileo, of Newton, of Einstein, we are clearly appreciating the achievements made possible by their higher-order rational capacities. But what are we doing when we appreciate the achievements of the great tragedians, of Homer, of Sophocles, of Shakespeare? Is it not their capacities to value in such a way that expresses a tragic sense? There seems, therefore, to be some difference between the higher-order rational capacities of the first group and the higher-order valuing capacities of the second, with the latter tied to tragedy in a way that is not exhausted by the former. The irony may well be that we are more like other animals than we are different from them and that, contrary to our rationalist tradition, it is our emotional capacities – capacities that make us vulnerable to tragic loss – that are our most distinctive qualities. Truly human, then, is the capacity to take loss to the level of the tragic.

Of course, not every bad happening that results in loss is a tragic event, nor is every decision with bad consequences a tragic choice. Some are too trivial to rise to the appropriate level. Others, though not trivial, could easily have been avoided. Nor is every tragedy or tragic choice to be analyzed in the same way. What is the same about Agamemnon's relationship with his daughter and Oedipus's relationship with his mother may be far less important than what is different about them. So, too, with real-life tragedies. Moreover, the tragedies of the modern condition may be far different from those of antiquity. But whatever the difficulties involved in giving an account of tragic experience, one thing should be clear: our recognition of tragedy is a function of our valuing. If we valued in other ways, we would not recognize the tragic dimensions of life. The guiding thought of this book is that our tragic sense can teach us a great deal about the nature of value and human valuing. The contribution I most wish to make here regarding the problem of tragedy is advancing our understanding of how our values give rise to a tragic sense. Since our experience of tragedy is made possible by our higher-order valuing capacities, a part of the current inquiry is to discern what these capacities are and what they are like. Are they a function of the higher-order rational capacities that distinguish us from other animals, or are they a function of capacities that we share with other animals?

Some of our beliefs about values and human valuing are false. Moreover, we can know that they are false for the simple reason that if they were true, there would be no tragedy, and few things are more evident than that life, not just literature, is pervaded with tragedy. What these thoughts reveal is that a theory of value should ha power, and if it lacks explanatory power, then it is false. I the ways in which we have thought and continue to thir are false. They lack the power to explain our tragic sens

Some theories of value fail because they do not reco at all; others fail because they do not recognize the ful of tragedy. We can learn from all these theories by recognizing the explanatory power they do possess, and we can improve them by altering them in ways that increase their explanatory potential. Currently, we do not have a theory of value with explanatory power adequate to account for the full phenomena of tragedy. Nor will the door close on that subject with what is said here. The goal is to advance the subject, not to have the last word.

The central thesis of this book is that an adequate tragic sense requires a conception of value that says that values are plural, conflicting, and sometimes incomparable and that nothing is of unqualified value. It also requires a view of the human condition according to which tragic losses generated by these values are pervasive and perpetual. To say that values are plural is to say that there are many things that we value for themselves in ways that make them worthy of commitment and that there are many irreducible ways of valuing them. To say that values are conflicting is to say that sometimes they are incompatible in the sense that the realization of one precludes the realization of another.[3] It is to say that loss, contrary to some forms of the pernicious fantasy, is an inevitable function of human valuing. To say that values are incomparable is to say that sometimes we are faced with decisions in life in which comparison of alternatives is essential for choice but where comparison is impossible. Finally, to say that nothing is of unqualified value is to say two things: first, that there is nothing of such a value that it cannot in some context be traded off for the value of something else; and second, that what is good and what is bad are in an important sense inseparable. If this is true, then there is absolutely no value that is not subject to loss, even given rational choice. Without all four of these elements and a view of the human condition involving

[3] See James Griffin, "Incommensurability: What's the Problem?," in *Incommensurability, Incomparability, and Practical Reason*, edited by Ruth Chang (Cambridge, Massachusetts: Harvard University Press, 1997), 36.

pervasive and perpetual tragic loss, I will argue, there are important features of tragedy for which we cannot account. I will not argue for the more ambitious thesis that these features can account for all tragic experience.

The focus will be on tragic choice and how practical reason – our capacity to reason about how to act and live – is affected by the tragic dimensions of life. Just as a theory of value is falsified if it cannot account for salient features of our tragic sense, a theory of practical reason is falsified if it falls short in the same regard. Framed, then, in terms of choice, this book is about how the comparisons we have to make when considering the practical options we face in life yield a tragic sense.

Sometimes tragedy is the result of choosing evil over good. Sometimes it is the result of choosing a lesser good over a greater good. But, as strange as it might sound, sometimes tragedy is the consequence of choosing the greater good over a lesser good. In these cases, it is rational that the greater good prevail, but what is tragic is that significant good is nevertheless lost: what is contained in the lesser good is significant but not contained in the greater good. These are occasions for reason's regret but not reason's grief. The regret is that significant good had to be lost, but it is lost for a reason, namely, for the greater good. There is, then, the consolation of reason for tragic losses of this sort.

Two observations about such losses are crucial. The first has to do with loss as waste. One of the great insights of A. C. Bradley's analysis of Shakespearean tragedy, especially of Macbeth, is the way in which he ties a sense of waste into the tragic effect of the plays.[4] Unless you feel the impact of the good that is wasted in Macbeth, you have yet to experience the kind of loss involved at the heart of the tragedy. This is a powerful observation and has wide application in real life. But Bradley is wrong to generalize tragic loss as waste. Why? Because in cases where the greater good prevails over the lesser good and where what is contained in the lesser good is amply significant but not contained in the greater good, the lesser good is lost but not wasted,

[4] See A. C. Bradley, *Shakespearean Tragedy: Lectures on Hamlet, Othello, King Lear and Macbeth*, (New York: Penguin Classics, 1991), 23–52 and 305–66.

which is why the tragic sense has some consolation in these cases even though the sense of tragedy remains.

The second observation is about incomparability. Where incomparability obtains and significant values are at stake, plurality and conflict bring loss for which no comparative reason can be given. This sense of loss is not that of regret, nor of waste or consolable loss, but of grief. It is loss without the consolation of reason or the aid of philosophical and religious opiates. This is reason's grief.

It is reason's grief because choosing between practical options requires comparing the conflicting options and judging which is most important and, in that sense, what is best. Without the thought that intrinsically important things in life are at stake and that it is important that we choose what is best in this sense, thoughts that evil might be chosen over good, or the lesser good over the greater good, or that what is lost in the lesser good is not included in the greater good, have no place. And without a sense of comparison, our tragic sense loses its shape. The impetus to compare in this sense, therefore, is central both to our ability to reason practically and to our capacity for tragic experience. Incomparability, then, obtains when we are faced with practical options in which one option is neither better than, worse than, nor equal to the others. Where incomparability obtains between options of great importance that are in conflict but where choice must be made, there arises a new tragic thought: that what is lost, no matter what we do, cannot be compared to what is gained in any of the options. This is reason's grief, the outer limit to rational choice, the end of the consolation of reason for loss, and a distinctive source of tragic experience that pernicious fantasies work to conceal. It is, as we will see, the emotional recognition of unintelligible loss.

The argument for these conclusions, however, will have to wait for later. For now, I want to say something about the argumentative strategy and structure of the book.

I will begin in Chapter 2 with a preliminary sketch of what I believe incomparability is. There is a growing body of philosophical literature on this subject and on the wider subject of incommensurability. My initial goal will be to present a general account of what incomparability is and how that account differs in important ways from current competing accounts. The key to understanding incomparability is not to be found in the metaphysics of value, as many philosophers believe, but in an understanding of what it is to value something vaguely, where the vagueness of our valuing is a direct function of our higher-order valuing capacities. If this is right, the study of incomparability is in part an empirical study, a study of our psychology, both neurological and pathological. In addition to the preliminary account, I will also provide a preliminary argument for the account of incomparability and how it relates to the pernicious fantasies that support the ubiquity of practical reason – the view that it is, in principle at least, always possible to be rational.

Having provided the preliminary account of incomparability, the argumentative strategy will be to show that any theory of value or practical reason that denies any of the four features listed earlier – the irreducible plurality of value, the conflicting nature of values, the sometimes incomparability of values, and the absence of anything of unqualified value – will fail to account for some important cases of tragic experience. Accordingly, successive chapters take up different views of value and their implications for providing an account of tragedy. Chapters 3 and 4 address dark views about value: nihilism and pessimism; Chapter 5 addresses various forms of monism, the view that there is only one kind of value; and Chapters 6 through 9 address various versions of pluralism. The final chapter addresses the avoidance of despair and the prospects for the future. The aim is to address each type of theory and evaluate its adequacy in terms of what it implies about tragedy and our tragic sense in contemporary circumstances. Another aim is to show how we must shift from a religious paradigm for understanding loss to a naturalistic one, one that sheds entirely its religious heritage.

Nihilism asserts that nothing is of sufficient value to merit our being committed to it. Rightly or wrongly, Nietzsche and later the existentialists have been associated with this view in the popular mind, and a good bit of twentieth-century art suggests it. Whether this is a correct interpretation of these thinkers is not the main concern. Nietzsche most certainly rejected nihilism and saw himself as fighting against it, though there are no doubt passages from his writings, to those who have only a cursory knowledge of his books, that seem to assert it. Sartre, at one stage or another in his development, seems to have both asserted it and denied it. Certainly, nihilistic interpretations of some of his literary works, particularly his novel *Nausea*[5] and his play *No Exit*,[6] are by no means implausible to the popular mind. Yet, rather than laboring over the correct interpretation of any particular thinker, the concern will be to articulate how we might understand a coherent version of what nihilism is. Chapter 3 will argue that there is a close connection between nihilism and nineteenth-century Romanticism, and that both suffer, oddly, from an inflated view of the human will and the creative role of art. Neither can possibly account for our response to the tragedies of the twentieth century. Reason may not be ubiquitous, but the Romanticism of the nineteenth century and its twentieth-century nihilistic counterpart have grossly and self-indulgently exaggerated its limits. It is our sense of tragedy that confirms this. If we are to take tragedy seriously, we must look to more mature views of the human condition.

Philosophical pessimism is such a view. Best articulated by Arthur Schopenhauer in the nineteenth century, it is particularly pressing at the beginning of the twenty-first. Pessimism does not assert, as nihilism does, that nothing is of value, but rather that there is not enough positive value to justify the continuation of human and animal suffering. Pessimism's main focus is on what it takes to be the tragedy of the human condition. Given that so much suffering is bound to dwarf the significance of anything else we value, the tragedy is that we are alive at all. We proceed only through self-deception about the nature and extent of suffering in the world or through the weakness of will to bring an end to our existence. That there is some joy and happiness, that there is value in personal relations, in the pursuit of excellence, in knowledge, in art and beauty, and in myriad other things, pessimism does not deny. What it asserts is that any sober assessment of the extent of suffering that is bound to accompany the future of humanity does not justify the continuation of human history. It asserts that while the existence of humanity is itself a tragedy, because the negative value of suffering undermines the positive values of human life, the continuation of human existence is a greater tragedy still.

Contemporary academic philosophy is almost silent on the problem of pessimism, which is a serious indictment of academic philosophy.

[5] Jean-Paul Sartre, *Nausea*, translated by Lloyd Alexander (New York: Norton, 1975).
[6] Jean-Paul Sartre, *No Exit and Three Other Plays* (New York: Vintage, 1989).

For centuries the problem of suffering has been recognized as a problem for theism and religious thinkers, yet academic moral philosophers who take a secular perspective are silent on this issue.[7] Most secular philosophers believe that the theistic belief in an all-powerful, all-knowing, wholly good God is undermined by the evidence of so much suffering in the world. What sober consideration of the history of human and animal suffering, say these philosophers, could lead anyone to seriously think that there is some divine plan that redeems it all? The pessimist, however, poses a similar question to the secular moral philosopher: what sober consideration of the prospects for human and animal suffering could lead anyone to seriously think that there is some human plan that can redeem the continued project of human history by promising a net surplus of good over bad? Any moral theory that takes this issue lightly should itself be taken lightly. Why? Because it fails to recognize the tragedy of human and animal suffering. The burden imposed by the pessimist on moral theory is to take seriously the tragedy of suffering and argue that it would be more tragic still just to end it all. I am not aware of any contemporary analytic theory that even attempts to meet this challenge.[8] I will argue, however, that pessimism gives us a distorted perspective on the question of suffering and that from another perspective there are some grounds for hope, if not optimism. In so doing, I will be arguing that pessimism gives us an inadequate account of tragic experience.

Unlike nihilism and pessimism, monistic theories of value are notoriously optimistic. They represent value as being about one thing, and there are two prominent versions. The first and historically most prominent version is hedonism, the view that pleasure is the only positive value and pain the only negative value. Epicurus, Jeremy Bentham, and John Stuart Mill advocated three different versions of hedonism. The second version of monism is perfectionism, most recently articulated by Thomas Hurka.[9] It is the view that the only thing of intrinsic

[7] A recent exception is Susan Neiman's *Evil: An Alternative History of Philosophy* (Princeton, New Jersey: Princeton University Press, 2002).

[8] Jamie Mayerfeld's *Suffering and Moral Responsibility* (New York: Oxford University Press, 1999) at least recognizes the problem, though it does not address it in a systematic way.

[9] See Thomas Hurka, *Perfectionism* (New York: Oxford University Press, 1993).

value is the development of our human capacities and that negative value is simply the privation of such development.

Like pessimism, both types of monism make contributions to our understanding of value and human valuing, and it is important to see what these contributions are. Pessimism establishes that any theory of value must recognize that suffering is a distinct negative value; monism in its hedonistic forms establishes that pleasure is a distinct positive value; and perfectionism establishes that the development of human capacities is a distinct positive value. These are all important contributions. The major limitation of even the most sophisticated versions of monism is that they cannot adequately account for our sense of loss, and this limitation is directly traceable to their lack of recognition of the plurality and conflicting nature of human values.

The resources available to the monist to account for loss are very limited. For the monist, loss can result from evil prevailing over good: pain over pleasure or the privation of human development over human development. Also, the lesser good could prevail over the greater good: one might irrationally choose a lesser instance of pleasure over a greater instance of pleasure or a lesser degree of human development over a greater degree of human development. What is not possible according to monism is that loss could occur as a result of the greater good prevailing over a lesser good. The reason this could not occur is that if monism is true, then there could be nothing of value contained in the lesser good that is not contained in the greater good. More pleasure is better than less pleasure, and there is nothing of value in less pleasure that is not contained in greater pleasure. So, too, with human development. Less human development does not contain anything of value that is not contained in greater human development, at least on a monistic understanding of human development.

Michael Stocker and others have argued that monism is false because we sometimes experience loss when we rationally choose the greater good over the lesser good.[10] The reason this is so is that there sometimes is value contained in the lesser good that is not contained in the greater good. This has become known as the argument from regret for the plurality of values. The idea is that it is possible for the

[10] See Michael Stocker, *Plural and Conflicting Values* (Oxford: Clarendon Press, 1990).

lesser good to contain value that is not contained in the greater good only if there are two distinct values involved.

Thomas Hurka has attempted to respond to this type of objection to monism, but I will argue that to the extent to which his response accommodates our sense of loss, it represents an abandonment of monism.[11] Not only does perfectionism fail to recognize the distinct negative value of human and animal suffering – and in this way fail to recognize one of the tragic features of the human condition – it also fails to recognize other distinct values and how the pursuit of human perfection can result in loss of these goods. Similarly, hedonism and its variants do not adequately recognize the distinctive value of human development and the way in which too much concern for how we feel can result in the tragic loss of nonhedonic goods. Why it is better to be Socrates dissatisfied than a fool satisfied cannot ultimately be given a monistic explanation of either a hedonistic or a perfectionist form.

I will show what tragic loss must come to for Epicurus, for Bentham, and for Mill, and show that all three thinkers fall woefully short, concealing the loss of important values that any adequate theory should reveal. Especially in the case of Epicurus and Bentham, their zeal to simplify value is a direct result of their aversion to conflict. All of these thinkers assume what the pernicious fantasy assumes – that ultimate value has a certain structure, namely, that it is the sort of value that could make heaven heaven or utopia utopia, a place where there is no occasion for sorrow. If we do not live in such a place, they believe, it is only because conditions prevent it. It is not because the structure of value brings tragic loss with it. This, however, is their mistake. Value is not singular but plural, and it does bring tragedy in its wake.

The recognition of pluralism, however, is not in itself enough to solve the problems haunting monism. Three versions of pluralism are worth considering – supreme value pluralism, best life pluralism, and tragic pluralism. All share the view that loss sometimes results from a rational choice of the lesser good over the greater good when something of value in the lesser good is not contained in the greater good. Both supreme value pluralism and best life pluralism limit their account of tragic conflicts between good and good to this claim. I will

[11] See Thomas Hurka, "Monism, Pluralism, and Rational Regret," *Ethics* 106 (1996): 555–75.

argue that all three versions clearly fail to account for some important dimensions of tragic experience. They all assume that value is a unity though not a singularity.

Supreme value pluralism rests on the claim that there is some value that is strictly superior to all other values. The most prominent version of such pluralism is that of Immanuel Kant, but it is also implied in many religious perspectives. Kant claimed that human dignity is strictly superior in value to any other value. To evaluate claims about the strict superiority of human dignity or any other value, we will have to consider a wide range of comparative judgments that we are willing upon careful consideration to make. When we do, we can then see that though we afford vast superiority to some values, we never afford strict superiority to anything. What we will find is that although we afford human dignity vast superiority to many other values, we sometimes rationally sacrifice human dignity to some other concerns in extreme contexts. Human dignity, then, is not always the greater of two goods, nor is anything else. Moreover, we will also see that living within the shadow of every good thing, even human dignity, are some very bad things. What we should conclude from this is that the tragic nature of the human condition is such that everything we value is subject to loss for the sake of something else. Value is neither a unity nor a purity.

Best life pluralism is associated not with Kant but with Aristotle and our Greek heritage. It will be important to understand how best life pluralism provides an interpretation of an Aristotelian perspective that is distinct from the perfectionist interpretation of Hurka. Best life pluralism is a certain interpretation of eudaimonism, the view that the fundamental choices of practical reason are about what kind of life to lead rather than most fundamentally about the rightness or wrongness of particular actions. On Hurka's perfectionist reading, the answer to the question about what kind of life to lead is to be found in the answer to the question of which kind of life most develops human nature. According to best life pluralism, the answer to the question about what kind of life to lead is to be found in the answer to the question of which kind of life most accommodates all of what a person values in the way that he or she values it. The view is pluralistic in two senses: first, perfecting our nature is only one among many things that we value, and, second, there are many different ways of life that can accommodate different goods in different ways. Best life pluralism asserts that one of these ways of life is superior to all others.

Best life pluralism has the resources to provide a great improvement over monistic perfectionism. Most importantly, it allows us to recognize forms of loss not available on views previously mentioned. Though Aristotle himself seemes to have believed that the best life available to us could, with a modicum of good luck, accommodate all the things we value in the way that we value them, best life pluralism need not assert this. In fact, it cannot assert it and recognize the tragic fact that even the best of lives involve tragic loss on a regular basis. This is one of the dimensions of life that keeps tragic concepts on center stage in a way that the Classical Greek tradition, including Aristotle, was inclined to move away from. What best life pluralism can assert is that there is a best life, though even in the best life some things of high value are routinely lost.[12] If we pursue the political life, the loss in intellectual and personal life is real and substantial. But if we choose the intellectual life, the loss of political and personal engagement is equally real and substantial. The same thing can be said about other ways of life and other goods, or so I hope to show. What best life pluralism insists upon, however, is that though the pursuit of the best life involves the tragic loss of some goods, it carries with it the consolation of reason that it is good and is the best of what is available. I will argue in Chapter 8 that even if there were a best life, it would contain a tragic value deficit in what is lost in the lesser good, and I will illustrate the point by considering two paired sets of values that we hold dear: (i) liberty versus security and (ii) equality versus cultural excellence.

In Chapter 9, however, I will argue that best life pluralism is false because among the most plausible forms of life there is no best life, nor are the best lives either roughly or strictly equal. Rather, they are incomparable. I will argue this in regard to ways of life that attempt to reconcile the paired set of values already mentioned – liberty versus security and equality versus cultural excellence. Now, if this is true,

[12] That Aristotle might have allowed that there are losses of this sort, even within lives built on a modicum of good luck, is one thing. That is a case that Nussbaum might succeed in making out (though I take no position on it here as an interpretation of Aristotle). But it is an altogether different thing to assert that Aristotle believed that the best life for humans under conditions of relative good fortune is riddled with tragedy. That is my claim.

the implications for loss are significant, especially when generaliz to apply to a broad range of other values. Being human, we are bound to live in such a way that important things are lost to us for which no comparative reason can be given. These losses are not cases of evil prevailing over the greater good, or of the lesser good prevailing over the greater good, or even of the greater good prevailing over the lesser good. Extended to culture as a way of life, the point is that the development of one form of culture precludes the development of another form of culture. Cultures are plural and conflicting. Moreover, some forms of culture are incomparable. Precluding some forms of culture by developing our own form of culture cannot be done for a reason. Because of its consequences, this is perhaps the greatest tragedy of all. What is left is reason's grief.

All forms of monism suffer from the pernicious fantasy that ultimate value is the kind of value that makes heaven heaven, a place where there is no occasion for sorrow. The forms of pluralism that deny incomparability suffer from a less destructive delusion, namely, that value is such that though sorrow is internal to our values, there can always be, if we are rational, a consolation for loss. I will argue that because of incomparability, this is false. The consolation of reason is often available to us, but often it is not.

The conclusion, then, will be that we should accept a form of pluralism called tragic pluralism, with the understanding that tragic pluralism asserts that values are plural and conflicting, that there is nothing of unqualified value, that values are sometimes incomparable, and that tragic loss is pervasive and perpetual within the human condition. I will try to show in the final chapter how grief is distinct from both regret and despair and leaves room for joy. Despair is where evil prevails over the greater good. I will suggest that we are not at the point in history in which despair is in order. In this regard, I will show that the concept of tragedy can provide the basis for a new paradigm for understanding our place in history, a topic almost completely abandoned by analytic philosophy. In so doing, I will discuss some of the conflicts emerging between the United States and Europe and between the developed world and the world of Islam by considering some of the views of the direction of history taken by recent thinkers such as Francis Fukuyama and Samuel Huntington. Joy can be had, but not ultimately through old ideas of progress. Rather, a new, tragic-sensitive idea of progress is needed, one that does not project utopian expectations onto the future but marvels that there is good and maintains hope that both personally and globally the good might still outweigh the bad. This is not the old joy of ubiquitous reason founded on pernicious fantasies, but a new, more sober joy tempered with sorrow. This must be the new hopefulness.

One final comment about the structure of the argument. Philosophy, on my view, is an instrument of culture, not a narrow academic specialty. What I mean by this is that the problems of philosophy must be viewed as problems faced by a culture. In this sense, philosophical problems are historical problems, problems in the history of ideas. Those who do not believe that ideas are important think that they are either relics to be studied by people who are fond of museums or fifth wheels pulled along by the real forces of history. Those of us who do believe in ideas think that how we understand things, including our place in nature and our relationship to the past and the future, is itself an historical force. Philosophy will persist as long as there are crises among our ideas, crises about how to understand where we have been, where we are, and where we are going. As we stand at the beginning of the twenty-first century, we do not understand the twentieth. History, like a book, is hard to read when eyes are close to the page. Yet one thing is clear: we do not know how to make sense of the awful tragedies of the twentieth-century and those that loom in the century ahead. Our crisis is that our cultural heritage has not yet provided us with a conceptual scheme – a network of ideas – to make sense of the tragedies we have witnessed and the decisions we have faced. All this means that the problem of tragedy is not a minor philosophical problem, one of interest only to those with a literary bent. It is, I contend, perhaps the philosophical problem of the moment, at least as important as the problem of justice, about which so much has been written over the last thirty or so years. One of the tasks of philosophy is to explain how we are now in intellectual crisis regarding tragedy; another is to recommend a way into the future. For this we need a tragic ethics, an ethics that recognizes the perpetual and pervasive presence of tragic loss.

We Westerners bring to our experience of tragedy at least four great traditions: a religious tradition born of Judaism, Islam, and Christianity; the classical tradition of Greece and Rome; the Enlightenment tradition of the seventeenth and eighteenth centuries; and the Romantic tradition of the nineteen century. We can understand our current values only by understanding how the problem of tragedy that faces us early in the twenty-first century has been shaped by these traditions. And if there is a crisis in our thought regarding tragedy, all these traditions are lacking in some important respect, meaning that one of the most pressing tasks now facing philosophy is to provide a revision in our understanding of tragedy that is appropriate to our times. For this reason, the argumentative strategy will include a recurring discussion of the roles of these traditions in our thought.

2

The Dubious Ubiquity of Practical Reason

> It is their abhorrence of incommensurabilities that makes rationalists what they are.
>
> Joseph Raz, *Engaging Reason*

> Thus conscience does make cowards of us all.
>
> Shakespeare, *Hamlet,* act 3, scene 1

There is a way of having faith in something, a way of believing in something, that is more akin to a well-entrenched hope or expectation than an attitude that is the product of inquiry. Life, it seems, requires a framework of hopes and expectations that make it both coherent and meaningful. Believing that someone loves you can be like this. The thought of not being loved might be so hard to entertain that you take being loved for granted. It is like the air you breathe: you fail to notice it until it is in short supply. Of course, faith in other things can be similar. For example, you might believe that you have the talent to embark on a medical career, never questioning your ambition until you attempt to master the science involved. Or you might have faith in your own character, until temptation becomes a possibility you thought you would never entertain. Consider also the shock of learning of someone you thought to be an ordinary person doing something extraordinarily bad. Was it that you had good reasons for thinking that such horrible behavior was beyond the pale of everyday people, or was the faith in the decency of ordinary folks a background belief that made life palatable?

These are common examples of a kind of trust in something that is crucial to living but that can be dashed. The truth is that a certain amount of confidence or faith in some things of this sort is essential to a coherent and sustainable human outlook on life. The problem is that we begin our intellectual and emotional lives in naivete, and somewhere along the way confidence in our hopes is challenged. When the evidence becomes just too compelling for our faith to sustain itself, we face a crisis of belief and have to rebuild on firmer ground. When we are able to do this as the result of inquiry, we have a different, less naive way of believing or trusting in these things. Moreover, when such a crisis arises, we have no intellectual option but to build hope on some sort of foundation. In this regard, the intellectual and emotional life is a constant work in progress, a process of adjusting faith to what seem to be reasonable grounds for hope.

This is no less true of cultures than it is of individuals. The intellectual crisis that precipitated the Enlightenment of the seventeenth and eighteenth centuries started out in naivete about authority. It ended with a conversion, very much like a religious one, to faith in human reason regarding almost every aspect of life, whether theoretical or practical.

It is hard for us to imagine a cultural outlook in which matters of fact are settled by appeals to authority. But this was just the case in the Christian West regarding astronomy prior to the time of Copernicus and Galileo. The Ptolemaic universe in which the heavens revolve around the Earth was backed not by sophisticated science but by authority. Of course, the absence of sophisticated science was a crucial factor in the ability of that faith to sustain itself. Still, the cultural view was that one learns about the heavens through biblical and ecclesiastical authority. Why? Because some things are mysteries that only God can reveal. Moreover, in the absence of the kinds of explanation that we now take for granted, it seemed self-evident even to intelligent people of the time that the heliocentric view of the universe was absurd. After all, anyone could plainly see the sun come up in the morning and go down in the evening in its daily rotation around the Earth. It ultimately took someone of Galileo's intelligence and diplomatic skill to start the fissure that eventually caused the authority view to crumble. Doubt was first cast on old expectations by Copernicus, but the ultimate turn away from authority was made possible by Galileo. What he provided was a way of thinking that allowed people to make sense of things differently than they had before. Before they could turn to the heliocentric view, they literally had to have a different way of making sense of the difference between night and day. This is what Galileo and his telescope provided.

This change in thinking was huge. It not only opened up many new questions about the size and nature of the universe, it freed human inquiry from its religious and metaphysical chains. The effect on intellectual ambition was enormous, and the advances, especially in physics, during the Enlightenment were the immediate results. The central change was from dour devotion to authority to giddy confidence in method. To borrow from Shakespeare: the method's the thing. It was the discovery of method – not the particular change from the Ptolemaic to the Copernican system – that was the more central revolution in thought.[1] What was discovered was that there is a method of inquiry that can yield great intellectual dividends. The ensuing success ensured that for the West, the rationalist turn away from authority regarding matters of fact was complete.

Looking back from the middle of the twentieth century, Isaiah Berlin characterized the brimming confidence of the Enlightenment in terms of three central principles.[2] The first is that all genuine questions can be answered: if a question cannot be answered, it is not a genuine question. What leaders of the Enlightenment meant by this was not that we have all the answers, but that if there is not some truth about a matter, then there can be no real question about it. The second principle is that all these answers are knowable. What they meant by this was that we have the methods whereby we can eventually get the answers, and that there are no genuine questions about matters that are inaccessible by these methods. The third principle is that all answers must be compatible with each other. Truth is a unity and knowledge a seamless web; otherwise, all is chaos. Intellectual disorder is the

[1] See Arthur O. Lovejoy, *The Great Chain of Being* (Cambridge, Massachusetts: Harvard University Press, 1936 and 1964), 99–143, for a correction to the standard view that the medieval mind saw the universe as so human-centered that the major effect of heliocentrism was a sense of how small and insignificant the Earth might be in comparison to the rest of the universe.

[2] See Isaiah Berlin, *The Roots of Romanticism*, edited by Henry Hardy (Princeton, New Jersey: Princeton University Press, 1999), 21–2.

result of ignorance, superstition, or lack of intelligence in employing rational methods. The goal of the Enlightenment was to advance as close as possible to a kind of intellectual utopia in which ignorance and superstition about matters of fact are replaced by a seamless web of beliefs verified by rational methods. This is a far cry from the religious attitude of the scholastic era of devotion to biblical authority and spiritual contemplation. If you want truth, you will have to earn it through rigorous rational methods; it will not come through prayer and grace.

The rigors of inquiry require the mastery of method, but once mastered, the methods are more than worth the effort. Moreover, they are available to anyone who has the character, intelligence, opportunity, and resources to employ them. In this sense, they are universal and democratic. All that they require in addition to intelligence, opportunity, and resources are the intellectual virtues, the most cardinal of which is an impartial mind, one willing to go wherever the methods of inquiry lead. Such was the new attitude toward matters of fact.

As to matters of value, transition was a bit slower but nonetheless certain. Discovering the power of human intelligence and rational method, it did not take long for thoughts of moral liberation from authority to engender an optimism about rational solutions to moral problems that paralleled the euphoria over the scientific method. Galileo himself remained a devoted Catholic in religion and ethics to the end.[3] But Hobbes and Locke and the full cast of moral and political thinkers of the Enlightenment soon set a new goal of inquiry: just as Galileo had made new sense of the difference between night and day, they would now make new sense of the difference between right and wrong. If the questions of morality were genuine questions, as they surely were, then the answers were knowable and accessible through an impartial method of inquiry. Moreover, since truth is a unity, there must be moral truths that are universally accessible to all those who have the intelligence, opportunity, resources, and character to pursue them employing a rigorous, impartial method of inquiry. Just as theoretical reason is governed by the principle of sufficient reason, there must be some analogue governing practical reason. Unless reason is ubiquitous in both theory and practice, the moral and intellectual hopes and expectations of the Enlightenment are

3 See Dava Sobel, *Galileo's Daughter* (New York: Walker & Company, 1999).

unthinkable. Christianity had its heaven, and modernity must have its utopia. Such was the orthodoxy of the new era. And so, for many, does it remain.

Some people once argued that science is possible only on the assumption that reason is ubiquitous in the sense that the principle of sufficient reason is true, that is, that every event has a cause and every matter of fact an explanation. Others now argue that we know from science that this is not true. Why? Because we can know what would have to be the case for the principle of sufficient reason to be false, and we know as a matter of fact, by using rigorous scientific methods, that this is the case. Of course, if the principle of sufficient reason is false, there must be something that makes it false. So, no matter what one thinks of theoretical reason as far as its ubiquity goes, it is important to ask whether it could be false, and, if so, what would make it so. There is, then, no valid way of insulating confidence in the ubiquity of theoretical reason against doubt by making the principle of sufficient reason an a priori truth.

Something similar is true regarding beliefs about practical reason. Some people believe that practical reason is ubiquitous. They believe that for every situation involving choice that any person faces, there is always at least one response that can be justified by a reason.[4] It is this belief that is the practical analogue to the role of the principle of sufficient reason regarding matters of fact. Of course, if every physical event has a causal explanation and every human action can have a rational justification, then reason is ubiquitous, both theoretically and practically. In some sense, then, people who believe in the ubiquity of both theoretical and practical reason believe in the possibility of a perfectly ordered universe. This is the most basic and fundamental form of Enlightenment hope: a world that is friendly to human reason.

Ultimately, much of the negative reaction to this hope and many of the attempts in the nineteenth and twentieth centuries to dash it are misguided by a Romantic ideal. Nevertheless, in the end, the Enlightenment hope is badly misplaced and undermined by the

4 See Donald Regan, "Value, Comparability, and Choice," in *Incommensurability, Incomparability, and Practical Reason*, edited by Ruth Chang (Cambridge, Massachusetts: Harvard University Press, 1997), 129–50.

truth. Ultimately, I will argue, it is a version of the pernicious fantasy that renders invisible tragic loss that we cannot afford to have concealed. At any rate, intellectual honesty and human experience require that we question it. We should not take a religious or political attitude toward the ubiquity of practical reason but ask whether it could be false, and, if so, what could make it so. Of course, we then should ask whether the conditions that could make the ubiquity claim false actually obtain. It seems to many that it is highly implausible from the start that practical reason is ubiquitous. What would make anyone think prior to inquiry that it is? Surely, it is not a necessary truth that in every practical context there is always something one can do that is justified by a reason. What is there about the universe and the place of humanity in nature that would lead anyone to think that the conditions for human life would be that neat? What is it that we know about human psychology that would lead us even to entertain such optimism? What follows is a preliminary account of what makes it false that practical reason is ubiquitous and what makes some kinds of tragic experience possible. The short answer, as already indicated, is that sometimes values are incomparable. This chapter will provide a preliminary sketch of what incomparability is. Confidence in one hope must wane before a new hope can emerge.

The object here is to say enough about what incomparability might be to call into question the ubiquity of practical reason. In later chapters, I will argue that such incomparability does obtain and is more pervasive than we want to believe; I will show abstractly where it obtains in the structure of our values; and I will illustrate concretely how it tragically appears in our contemporary lives.

So what might incomparability be such that it could undermine practical reason?

It has to do with vagueness, but not in the way that current philosophers treat vagueness and value. Current debates about vagueness and incomparability treat the issue as largely an issue in the semantics and metaphysics of value. On this approach, arguments for incomparability go in one direction, and arguments for vagueness go in another, making the two kinds of argument mutually exclusive.

The arguments center on what philosophers have called the trichotomy thesis, which asserts that for any pair of value bearers, A and B, A is either better than, worse than, or equal to B relative to some covering value.[5] A covering value is simply a value in terms of which practical options are compared. When choosing a dessert, I might make the choice between cake and pie in terms of taste. Taste would be the covering value. Or I might choose on the basis of diet, or cost, or even something else. Whatever the covering value for the choice is, the trichotomy thesis asserts that there are only three value relations that can obtain between the cake and the pie (or anything else) in regard to any covering value. One of the options is either better than, equal to, or worse than the other. The idea is simple but fundamental; there are only three general types of value relations that can obtain between practical options: the superiority relation, the equality relation, and the inferiority relation. And recall that it is in terms of these relations that we distinguish different forms of tragic choice. When evil is chosen over the good, there is a loss of the superior and better to the inferior and worse. When the lesser good is chosen over the greater good, the same thing occurs to a different degree. When the greater good is chosen over the lesser good, the superior good is gained but the inferior good is lost, which might still be of tragic significance. And even where we choose between options that are equally good, what is lost in the good forgone might not be included in the good that is gained. So the trichotomy thesis is crucial to understanding different forms of tragedy that can occur. It is also crucial to understanding the very possibility of rational comparative choice between options. Being rational means choosing what is best or at least as good as any other option in the circumstance of comparative choice. These are simple but fundamental thoughts about both tragedy and practical reason.

Yet, despite the immense plausibility of the trichotomy thesis, many contemporary philosophers, including myself, reject it, and a great deal of real importance to how we are to think of our values turns on this issue. It is not a mere "academic" debate, but one of crucial importance to contemporary culture, as I hope to show.

Current philosophers who reject the trichotomy thesis tend to give one of two different kinds of arguments. On the one hand, incomparability arguments assert that for some such pair of value bearers,

5 See Ruth Chang, "Introduction," in *Incommensurability, Incomparability, and Practical Reason*, 4.

the trichotomy thesis is false.[6] On the other hand, arguments from vagueness assert that for such a pair of value bearers, the trichotomy thesis is indeterminate, that is, it is neither true nor false.[7] Since the trichotomy thesis cannot in the same instance be both false and indeterminate, the arguments are mutually exclusive.[8] Those who are metaphysically inclined on this issue then find themselves wondering what the semantic debate says about realism and the metaphysical status of value. There, as in so many cases involving metaphysics, the debate bogs down. In contrast to this, I offer a better, less metaphysical way of conceptualizing the problem that employs a kind of argument from vagueness to get the conclusion of incomparability without attempting to square the circle.

In making sense of how incomparability could obtain because of vagueness, I will use two notions of incomparability and a different notion of vagueness than the one employed by the advocates of indeterminacy. The difference between my approach and that of other philosophers is that other philosophers frame the issue metaphysically and semantically, whereas I frame the issue as being more empirical and psychological.

To motivate the need for such a view, suppose you believe that our very ability to make rational choices between practical options turns on our ability to compare the importance of the options, that is, to determine whether one is more important than, less important than, or equally important as the other. Call this the tracking thesis. The thought is that practical reason tracks our ability to compare the importance of practical options. Now suppose you believe that

[6] Joseph Raz is perhaps the leading advocate of this kind of argument. See his *The Morality of Freedom* (Oxford: Clarendon Press, 1986) and his "Incommensurability and Agency," in *Incommensurability, Incomparability, and Practical Reason*, 90–109.

[7] John Broome is the leading advocate of the argument from vagueness. See his "Is Incommensurability Vagueness,?" in *Incommensurability, Incomparability, and Practical Reason*, 67–89. See also his book *Weighing Goods* (Oxford: Basil Blackwell, 1991) for further discussion of incommensurability.

[8] Ruth Chang wants to defend the notion of parity, which she says is a comparative relation distinct from the usual three. See Chang, "Introduction" 23–7. She defends this further in "The Possibility of Parity," *Ethics* 112 (July 2002): 659–88. In this way, she rejects the trichotomy thesis in favor of what we might call a quadrochotomy thesis, which asserts that A might be better than, worse than, equal to, or on a par with B. I believe that the parity relation is just a form of equality. If so, then we are back to the trichotomy thesis.

practical reason is ubiquitous, that is, you believe that there is no context in which if we deliberate properly under favorable epistemic conditions, where we have all the information relevant to the choice, we cannot come to a rational choice in the sense that we have a comparative reason for doing what we decide to do. (In some cases, this reason might be no more than that we have equally good reasons for doing one thing rather than another.) If you believe both the tracking thesis and the ubiquity thesis, then you believe that in principle rational choice is always possible because in principle comparison is always possible. The trichotomy thesis, then, is a claim about the limited number of comparative choices you have between options. But suppose you believe, as I do, that the tracking thesis is true but that the ubiquity thesis is false. What you must believe is that the ubiquity thesis is false because of a failure regarding comparability; otherwise, practical reason does not track comparability. You must then reject the trichotomy thesis, and I do because I believe it is false. Though this may seem just an abstract academic issue, it turns out to be crucial to understanding the structure of our values and our experience of tragedy in the twentieth and twenty-first centuries. Whether we can make sense, then, of the tracking thesis being true and the trichotomy thesis (and thereby the ubiquity thesis) being false is crucial to understanding the problem of tragedy and whether pernicious fantasy is fantasy after all, rendering invisible losses that we cannot afford to ignore.

How are we to do this?

First, there are two notions of incomparability at work here, one semantic and the other psychological. Moreover, one explains the other. The more fundamental notion is the psychological notion. The trichotomy thesis, I believe, is false rather than true or indeterminate. So I reject a certain account of vagueness, the semantic notion of indeterminacy. The crucial question is this: if the trichotomy thesis is false, what makes it false? The answer is that it is false just because even under favorable epistemic and psychological conditions, rational people cannot always compare the value of options in a way that allows them to choose.[9] Incomparability in this sense is not fundamentally

[9] I assume here the standard view of favorable epistemic and psychological conditions. Favorable epistemic conditions are conditions that allow us to determine all the relevant facts and logical relations. Favorable psychological conditions are conditions that exclude any kind of psychological encumbrance that would prevent a rational consideration of the relevant options.

a semantic fact or a fact about normative language at all. It is a fact about our higher-order valuing capacities. We care about things and value them in a variety of ways. We sometimes value one thing more than another; we sometimes value one thing less than another; and we sometimes value two things equally. But sometimes we value two things in a way that renders choice between them impossible because we cannot value them in a way that makes one of them superior, inferior, or equal to the other. These are comments about our higher-order valuing capacities. They are comments about our psychology. If the trichotomy thesis is true, it is true in virtue of some nonsemantic fact about our higher-order valuing capacities as practical reasoners. Similarly, if the trichotomy thesis is false, it is false because of some nonsemantic fact about our higher-order valuing capacities as practical reasoners. So, on the one hand, it makes perfect sense to assert that the trichotomy thesis, the ubiquity thesis, and the tracking thesis are true if we believe that when the higher-order valuing capacities of practical reasoners fail to determine choice, this is only because of unfavorable epistemic or psychological conditions of choice. On the other hand, by parity of reasoning, it makes perfect sense to say that the tracking thesis is true but that the trichotomy thesis and the ubiquity thesis are false if we believe that sometimes under favorable epistemic and psychological conditions, practical reasoners cannot choose. Just as the ubiquity of psychological comparability would explain the truth of the trichotomy thesis and the ubiquity thesis, the failure of psychological comparability would explain the falsity of the trichotomy thesis and the ubiquity thesis and establish the semantic point against vagueness as indeterminacy.

Before turning to the notion of vagueness that I believe is at work in incomparability, one source of objection must be removed. As Ruth Chang has pointed out, there is a difference between incomparability and noncomparability.[10] Noncomparability obtains when a covering value does not apply between two value bearers. Concepts and cookies do not compare in taste, simply because they are not both the sorts of things that can be tasted. This is noncomparability. Incomparability would have to involve a case in which the covering value applies but the options cannot be compared in regard to it. Incomparability in

[10] See Chang, "Introduction," 27–34.

this sense just is the inability of a practical reasoner to choose under favorable epistemic and other psychological conditions.

Think of love and its different forms. We sometimes love two people equally. With our children, this is often the case. Our children sometimes ask which we love most, and we have no trouble saying that we love them all equally. The same is sometimes, but not always, true about our love for our friends. But there are clear cases where we love two people unequally, and this is sometimes because we love them in different ways. One might really love one's neighbor (a member of one's community), but, comparatively speaking, we have no hesitation in saying that we love our children more than our neighbors. These are cases in which comparison is clear and unproblematic. Now consider choosing between saving the life of your spouse and the life of your child or parent. It might be very clear that you love one more than the other, but it is anything but clear that this would always be so or that you would love them equally. For most of us, our love for our children is distributed equally among them but superior to our love for our neighbors. But which is superior in general: our love for our children, our love for our spouses, or our love for our parents? This question is much harder to answer. Imagine that you dearly love your parents, you dearly love your spouse, and you dearly love your children. Which do you love more, and which in this sense is superior in terms of love? Notice that life can put us in a position of having to answer this question. This means that the relation between the value bearers is not that of noncomparability. Moreover, the psychological anxiety the question generates when taken seriously presents at least a preliminary case for incomparability. Why so? Because it suggests that there are contexts in which we could not choose. If this occurs under propitious epistemic and psychological conditions, then this just is a case of incomparability in the psychological sense. It is not a case of noncomparability.

One consequence of this way of conceptualizing the matter is that the issue of incomparability should turn on evidence. And that evidence should turn on what our higher-order valuing capacities are under favorable epistemic and psychological conditions, not on the semantics of normative language or metaphysical speculation.

Some might worry that to have to make a choice between saving one's child or one's spouse would itself impose unfavorable psychological conditions. True, the worry might go, one might be unimpeded epistemically – one might know all the relevant facts – but the stress of the choice itself would count as an unfavorable psychological condition.

This cannot be the case.

Not all forms of being under stress can count as a psychological encumbrance. The values that eventuate the choice are themselves such that they bring the stress. Important things are at stake. Which will it be? These are the very components of any important choice. Only stress that blinds one to what is at stake or independent psychological factors that precede the choice situation can count as unfavorable psychological encumbrances. The stress that is brought by the conflict of the values at stake cannot.

Of course, psychological forces other than stress may be at work. There may be character flaws like self-deception or weakness of will. Unlike the forms of stress that issue from the values at stake, these must count as encumbrances, the former with an epistemic dimension not found in the latter. Moreover, it cannot be denied that self-deception is often an understandable mechanism for rendering tragic loss invisible and thereby psychologically bearable. The problem is that the invisibility provided by self-deception often conceals what must at some point be faced, compounding the tragedy by delaying the recognition of what must be seen for what it is. But be this as it may, no one, on reflection, would want to claim that all cases of inability to decide are attributable to self-deception. On the contrary, self-deception often explains why people can decide. By blinding people to what is at stake, self-deception allows choice to proceed unproblematically in situations where we would expect it to be problematic.

There remains weakness of will. One might think that in every decision context any person who does not suffer from a lack of relevant information, self-deception, or some other psychological condition that distorts what is at stake knows clearly how much she values one thing in regard to another and that if she cannot decide, she suffers from weakness of will. For example, consider the awful choice cruelly imposed by a Nazi officer on the protagonist of William Styron's novel *Sophie's Choice*. Sophie was forced to choose which of her two children would have to go to the ovens and which to a labor camp with some small chance of survival. Suppose she could not see any way to choose between them in terms of their comparative importance. It might still be thought that she had a way of making a comparative choice, namely, that it is better to arbitrarily choose between them than not to choose. This would at least give one of the children a chance to live, and that is better than having both of them die for certain. But suppose such a thought could not direct her to choose. Does it follow that she was suffering from weakness of will to do what was better, however understandably difficult? That would certainly be one kind of tragic choice, one that we should not take lightly. Moreover, it makes no appeal to the issue of incomparability, but only to the understandable difficulty of doing what is best in horrible circumstances.

But couldn't Sophie be trapped between the thought that it is better to try to save one of her children than to let both die and the thought that it is best for both to die given the slight odds that one would survive and the fact that the other would feel betrayed by her choice? If so, her inability to choose would not be weakness of will but the inability to compare the options. If it is the latter, then to insist on weakness of will is to conceal a kind of tragic loss that is different from the kind incurred where weakness of will is at work. Conceptually, these are two clearly distinct possibilities.

If Sophie's case is not convincing, consider the following question that I will use to haunt the reader from time to time: just how many decent people is your most cherished loved one worth to you? If you had the awful and inescapable responsibility of saving your loved one or some number of other decent people – individuals who are no better or worse as persons than your loved one – what would be the mathematical equation for the choice? Certainly, even where the probabilities for saving the other people are to some degree in their favor, the ratio would not be 1:1: one loved one for one equally worthy person. Nor would it be 1:2 or anything close to it. Yet at some point, if you care about both your loved one and these other people in the way that we normally do, the numbers on the right of the equation would build to the point that your loved one would have to be sacrificed. To save the rest of humanity, for example, most of us feel that we would have to sacrifice our most cherished loved one. That such a sacrifice is something that we might lack the will to do, even in the face of a clear comparison, is understandable. But are there not other kinds of cases? Is there no grey zone in which it is not weakness of will that prevents us from making the choice but the inability to judge that the numbers are sufficient for the sacrifice? Could we not be trapped between the thought that the numbers are sufficient and the thought that they are not without suffering from weakness of will or being forced to the conclusion that we have yet to understand just what the mathematical formula for such choices is? This is the kind of question that must haunt those who would deny incomparability.

The difficulty is that of understanding why anyone would believe that weakness of will must be at work in cases like these. Is this supposed to be a conceptual truth? If so, what is the analysis of the cases that shows incomparability to be impossible and weakness of will necessary? Of course, if practical reason is ubiquitous and these other conditions obtain, then Sophie suffers from weakness of will, and so do you when you cannot decide how many other worthy people your most cherished loved one is worth. But whether practical reason is ubiquitous is the very issue at stake. Ubiquity, therefore, cannot be a criterion for settling whether ubiquity obtains. This would be somewhat like refuting Galileo by pointing out that the sun rises and falls. So the only way that the ubiquity thesis could be falsified and for the tracking thesis to be true is for something to count against comparability. The crucial question is, What must incomparability be?. The answer given here is that incomparability just is the inability to choose under favorable epistemic and psychological conditions. One cannot eliminate this possibility with an a priori commitment to the view that if a person cannot decide it must be because of a lack of information, a psychological encumbrance, or a character flaw. To insist on this is to insist on a conceptual scheme that necessarily conceals what is clearly a possibility, and as I will later argue, a fact of our lives. If this is right, then to insist, no matter what, on a conceptual scheme that construes the inability to decide when epistemic and psychological conditions are favorable as necessarily being due to a character flaw is to nurture a fantasy for the solace it provides, which, ironically, is itself a character flaw, a form of philosophical self-deception that renders invisible tragic losses that it would be better for us to see and understand for what they are. And if we refuse to make visible what we realize must be seen, it is again ironic that we will be preserving a conceptual scheme because of the weakness of will to do what is understandably difficult but better.

But if incomparability just is the inability to decide under favorable epistemic and psychological conditions, what role can vagueness play in explaining it? It cannot play the role assigned to it by the advocates of semantic indeterminacy. Otherwise, semantic incomparability could not obtain. Therefore, if vagueness plays a role, it must be a different notion of vagueness than the semantic notion. I will argue that there is a kind of vagueness – value vagueness, I will call it – that explains psychological incomparability. It explains why we cannot always, even under favorable epistemic and psychological conditions, determine choice. If there is such vagueness, then the trichotomy thesis is false because such vagueness prevents choice under favorable conditions, and the pernicious fantasy that there is a rational reconciliation of all our values is indeed a fantasy.

What kind of vagueness, then, is value vagueness?

Consider both an analogy and a disanalogy with a case involving perception. You are driving in a rainstorm that worsens as you drive, making it more and more difficult for you to see well enough to continue. At first, but with some difficulty, you can make out what you are approaching as you drive ahead. For example, you can vaguely see a person on the side of the road, but you cannot tell whether it is a man or a woman. As the rain increases and as you continue to drive, you vaguely see something on the side of the road, but you cannot tell whether it is an animal or a person. Just a bit later, you vaguely see an object but cannot tell whether it is animate or inanimate or whether it is in the road or beside it. Finally, your vision is so impaired that you can only vaguely tell where the road is, and so you decide to pull over and wait for a change in the weather.

Certainly, the notion of vagueness in all these cases makes perfect sense; yet clearly none of the cases implies the linguistic vagueness of semantic indeterminacy. Suppose as you drove along you guessed at whether the first object was male or female, whether the second was an animal or a person, and whether the third was inanimate or animate, in the road or beside it. The propositions that express the guesses would all be straightforwardly true or false rather than indeterminate. Vagueness here is not a feature of language but of perception, a capacity of your cognitive psychology. When we are not in favorable conditions for perception, we sometimes perceive vaguely in the sense that we can determine some things about the object but not others.

When the weather clears, so to speak, the vagueness evaporates with the clouds. Our perceptual capacities can then determine unproblematically beliefs about objects in the world.

With valuing, things are both similar to and different from perception. The similarity with the perception case is that if our ability to compare is impeded enough, we cannot choose, just as we cannot continue to drive when the rain impedes our perceptual abilities past a certain threshold. Sometimes our valuing abilities are impeded by unfavorable epistemic or psychological conditions. For example, sometimes we cannot compare one wine to another because we have not tasted one, or because we have tasted both but with our taste buds under the influence of another powerful taste. At other times, we cannot compare one wine to another because we are so preoccupied with problems at work that we cannot pay attention. These are cases of incomparability that are due to epistemic or psychological impediments. They are cases in which we cannot tell how important the options are to us because our higher-order valuing capacities are not working under favorable conditions. Just as vagueness of perception is the inability to tell with enough precision *what* something is, vagueness of value is the inability to tell with enough precision *how important* something is to choice. In the cases in question, we value vaguely due to unfavorable epistemic and psychological conditions of choice, but when the conditions return to a favorable state, we can compare–we can tell how important the options are – and make the choice. In these cases, the vagueness of value can be treated somewhat like the perception case of vaguely seeing something on the road ahead.

Now for the difference. Sometimes we value vaguely under favorable circumstances. Despite the fact that we have adequate information and are not psychologically encumbered, we know *that* the options are important to our choice; we know *why* they are important to our choice; but we cannot tell *how* important they are to our choice.

Moreover, not knowing how important two things are to our choice is not so much a matter of knowing as a matter of feeling. It is simply the felt inability of one's forms of caring about the objects of choice to resolve choice. Conversely, knowing how important two things are to our choice is the felt ability of one's forms of caring about the objects of choice to resolve choice. Put another way, knowing how important two things are to choice is the felt integration of the objects of choice into a projected and coherent future or way of life; not knowing how important two things are to choice is the felt inability to integrate the objects of choice into a projected and coherent future or way of life. What one is doing in forming a practical decision is trying to resolve a problematic situation that has arisen in the context of one's life in a way that allows one to proceed into the future. That is what practical reason is about. To lose sight of this fact, which is something that occurs all too often among philosophers, is to lose sight of what issues are at stake in debates over our values. What makes the trichotomy thesis false is just this kind of psychological limitation on the ability of our higher-order valuing capacities to resolve certain kinds of conflicts among the things we care about. The incomparability of values just is this feature of our higher-order valuing capacities.

Consider an extension of the analogy. Imagine, what is no doubt true, that we sometimes fail to perceive something because of the structural limitations of our cognitive capacities.[11] For example, perhaps we misperceive the speed at which an object is traveling because we cannot detect certain light waves. People who are very good at hitting a baseball traveling at ninety miles per hour seem to have perceptual capacities that most of us lack. But imagine that if there were structural changes in our cognitive capacities there would then be things that the average person could perceive that even the most perceptive person currently among us cannot now perceive. A crucial question would be whether the structural changes would come at some perceptual cost. In some cases, they probably would. If we could see like hawks, we might not be able to see the range of colors we now see, and if we could hear like deer, music might lose its harmony. Analogously, consider the possibility that something similar is true of our valuing capacities. Perhaps the structure of our valuing capacities is such that though we are now unable to determine choice in some contexts that are epistemically and psychologically favorable, if there were certain structural changes in our psychology and in the way we care about things, then we could in those contexts determine choice. For this to be the case, there would have to be changes in our noncognitive psychology (in our feelings and emotions), in addition to whatever changes were involved in our cognitive capacities. Moreover, as with the case of perception, a crucial

[11] My thanks to Paul Davies for discussion on this point.

question would be whether the structural changes would come at some valuational cost. Would we lose forms of caring as we gained the ability to decide? If we could love like the Christian God and decide everything, could we care as we do now, or would the cost be too high? I believe it would.[12] Framed in this way, a well-formed thesis about the incomparability of values is a psychological thesis, a thesis about the structural features of our cognitive-affective-conative psychology.

If the incomparability of values is a psychological thesis, its truth will have among other kinds of explanation a neuropsychological one. And from what we already know about neuropsychology, the explanation will not be made just in terms of what we now call our cognitive capacities but in terms of our affective and emotional capacities as well. The old cognitive psychology modeled so much on computers has been superseded by one that takes the brain in its wholeness seriously. Moreover, the old neuroscience that focused almost exclusively on cortical analysis has been superseded by one that recognizes that the more ancient subcortical regions, especially the amygdala, are crucial to understanding both cognition and emotion. The reason that emotional capacities will play a central role is that our emotions are the basis for many (perhaps all) of our forms of caring and valuing. Consequently, some failures of comparison will not be like failures to detect relevant information or like failures to detect relevant differences in the objects of value, but failures of affective and emotional integration in incorporating the objects of our values into our lives. Failures of comparison at this level will be failures in which what we now call noncognitive elements of our psychology play a substantial role. Such failures of comparison will not be the *result* of a lack of integration, and lack of integration will not be the *result* of failures of comparison. Rather, failures of comparison *just will be* failures of the kind of emotional homeostasis requisite to choice, with the understanding that the failures occur under favorable epistemic and psychological conditions.

If this is right – and there is no a priori conceptual reason for thinking that it is not – then we should look to understand what both the comparability and incomparability of values are in terms of what we

12 I have argued this extensively in my book *Dignity and Vulnerability: Strength and Quality of Character* (Berkeley: University of California Press, 1997).

can learn about clinical psychology and neuropsychology. We should look to neuropsychology because we need to understand which neural systems and their functions are at work when comparison succeeds and which are at work when comparison fails. For example, if we know neurologically what counts as weakness of will as a response to stress, and if we know that a subject is not in that neurological state and is well informed and that other psychological variables are controlled, we have good empirical grounds for concluding that if the subject cannot decide, we have isolated neurological systems at work in cases of incomparability. We will then know more about what roles higher-order cognitive functions play and what roles various emotional functions play in our higher-order valuing capacities.

We should look to clinical psychology for several reasons. Very generally, we need a concept of what it is for a psychological system to be in a state analogous to biological homeostasis. Since clinical psychology deals with personality disorders in which personality is disintegrated in various degrees, it deals with the kinds of phenomena crucial to this enterprise. Protracted inability to choose is just the kind of state that has the kinds of clinical dimensions suited to clinical psychology. More specifically, we need clinical psychology in order to diagnose subjects and classify them on behavioral criteria so that they can be studied by neuropsychologists. In addition to the ususal clinical diagnostic classifications of depression and schizophrenia and the like, we need the clinical psychological means of diagnosing self-deception and weakness of will. We need to be able to observe behavior and on those observations have good empirical reasons for at least some broad classifications of different levels of personality integration and disintegration, some of which have been of traditional interest to philosophers. We need then to match those broad clinical classifications with corresponding neurological analyses. In so doing, we will be mapping the neurological bases for human souls and their values. If this is right, comparability and incomparability are more like feelings that attend psychological states involving the emotions than thoughts that constitute or produce them. Ultimately, neuropsychology will either confirm or disconfirm this by isolating the neurological systems involved in emotion. If neuropsychology ultimately confirms the existence of incomparability, then we will have one aspect of the Enlightenment disconfirming another aspect. Science will have disconfirmed the ubiquity of practical reason and will have shed light on the neurological underpinnings of our tragic sense.

For now, however, why think, as was suggested earlier, that the ubiquity thesis is implausible from the start?. There are two reasons. First, it seems utterly implausible that our psychology would have been so fine-tuned by evolution that no matter what variations occur in the human environment, we would be psychologically equipped to integrate ourselves in such a way as to have a response. That we would be equipped so as to allow for sufficient integration to beat out our rivals reproductively is one thing; that we would be equipped to beat out all rivals in all possible environments is another. Moreover, it is doubtful that any creature that could beat out any possible rival would be one that we, with our current psychology, could look upon with favor. There is also the further possibility, which itself has some plausibility, that the current limitations of our integrative capacities, which include our limitations to compare our values, are actually crucial to our having beaten out the rivals we have actually had. It may be, after all, that what allows for ubiquitous integration is a simpler rather than a more complex psychology than ours. Some of our evolutionary ancestors were specialists in the sense that they were designed to succeed in a special kind of environment. It is doubtful that they were capable of the psychological stress that can befall us. But, then, it seems to be the fact that we are not specialists that led us to victory over those ancestors. On the other hand, if we are ever pitted against the common roach for survival, we will likely lose, but it will not be because their psychologies are more complex than ours.

The second reason the ubiquity thesis seems implausible is that it seems quite clear that we are in fact sometimes unable to decide under favorable conditions of choice. Like deer caught in the headlights of a car, we are transfixed by our options, compelled by the necessity of choice, but at the mercy of chance. This is one source of both tragedy and hysteria – the desperation of reason's grief, which will be the subject of much that is to follow in later chapters.

It will not do, then, to object, as Donald Regan has, that if incomparability were true some choices would be unintelligible to us.[13] Why? Because some choices are unintelligible to us, which is why we cannot

[13] Regan, "Value, Comparability, and Choice."

make intelligible a formula that answers the question, How many decent people is a loved one worth? Reason's grief is the emotional expression of such unintelligible choice when the stakes are sufficiently high.

What I propose to do in Chapters 3 through 8 is to see how much of our tragic sense can be explained *without* appealing to incomparability. The point is to demonstrate, against exaggerated claims regarding the essential irrationality of life, how reliable comparative reason can be. It is also to illustrate the strengths and contributions of various theories of value and what we should learn from them. I begin with two theories, nihilism and pessimism. If either were true, despair rather than grief should be reason's response to our tragic condition. But the dashed hopes of the Age of Reason do not have to lead to an age of despair or self-pity. Or so I hope to show, beginning with the discussion of nihilism.

3

Nihilism

We have our highest dignity in our significance as works of art.

Friedrich Nietzsche, *The Birth of Tragedy*

To-morrow, and to-morrow, and to-morrow,
Creeps in this petty pace from day to day,
To the last syllable of recorded time;
And all our yesterdays have lighted fools
The way to dusty death. Out, out, brief candle!
Life's but a walking shadow; a poor player,
That struts and frets his hour upon the stage,
And then is heard no more: it is a tale
Told by an idiot, full of sound and fury,
Signifying nothing.

Shakespeare, *Macbeth*, act 5, scene 5

Dark values often loom in the shadows of desire. When they do, frustrated hopes and ambitions can lead to desperation only to reemerge to take a disguised but fatal form. Sometimes old lovers can make good friends, but often the attempt to simulate friendship where passion is lurking in one but not the other is just a desperate attempt to hang on and not let go of something that is past its time. When the truth sets in, things can then get ugly and mean before the loss is accepted for what it is. In this regard, there is a sense in which the rise and fall of both the Enlightenment and Romanticism is like the rise and fall of Macbeth. It is a witches' fable of blind ambition, leading inexorably to the birth of nihilism, a bastard child of extravagance and despair. In the case of the Enlightenment, the extravagance was the naive assumption that the liberation of the human intellect from religious authority would pave the way for human autonomy to usher in utopia. The despair was the wretched state of the cities that the technology and science of the Enlightenment made actual and that both Hugo and Dickens were to depict so bleakly. In the case of Romanticism, the extravagance was an inflated notion of the human will and its creative powers. The despair was the recognition that the human will is not up to the Romantic task of creating value and meaning ex nihilo. When the Romanticism of the nineteenth century confronted the horrors of the twentieth, its pathos soured and became the whimper that is nihilism. The recovery of what is good in both the Enlightenment and Romanticism – and there is much that is – must await an assessment of where they went wrong. For now, it is important to see how the exaggerations of Romanticism led to the nihilistic attempt to deny the first feature of our tragic sense, namely, that there is high value, that there are things that we value in a way that makes them worthy of deep commitment.

The importance of assessing Romanticism and its relationship to nihilism for the current project is hard to underestimate. Not only must these views be evaluated in terms of their implications for an account of tragic sensibilities, it is also important to see in what sense the view to be developed here, tragic pluralism, is distinct from traditional Romanticism. Why? First, because Romanticism asserts, as does tragic pluralism, that values are plural and conflicting and sometimes incomparable and that reason is anything but ubiquitous; and second, because, at least in its historical form, Romanticism is a project of massive self-deception and self-absorption for which tragic pluralism is intended as an antidote.

Isaiah Berlin said about the importance of Romanticism "that it is the largest recent movement to transform the lives and the thought of the Western world."[1] It was, he said, "the greatest shift in the consciousness of the West that has occurred . . . in the course of the nineteenth and twentieth centuries. . . ."[2] A revolution, he called it, comparable in

[1] Isaiah Berlin, *The Roots of Romanticism*, edited by Henry Hardy (Princeton, New Jersey: Princeton University Press, 1999), 1.

[2] Ibid., 1–2.

historical significance to the industrial, political, and economic revolutions of the modern era. He then set out to provide an understanding of what Romanticism was by tracing its origins and development. Something of the same will follow here, though in much less detail and tailored to current purposes.

As a reaction to the Enlightenment, Romanticism was a counterrevolution, and understanding it requires understanding what it opposed in the Enlightenment and what the Enlightenment opposed that Romanticism sought to restore. Much of the twentieth century can then be seen as an extension, though a negative one, of the Romantic movement. When the bloom was off the Romantic rose, nihilism was the result.

Any significant revolution or movement of lasting consequence constitutes an historical turn, a turn away from something and a turn toward something. As we have seen, the Enlightenment was a turn away from religion and authority and a turn toward reason and science. Many in France and England found this liberating, but others, especially in Germany (and later in England and still later in France) found it confining and alienating. Most fundamentally, what the Romantics found abhorrent about the Enlightenment was that it took, or sought to take, the mystery out of life. In seeking to understand the universe, it somehow, from the Romantic's perspective, reduced the universe to something ordinary. Bothered less by the awesome authority of God than by the irreverence of science, the Romantics focused their scorn on what they took to be the arrogant assumption that the ultimate truth about things is accessible to method. The method's the thing all right, thought the Romantics – the thing most wrong with the eighteenth century.

Each of the three central principles of the Enlightenment was the object of complete opprobrium. Are all genuine questions ultimately answerable because there is some objective truth about reality waiting to be discovered? No. Subjective, not objective, truth is at the heart of what matters. Is the truthful answer to all genuine questions accessible to the methods of human reason and experience? Just the opposite. Only trivial questions have answers that are accessible to the intellect. Science, then, can only be about the ancillary aspects of life. Ultimate questions, questions about ultimate reality and value, are not questions of the intellect at all but issues of the will. Is truth a unity and a seamless web? No. It is more like a storm than a placid lake, for clash and conflict are essential to the existence of will. Were truth a unity, will would not be possible. And the will's the thing. In this sense, Romanticism did not seek peace but a sword.

Of course, this is all very religious in its roots, which is why Romanticism was a counter-revolution, a return to a religious perspective – not the same perspective as the religion of scholasticism, but religious nonetheless – and it continues in many quarters to this day. As Berlin pointed out, Romanticism had its birth in German pietist soil. It was Kant, a railer against Romanticism, who provided a sophisticated intellectual opening for lesser thinkers to mount the assault on the intellect and to promote the glorification of the will. To be sure, Kant abjured the emotions and sang the praises of reason. He sought to reconcile the Enlightenment with religion by making faith, as Locke had suggested, a species of reason – and reason alone. But unlike his rationalist predecessors, Kant was to appeal to practical rather than theoretical reason as the basis for faith. Matters of faith cannot be settled by appeal to theoretical reason. This is a central Kantian message, one the Romantics heartily approved. The limitations of reason, Kant claimed to have shown, make room for faith. How so? Through the will. This, too, the Romantics were to approve. But, for Kant, the will is practical reason, the ability to legislate rational laws for self and others, and therein lies human freedom. Spirituality and the Enlightenment are reconciled through the categorical imperative.

This the Romantics rejected completely. The will is not practical reason; practical reason is the will. And at the heart of the will are the emotions, with their multiplicity, their conflict, their pain and sorrow, their ecstacy, their unpredictability, and their creativity – above all their creativity. We are what we feel and do, not what we think; and there can be no rational formula for what we feel and do. Though Hume also insisted that emotion and sentiment were at the heart of the will and that reason was only their servant, he thought that they could be rationally ordered. Hume, then, was just as blind to the ultimate nature of things as his Enlightenment counterparts. He lacked spirituality, as did Voltaire and Kant and all the rest of the Enlightenment crowd. They all placed their faith in the employment of a method that would reveal a formula for morality analogous to the laws of physics that Newton had discovered through the methods of science. What the Enlightenment thinkers could not understand was that life is ultimately spiritual and

that spirituality is the active life of the emotions under the creative expression of the will. Science and reason can neither understand nor express this. Spirituality is reborn as art. Just as scientists had replaced the priests of the ecclesiastical regime preceding the Enlightenment, the new priests of Romanticism were the artists. Germany had its composers, France its painters, and England its poets.

Within the Enlightenment, there was a division of labor in which scientists and artists had their own roles. It was the purpose of the aestheticians of the Enlightenment to clarify and above all to explain the nature of aesthetic experience and the proper role of the artist. Everything has an explanation, and the important thing to see was that the workings of the human mind, whether rational or aesthetic, are different but compatible. Just as the goal of science and rationality is truth, the goal of art is beauty (and the sublime). This theme emerges from the developments in aesthetics during the eighteenth century from Boileau through Shaftesbury, Addison, Hutcheson, Burke, Hume, Gerard, Lessing, Reynolds, Alison, and Kant.[3] When the developments in epistemology and metaphysics, in aesthetics, and in moral and political philosophy are considered, the eighteenth century reveals a conceptual scheme that reflects a deep confidence in the unity of truth, goodness, and beauty.

So deep was the confidence in the unity of truth, goodness, and beauty that it yielded almost a religious attitude toward human intellectual powers. Though the hymn is to God, one can easily imagine Browning's theistic confidence of the Victorian era applying in a humanistic version to eighteenth-century Enlightenment thinkers:

> The year's at the spring
> And day's at the morn;
> Morning's at seven;
> The hillside's dew-pearled;
> The lark's on the wing,
> The snail's on the thorn;
> God's in his heaven –
> All's right with the world![4]

3 Alexander Sesonske, ed., *What is Art? Aesthetic Theory from Plato to Tolstoy* (New York: Oxford University Press, 1965).

4 Robert Browning, "Songs from Pippa Passes," in *The Literature of England*, edited by George B. Woods et al., fourth edition (Chicago: Scott, Foresman, 1958), 657–8.

What God could create, the scientist could explain; what heaven could reward, the good person could deserve; and what nature could display, the artist could embellish. Moreover, there is no principled reason why a person of intelligence and talent cannot have knowledge, character, and taste. It was indeed believed that in the history of the mind, it was spring and the dew was still on the method. The liberation of the human mind was in its infancy. What truth, what goodness, what beauty lay in the future waited only the workings of the human intellect to provide.

Moreover, just as there is method to reveal truth and goodness, there is method to produce beauty. Of course, there is much more disagreement about method when it comes to goodness and beauty than with truth, and there is more disagreement about method regarding beauty than with goodness. Still, Enlightenment thinkers feel compelled to address the issue of what principles the artist employs to effect the beautiful and the sublime. They feel compelled to explain the marvels of human intellectual powers to appreciate and produce beauty. By the time this issue gets to Kant, the concept of genius is introduced to save the appearance of unity and the ubiquity of method. The artistic genius creates without rules but becomes a rule for others.[5]

The Romantics were to take up the genius motif and develop it. One of the ways in which they did was with the radical notion that truth is subjectivity, and genius the means of access to it. If objective truth is a matter of thinking the world as it is, subjective truth is a matter of feeling the world as it could be felt at the highest levels of feeling. The point of painting is not to copy nature but to feel it and to engage it aesthetically. Even a glance at David Friedrich's *The Wanderer above the Mists* or *Monk by the Sea* confirms this. Similarly with the other arts; the goal is not for the subject to cognize an object but to engage it emotionally. "Poetry," said Wordsworth, "is the spontaneous overflow of powerful feelings."[6] And speaking of the different functions of the language of reason and science on the one hand and of art and poetry on the other, Burke explained, "The one describes a thing as it is; the

5 Immanuel Kant, "From *The Critique of Aesthetic Judgement*," in *What is Art? Aesthetic Theory from Plato to Tolstoy*, 196–244.

6 William Wordsworth, "Observations Prefixed to 'Lyrical Ballads'," in *What is Art? Aesthetic Theory from Plato to Tolstoy*, 263.

other describes it as it is felt."[7] The true artist is the person who, without rules or formulas, is emotionally adept at living and at feeling the world rather than thinking it. Creative emotional expression, then, rather than patterned intellectual inquiry is at the heart of what matters.

Though there was much concern for the sublime, the significance of beauty to subjectivity played an important role in the evolution of the Romantic vision. Keats, of course, was famous for the last lines of "Ode on a Grecian Urn":

> When old age shall this generation waste,
> Thou shalt remain, in midst of other woe
> Than ours, a friend of man, to whom thou say'st,
> "Beauty is truth, truth beauty," – that is all
> Ye know on earth, and all ye need to know.[8]

And the opening lines of "Proem from Endymion ":

> A thing of beauty is a joy forever;
> Its loveliness increases; it will never
> Pass into nothingness; but still will keep
> A bower quiet for us, and a sleep
> Full of sweet dreams, and health, and quiet Breathing.[9]

The connection between beauty and truth as subjectivity is that the appreciation of beauty is the highest form of human reality. For Schopenhauer, the misery of life could never be compensated by pleasure. Were a hedonistic calculus used to measure the meaning and prospects of life, life would not be worth living. Pain avoided, then, is far more important than pleasure attained. Still more important is relief from both will and intellect through a kind of experience that is neither theoretical nor practical. This is the experience of beauty, an experience Schopenhauer thought was best had through music.[10]

For both Keats and Schopenhauer, beauty is the solution to a philosophical problem, the problem of suffering and tragedy. Were it not

7 Edmund Burke, From "Philosophical Inquiry into the Origin of Our Ideas of the Sublime and Beautiful," in *What is Art? Aesthetic Theory from Plato to Tolstoy*, 153.

8 John Keats, "Ode on a Grecian Urn," in *The Literature of England*, 281.

9 John Keats, "Proem from Endymion," in *The Literature of England*, 278.

10 Arthur Schopenhauer, *The Will to Live: Selected Writings*, edited by Richard Taylor (New York: Ungar, 1967).

for beauty, life would be unbearable. Beauty is the compensation for the pain, suffering, and tragedy of life. Both thinkers endorse the comparative judgment that on balance A contains more good than bad and B does not, where A is our world with its pleasure, its suffering, and its tragedy as well as its beauty, and B is our world with its pleasure, suffering, and tragedy but without its beauty.

The comparison is ambiguous and suggests two ways of understanding the relationship between beauty and tragedy on the Romantic view. The first way understands beauty as something experienced independent of tragedy that compensates for the suffering of life. Think of the experience of beautiful colors or the experience of a playful melody. There need be no recognition of tragedy or suffering when having these experiences. Indeed, such experiences offer relief from the tragic dimensions of life by deflecting the mind away from the practical to the aesthetic in a certain way. On this view, the experience of tragedy is one thing, the experience of beauty another. The second way of understanding the relationship between beauty and tragedy employs a notion of beauty that incorporates tragedy itself; that is, it employs a notion of tragic beauty. According to this view, what makes tragedy and suffering bearable is the beauty in it. Of course, not all suffering and tragedy involve beauty, but some does, and the Romantic goal is to live a life that, however tragic, is beautiful in virtue of its tragic dimensions. In this way, Romantic tragedy and beauty are essentially intertwined. For example, music that truly captures the beauty of life is played in a minor key.

Understanding Romantic tragedy, therefore, requires understanding what constitutes tragic beauty or what is beautiful about some tragic loss. Consider in this regard Goethe's *The Sorrows of Young Werther* (1774),[11] Schiller's *The Robbers* (1781),[12] and *Tristan and Isolde*,[13] both the medieval epic and Wagner's opera (1859). Though there are several Romantic themes (sometimes conflicting themes) that run through these works, it is instructive to draw attention only to those that bear on beauty and tragedy.

[11] Johann Wolfgang von Goethe, *The Sorrows of Young Werther: And Selected Writings*, translated by Catherine Hutter (New York: Signet Classics, 1962).

[12] Friedrich Schiller, *The Robbers and Wolstein*, translated by F. J. Lamport (New York: Penguin, 1979).

[13] Gottfried von Strassburg, *Tristan*, translated by A. T. Hatto (New York: Penguin, 1967).

One very important thing to note is that these works are all love stories, whatever else they are. In this regard, they emphasize a central theme of at least one branch of Romanticism, namely, that the most important things in life are personal. The cause of the revolution, the elimination of tyranny, the impersonal devotion to science, the realization of utopia – all pale in comparison to the significance of personal devotion and love. To be sure, the Romantic protagonist is often a rebel. Young Werther rebels against classical learning and the society of taste, against convention and constraint, and against aristocratic pretentiousness and class snobbery. And Karl Moor, in a more violent fashion, rebels against patriarchal dominance and the confining power of the state. As a rebel, the Romantic hero values freedom from the forces that inhibit and constrain a life of passion and creativity. But what is most common to Werther, Moor, and Tristan is that they are all lovers. They all believe, as Werther says in one of his letters, that: "Nothing justifies a man's existence like being loved."[14]

Moreover, from the Romantic perspective, the value of their lives is in the beauty of their love, even when their lives and loves are unavoidably tragic. That they love passionately and unrestrained by the prospects of loss is to be viewed as a beautiful work of art. Without the tragic dimensions of their love, their lives would not be beautiful in the way the Romantics saw these figures. Werther's suicide was romanticized as a creative expression of the value of passionate love and the capacity for being destroyed by unrequited affection. Moor's killing of Amalia and surrendering himself into the hands of the law was both an act of love and a rebellion against hatred, a rebellion that redeemed his life through love by making what beauty it could of a life so terribly lived. Romantics love their rebels, but they love their lovers more. This could not be clearer than in the lives and deaths of Tristan and Isolde.

Cheated by fate and tormented by divided loyalties, they refused to retreat from their love for each other (as well as for King Mark) despite the misery their love brought. Given their predicament, they could have accepted conventional alternatives in order to achieve tranquility in lieu of their passion for each other. Isolde could have resigned

[14] Goethe, *Werther*, 63.

herself to the lofty status of being queen, and Tristan could have settled for a substitute for Isolde by resigning himself to a marriage with a facsimile of his love, Isolde of the White Hands. But a central romantic tenet is "never settle." To have settled for Stoic tranquility over love would have been both cowardly and ugly. Without a moral formula and without conventional guidance, Tristan and Isolde became artists in constructing a narrative for their lives that reflected their deepest values in a way that radiated beauty. To miss the tragedy of their lives, then, is to miss the beauty in what matters most in life. This, I believe, is one of the most central themes of Romanticism. We must accept as fate that things matter to us personally, and we must give ourselves to our values passionately. We must then will to live beautiful lives in an often ugly world. In turning the suffering of the world into a tragic but beautiful work of art, we must be artists with near divine powers of creativity. No wonder the artists were the priests of Romanticism.

One of the things wrong with this is that artistic efforts, even by excellent artists, most often fail. Goethe's novel about young Werther, though beautifully written, is an excellent example of how to live a pathetic life, and pathetic lives are not beautiful. Of course, one of the reasons they are not beautiful is that they lack the kind of pathos that rises to the level of the tragic. Werther's suicide is ridiculous, and his attachment is infatuation rather than love. It is infatuation because it depends on false beliefs about an idealized Lotte, the object of his pathetic desire.

Goethe himself was shocked by the reaction to his novel. That young men in droves were dressing in blue coats and yellow trousers like those of Werther and that many were committing suicide were facts Goethe thought reflected a tendency in some more toward melancholy than toward authentic human feeling and passion.[15] Despite the veneration of Goethe by the Romantics, he seemed to have taken the view that Romanticism was a disease of shallow intellect and morbid personality.

It was a central feature of the romanticizing instinct to exaggerate the value of its objects. Indeed, Romanticism often seems to require false beliefs to sustain its passion. When recommending its version of an ideal emotional life – a life properly felt rather than

[15] Ibid., 132–55.

thought – the Romantic picture is that of a life lived either on the crest of a wave of passion or caught in the throes of reverie. Such an ideal puts tremendous pressure on the Romantic's belief system. What kinds of belief would it take to sustain an emotional life of that sort? Must I believe that my lover is the most beautiful to have ever lived to have a sustainable passion for her? Must I be incapable of smelling bad breath in the morning? Must I believe that, unlike others, she has eyes only for me? Must I believe that she is beneath the vices that tempt the rest of humanity? Must I believe that the poor are pure whereas the successful and talented are soulless and would do anything for their own advancement? Must I believe that humanity is neatly divided into the oppressors and the oppressed, between the good and the evil, between the beautiful and the ugly, between the conventional and the authentic, between youth and old age, between a golden age of the past and the shallow present, between benign nature and ominous technology? Must I be kept in ignorance of the fact that there was never a poet named Osian, though there was most surely one named Homer? Must I believe that every fit thrown by an artist is an expression of authenticity? Is a desire to have an emotional life dominated by a longing for purity and a dreamlike state in awe of the unattainable worth its cost in stupidity?

Sooner or later, the truth comes home to roost. This is a part of the Enlightenment that we cannot escape. When the truth does make itself painfully clear, the emotional life that is predicated on the denial of reality will collapse inwardly. And there is no artistic talent that can transform some of the ugly truths of life into beauty. It is not a power of the human will to deny some aspects of life indefinitely or to construct a tragic narrative about those facts as a story that radiates beauty. Moreover, the emotional response to these ugly facts is not reverie or even the passion of anger but horror and grief.

The Romantics were right to emphasize that the point is not simply to think or cognize life but to feel it. This is something about Romanticism that we must insist on as an important point about the human condition. But what is it to feel life rightly? Can one get it wrong, or is feeling life a matter entirely guided by one's imagination and will?

The fact is that one can get it wrong, and the bloody history of the twentieth century proves it. Consider in this regard two grand narrative views of history. The first is the product of Romanticism and has its lineage from Herder and Fichte through Wagner to the Third Reich. Herder believed that cultures were incomparable, that the conceptual schemes that defined different cultures could only be understood from within. According to Herder, we simply cannot understand what it was like to be a member of pre-Classical Greek culture. Each culture has its own set of values – its own music, its own painting, its own literature – and its own historical calling.[16] Fichte then called Germans to the task of realizing the uniquely German "spirit" and their own grand narrative.[17] Wagner dramatically added anti-Semitism, and Naziism had the seed and egg of its conception.[18] As we buried the fifty million people who died in the Second World War, we also buried the grand narrative view of national destiny.

The second version of the grand narrative view of history sheds nationalism in favor of a universal form of utopia, a relic of the Enlightenment. On this view, history is on a course to a utopia where human nature will find its rest. But utopianism is just as dead as Romantic nationalism. Both were killed by the facts. Eighty-six million people died during the twentieth century from the violence of war alone. That is a hundred people an hour for every hour of the twentieth century who have died from the violence of war.[19] And this figure does not count the death and suffering that came from other forms of human violence. If the Romantic nationalism that gave us Nazi Germany killed a certain form of sentimentality, the purges of Stalin, Mao, and Pol Pot killed whatever was left of the ambitions of Marxist socialism as the realization of an Enlightenment utopia. When confronted with these ugly facts, unrealistic expectations often exhaust a positive emotional response. How is a life aware of such unspeakable horrors to be properly felt or thought? If this is not an important philosophical question, it is difficult to see how any philosophical questions are of any importance.

[16] Johann Gottfried Herder, *Herder: Philosophical Writings*, edited by Michael Forster (Cambridge: Cambridge University Press, 2002).

[17] J. Gottlieb Fichte, *Addresses to the German Nation*, edited by R. F. Jones and G. H. Turnbull (New York: Greenwood, 1979).

[18] Gottfried Wagner, *Twilight of the Wagners*, translated by Della Couling (New York: St. Martin's Press, 2000).

[19] Jonathan Glover, *Humanity: A Moral History of the Twentieth Century* (New Haven, Connecticut: Yale University Press, 1999), 47.

One emotional response to the ugly facts of the twentieth century clings to the notion that our valuing is a matter of our choosing. This is the response of nihilism. The move from "never settle" to "nothing matters" is not as great as it might seem. When passion for life is predicated on the requirement that the object of passion be utterly pure, utterly perfect, and utterly grand and that anything less is nothing, there is no gap between the grand and the grim. So what is a person to feel? "Very little" is the answer of nihilism. Nothing is worth getting worked up over. "Don't get attached" is the creed of both Stoicism and nihilism. Of course, not getting attached is difficult. Stoics recommend that we either extirpate or compartmentalize our emotions in order to preserve our virtue, the only thing of any real value that is worthy of commitment. Nihilists go even further than the Stoics in recommending a pruning of our commitments. In this sense, nihilism is Stoicism minus a value. Nihilists scoff at the very notion of commitment. Nothing, not even virtue, is worth caring enough about to be committed to it. This is the very point of nihilism regarding attachment. The nihilist therefore retreats into amusing himself. Nihilism is the view that at its best life might be slightly amusing, but if one gets bored there is always suicide, which itself has neither Romantic nor tragic value. The nihilist is the person who has tried Stoic and Enlightenment rationalism as well as Romantic sentimentality and found them unsustainable in a way that leads to the life of amusement as the life both properly felt and properly thought.

Not so strangely, the priests of nihilism are also artists. Like Keats and Schopenhauer and other Romantics, the nihilist recommends an aesthetic response to suffering. But unlike the answer of Keats and the Romantics, his response is not the rapture of beauty or the awe of the sublime. Rather, facts are to be felt as either amusing or boring. Anything else is mere Romantic sentimentality. Keats and his clan were naive fools: art is not about beauty but about the cleverness of artists. The world does not matter. The object does not matter. Art is about art, not about anything beyond itself. Of course, as an amusement, art might entertain itself by rubbing the noses of Romantics and dreamers of utopia in the misery of the world. But be assured, calling attention to such misery is not the expression of social conscience but a creative way of passing time. More and more during the twentieth century, art is about the artist, until even that disappears. The turn to subjectivity in

Romanticism has run its radical course to the point that the art object is not about the world or anything beyond itself, nor is it an expression of the subjectivity of the artist. Rather, the meaning of each art object is determined by the creative subjectivity of the observer, who is guided in her response only by what she can find amusing. The message here is that aesthetic experience is all we have going that is worth anything, and that is not much. The most any of us can be is an artist conceived as a constructor of a reality for our own amusement. This is why much of the response of twentieth-century culture to its horrors is to turn to entertainment. We are all waiting for Godot, and in the meantime, the show must go on. The more ridiculous the show the better, because the ridiculous is the only thing left that we can bear to both think and feel. The theater of life in the twentieth century is the theater of the absurd, where the value of human existence never exceeds the entertainment value of David Letterman's Top Ten List or the night's stupid pet tricks. The unavoidable conclusion of nihilism is that our tragic sense is a relic of Romanticism and that nothing is worth the feelings that a tragic sense evokes.

Of course, this is all hyperbole: we are not left with a choice between the sentimentality of Romanticism and the detachment and self-pity of nihilism. Nihilists are as bad at logic as they are at art. We need a view of the life best felt and thought, and any adequate theory of value, including tragic pluralism, must meet this requirement. What we need if we are to be Romantics is a Romanticism properly tempered by some of the values of the Enlightenment. And what we need if we are to save some of the important features of the rational capacities valued so highly by the Enlightenment is the ability to feel life even in the light of the facts.

In this context, it is important to bear in mind that survivors of the Holocaust insist that we must never forget. We must remember. As Primo Levi put it:

> You who live safe
> In your warm houses
> You who find, returning in the evening,
> Hot food and friendly faces:
> Consider if this is a man
> Who works in the mud
> Who does not know peace

Who fights for a scrap of bread
Who dies because of a yes or no.
Consider if this is a woman,
Without hair and without name
With no more strength to remember,
Her eyes empty and her womb cold
Like a frog in winter.
Meditate that this came about:
I commend these words to you.
Carve them in your hearts
At home, in the street,
Going to bed, rising;
Repeat them to your children,
Or may your house fall apart,
May illness impede you,
May your children turn their faces from you.[20]

This is the imperative to think, to think the world as it was and is. We must see the facts. As Enlightenment thinkers would insist, there are facts about these matters that reliable methods of inquiry can, with hard work, reveal. First, there are the facts about what really happened, and second, there are facts about human social psychology that explain why these things happened.

Consider in this regard the recent research on the role of the ordinary German citizen in the atrocities of the Holocaust. What are the facts? What happened, and why? One claim about what happened is that ordinary citizens were kept at a psychological distance from the gruesome details of the slaughter, and that this explains how such wholesale slaughter could take place. The problem is that rational inquiry does not support either this account of what the facts were or the explanatory power of the causal hypothesis. Whatever the failings of Daniel Goldhagen's account of these matters in his book *Hitler's Willing Executioners: Ordinary Germans and the Holocaust*,[21] turn out to be, one thing is clear: many German citizens knew in detail through their own participation of what was going on. They knew, because they were doing it.

20 Primo Levi, *Collected Poems*, translated by Ruth Feldman and Swann Brian (London: Faber and Faber, 1988), 9.
21 Daniel Jonah Goldhagen, *Hitler's Willing Executioners* (New York: Knopf, 1996).

One member of Police Battalion 101 gives the following account of one incident:

These Jews were brought into the woods on the instruction of [Sergeant] Steinmetz. We went with the Jews. After about 220 yards Steinmetz directed that the Jews had to lay themselves next to each other in a row on the ground. I would like to mention now that only women and children were there. They were largely women and children around twelve years old.... I had to shoot an old woman, who was over sixty years old. I can still remember, that the old woman said to me, will you make it short or about the same.... Next to me was the Policeman Koch.... He had to shoot a small boy of perhaps twelve years. We had been expressly told that we should hold the gun's barrel eight inches from the head. Koch had apparently not done this, because while leaving the execution site, the other comrades laughed at me, because pieces of the child's brains had spattered onto my sidearm and had stuck there. I first asked, why are you laughing, whereupon Koch, pointing to the brains on my sidearm, said: that's from mine, he has stopped twitching. He said this in an obviously boastful tone....[22]

Another incident is recorded by an eyewitness perpetrator:

Meanwhile, Rottenfuhrer Abraham shot the children with a pistol. There were about five of them. There were children whom I would think were aged between two and six years. The way Abraham killed the children was brutal. He got hold of some of the children by the hair, lifted them up from the ground, shot them through the back of their heads and then threw them into the grave. After a while I just could not watch this any more and I told him to stop. What I meant was he should not lift the children up by the hair, he should kill them in a more decent way.[23]

A more decent way? What is more jarring about this report: the actions of the *Rottenfuhrer* or the strange sentiment expressed in the perpetrator's report? Just what is the decent way to murder a child? What is the psychology that makes room for worrying about brutality and retains a concern for decency but does not blink at genocide?

Then there is the famous photograph of a German soldier taking aim with a rifle no more than six feet away from a Jewish mother holding her child during the slaughter of the Jews of Ivangorod.[24]

[22] Ibid., 219.
[23] Ibid., 401.
[24] Ibid., 407.

The soldiers would take mothers and their children individually into the field and shoot them at point blank range. They would then return to repeat the process over and over. These were not soldiers fighting an armed and faceless enemy. And in the two incidents just described, trained soldiers were not involved at all. This gives some indication of what the perpetrators' actions were like.

But what about causal hypotheses to the effect that the Holocaust was made possible by the benign evil of bureaucratic distance or by the complicity of fear? If Goldhagen is even close to being right, these hypotheses fail to explain a great deal of what happened. The members of the police battalions responsible for the two incidents described here were not well-trained killers. Nor were they coerced into their behavior. The truth is that many ordinary citizens voluntarily and enthusiastically participated in the slaughter and humiliation of other human beings, including mothers and their children. Many of the perpetrators were parents themselves. What we need is an account – an account provided by the best scientific methods that have evolved since the dawn of the Enlightenment – of what makes human beings do these things. We need to know the truth about our social psychology and what we are capable of. This extends not only to the horrors of the Holocaust but, as Jonathan Glover has recently insisted, to those of the purges of Stalin, Mao, and Pol Pot and to other forms of violence as well.[25] To insist on this is to insist on seeing the facts and that there is such a thing as thinking the world wrongly.

Art can play a vital role. Sometimes the aim of art is fact and truth rather than beauty and fiction. What the Holocaust was like for both the perpetrators and the victims is best told, not by the propositions of historians, though these are very important, but by the photographic history of the period. One thing left out of the Romantic view of the artist's role is the sensuous representation of objective rather than subjective reality. The point here is that realist art is indeed art, and art of the utmost aesthetic importance. Ugly truths are best represented in their starkness, without a sermon. Some art, then, forces us to think the world as it is, to see it in its stark sensuous representation. One failure of Romanticism in its vision of art is that it fails to recognize this function.

[25] Glover, *Humanity: A Moral History of the Twentieth Century*.

But what is it to feel the world rightly after having thought it as it is? The Romantic has one answer, the nihilist another. Neither is remotely correct for the horrors we are considering. Our tragic sense tells us that neither of these recommendations for how to feel the world is right when it comes to some of our history. The history of human atrocities is not a narrative that radiates beauty. Though one might find beauty in the tragic lives of both Achilles and Hector, the warriors responsible for the atrocities we have considered did not live in a way that could be both truly thought and redemptively felt. The Holocaust is not to be romanticized, and it is a mistake to understand those who insist that we must never forget to be suggesting any such thing. What they are prescribing is the starkest form of realism. By contrast, the only thing worse than romanticizing the Holocaust is finding it amusing or boring. So neither the Romantic nor the nihilist is right about how to think and feel this aspect of life. The response to such tragedy ultimately takes not an aesthetic but a moral form.

How anyone can see and think much of the twentieth century as it was and not view it with horror is beyond any *moral* comprehension. Yet some people feel no horror at all, even when they know the facts and see the photographic history. Are they not lacking some emotional capacity in a way that we find disturbing? To what stimuli do their affective capacities lie in waiting to respond? Are they merely aesthetically dense, or does their emotional insensitivity lie elsewhere? Nihilism can only appeal to someone for whom the capacity for horror is absent. Yet coping with the horror of the twentieth century is among our greatest tasks. To forget, to refuse to think our history in its starkness, is unforgivable. To feel it without horror is inhuman. For to be human is to have a tragic sense that makes us vulnerable to the destructive effects of horror. What cannot be overemphasized is that horror is one form of ethical tragic effect.

Of course, the same point applies to other periods of our history and to the history of those other than ourselves. Some estimates of the cost in human lives of the African slave trade put the numbers in excess of eleven million.[26] Husbands and wives, children and parents

26 Hugh Thomas, *The Slave Trade* (New York: Simon & Schuster, 1997), 804–5.

would be sold to different owners, destroying forever the historical bonds between families that we all take for granted and that provide much of the basis of our personal identity. The lynchings that persisted in the American South well into the twentieth century, the devastating effects of apartheid in South Africa, the cruelties of the Japanese in the rape of Nanking, the ethnic cleansing in the Baltic states, the incalculable loss to millions of nameless women whose lives were truncated by suffocating views of gender, the vitriolic hatred perpetrated against homosexuals that sometimes left its victims beaten and bound to fences, abandoned to die alone – all are facts to be thought in their stark reality and to be felt with utter horror. Any theory of value, therefore, that fails to account for the fact that for humans some things are horrible beyond description is doomed to failure. Some things are neither beautiful nor amusing. For this reason, the unpardonable sin of nihilism and the art it generates is the cardinal sin of superficiality.

Finally, with both Romanticism and nihilism in mind, consider the enigmatic death of Primo Levi. Primo Levi was an Italian Jew who spent a year as a prisoner in Auschwitz, the last year before its liberation. A chemist both before and after the war, Levi turned to writing as a way of bearing witness to the horror of the Holocaust. His writings reveal that one of the most crucial aspects of survival for many in the camps was the commitment to survive and tell the story, to bear witness for the dead so that the world would never forget. The psychological costs of such a commitment were often enormous. What one would have to endure in physical pain and humiliation had to be reconciled with the larger purpose, the imperative to survive to tell the story. For many, yielding to death as a release – "to touch the electric fence" – was a constant temptation. But more threatening than humiliation was something much deeper. Humiliation comes with the appearance before others of being something less than what you are. This is a horrible thing. What is worse is to become less than what you can tolerate being in the privacy of your own thoughts. It is one thing to stand naked before the enemy; it is quite another to steal undetected a bread ration that might have saved a fellow prisoner from starvation. As Levi put it in his first book, "Whoever waits for his neighbour to die in order to take his piece of bread is, albeit guiltless, further from the model of thinking man than the most primitive pigmy or the most vicious sadist."[27] And later in verse, not long before his death:

> Once more he sees his companions' faces
> Livid in the first faint light,
> Gray with cement dust,
> Nebulous in the mist,
> Tinged with death in their uneasy sleep.
> At night, under the heavy burden
> Of their dreams, their jaws move,
> Chewing a nonexistent turnip.
> "Stand back, leave me alone, submerged people,
> Go away. I haven't dispossessed anyone,
> Haven't usurped anyone's bread.
> No one died in my place. No one.
> Go back into your mist.
> It's not my fault if I live and breathe,
> Eat, drink, sleep and put on clothes."[28]

Here is a threat to one's integrity different from humiliation. Yet one might have to endure either humiliation or the dangers of self-contempt to survive. How much of what was done for survival was done for the purpose of bearing witness and how much for the simple relief from the agonies of hunger and other sources of misery? Answering this question meant facing the terrible gray zone in which the answers were not clear. Those of us who have not faced these problems can only begin to imagine the torture that is threatened by the gray zone and that persists as survivor's guilt or shame.

Early in his writings, Levi said that he came away from the experience of Auschwitz largely unscathed. He had been lucky, he thought. Lucky to have been sent to Auschwitz when the need for labor had reduced some forms of brutality in the camps; lucky to have had the skills of a chemist, which were useful to his oppressors; lucky to have been the recipient of citizen Lorenzo's humanity; and lucky to have been one of fifteen men and nine women to have survived out of the 650 people with whom he had arrived at Auschwitz. This is not to say that he had not suffered deeply from the constant humiliation,

[27] Primo Levi, *Survival in Auschwitz: The Nazi Assault on Humanity*, translated by Stuart Woolf (New York: Simon & Schuster, 1958), 171–2.

[28] Levi, *Collected Poems*, 64.

deprivation, and physical abuse to which others were subjected. Like others, he had endured the stresses of "selection," the cold of winter rain without shelter, and the ravages of scarlet fever. Yet he was able, at least for a while, to come away from the experience with an optimism others were unable to recover. He revived to enjoy an eye for beauty, an ear for poetry and music, a love of nature, a sense of humor, and close personal attachments. But he was haunted by the need and driven by the imperative to tell the story, and a heavy burden it was.

Read Levi in his own words from his last book, *The Drowned and the Saved*:

After my return from imprisonment I was visited by a friend . . ., the cultivator of a personal religion. . . . He was glad to find me alive and basically unhurt, perhaps matured and fortified, certainly enriched. He told me that my having survived could not be the work of chance, . . . but rather of Providence. I bore the mark, I was an elect: I, the nonbeliever, and even less of a believer after the season of Auschwitz, was a person touched by Grace, a saved man. And why me? It is impossible to know, he answered. Perhaps because I had to write, and by writing bear witness. . . .

Such an opinion seemed monstrous to me. . . . What I had seen and lived through proved the exact contrary. Preferably the worst survived, the selfish, the violent, the insensitive, the collaborators of the "gray zone," the spies. . . . I felt innocent, yes, but enrolled among the saved and therefore in permanent search of a justification in my own eyes and those of others. The worst survived, that is, the fittest; the best all died.

Chaim died, a watchmaker from Krakow, a pious Jew who despite the language difficulties made an effort to understand and be understood, and explained to me, the foreigner, the essential rules for survival during the first crucial days of captivity; Szabo died, the taciturn Hungarian peasant who was almost two meters tall and so was the hungriest of all, and yet, as long as he had the strength, did not hesitate to help his weaker companions to pull and push; and Robert, a professor at the Sorbonne who spread courage and trust all around him, spoke five languages, wore himself out recording everything in his prodigious memory, and had he lived would have answered the questions which I do not know how to answer; and Baruch died, a longshoreman from Livorno, immediately, on the first day, because he had answered the first punch he had received with punches and was massacred by three *Kapos* in coalition. These, and innumerable others, died not despite their valor but because of it.

My religious friend had told me that I survived so that I could bear witness. I have done so, as best I could, . . . but the thought that this testifying... could... gain for me the privilege of surviving and living for many years without serious problems troubles me because I cannot see any proportion between the privilege and the outcome.[29]

On April 11, 1987, the year after the publication of *The Drowned and the Saved,* Primo Levi died after tumbling over the railing of a stairwell in his home in Turin. Though his death was ruled a suicide only hours after he was found, others have denied that he could have taken his own life. He had spoken out against Jean Amery's views on suicide; his public declarations had seemed to dispel the notion that he was permanently scarred by his experience; and he had expressed an optimism about humanity despite the cruelty and cowardice he had seen. However, the tone of the last book and the record expressed in his collected poems can leave no doubt that he carried a heavy burden. Though he once expressed the view that "the aims of life are the best defense against death,"[30] it is not implausible that he believed that his story had been told or that it was no longer being heard and that his life, having no further aim, had lost its defenses. If so, then what are we to make of such a death and its tragic dimensions? How are we to think and feel it? Also, how are we to think and feel the deaths of people like Chaim, Szabo, Robert, and Baruch? How are we to think and feel the deaths of untold others who were neither the best nor the privileged? And what of those who did survive but could not witness because to speak about such things was to relive them?

Commenting on what he called a literary view of death as expressed in a claim reminiscent of the Romantics that "A beautiful death honors all of life," Levi said, "This boundless archive of defensive and thaumaturgic formulations in Auschwitz... was short-lived: Death in Auschwitz was trivial, bureaucratic, and an everyday affair. It was not commented on, it was not 'comforted by tears.' "[31] Certainly it is safe to say that the Romantic view of death does not apply to those who died by the millions and who were neither the best nor the privileged. And when we reflect on the everydayness of such death, we do not feel it with the solace of beauty, with the discomfort of boredom, or with the titillation of amusement. As to Levi's death (if it was a suicide) and

[29] Ibid., 82–3.
[30] Ibid., 159.
[31] Ibid., 148.

the deaths of people like Chaim, Szabo, Robert, and Baruch: there is tragic beauty there, though not enough to account for the full impact of the tragedy involved. As Levi himself had said, there is something missing in the proportion of the privilege and the outcome. We may admit, even enthusiastically embrace, the Romantic view that many of the things we value most involve inevitable, ineliminable loss, and that such loss can be lived beautifully, even as it crushes. To care is to suffer. The truth in Romanticism is that we know this but nevertheless embrace the caring and see its beauty in the midst of the pain and ugliness. Yet to feel the deaths of Primo Levi and the best who died in the Lagers is to be overwhelmed by the ugliness and the horror of a world that eclipses the beauty it produces. To feel this way is to be neither a Romantic nor a nihilist. It is to experience horror unrelieved by beauty. Unlike Keat's reflections on the Grecian urn, our reflections on Levi, the best, and the others who suffered and died in the Lagers do not "keep a bower quiet for us, and a sleep full of sweet dreams, and health, and quiet breathing." Nor do they leave us amused or bored. They leave us in horror in both thought and feeling.

Because tragedy is not always redeemed by beauty, Romanticism is incomplete in its view of the life best felt and thought. Because of its superficiality, nihilism is pseudo-intellectual, a theory of value for the emotionally vacuous. But there is another dark view about value that takes tragedy seriously and that must itself be given serious intellectual consideration. Unfortunately, it has not. It is the view of pessimism.

4

Pessimism

Le jeu vaut-il bien la chandelle?

Arthur Schopenhauer, *On the Affirmation of the Will to Live*

If we picture to ourselves roughly as far as we can the sum total of misery, pain, and suffering of every kind on which the sun shines in its course, we shall admit that it would have been much better if it had been just as impossible for the sun to produce the phenomenon of life on earth as on the moon, and the surface of the earth, like that of the moon, had still been in a crystalline state.

Arthur Schopenhauer, *Additional Remarks on the Doctrine of Suffering*

Pessimism is essentially a religious disease.

William James, *Essays on Faith and Morals*

The poor you shall have with you always.

Jesus Christ, from *The Gospel According to Matthew* (26:11)

By way of a thought experiment, make the following pessimistic assumptions about the near and far future. Assume that within the next century we will gradually lose the struggle to sustain the environment and that moderately scarce natural resources will become extremely scarce, due both to increased levels of expectation by the privileged and to increased population. Assume that within the next fifty years the world's population will double but then begin to level off. The best scientific assessment of our prospects for saving the environment in a way that will sustain even a quarter of that population over time (say, several centuries) turns out to be that it cannot be done. The damage done to the environment by industry and other sources of pollution will have taken us past the threshold of possible recovery on the most optimistic projections of voluntary population control. The decline will be slow, but it is clear to everyone that the course is irreversible. Assume also that we will gradually lose the battle with disease and that it will be clear to everyone that medical research cannot compete with the deteriorating conditions of scarcity and the mutation rates among the viral and bacterial sources of disease. Gradually, what cannot be accomplished through voluntary population control can and will be accomplished through disease, regardless of the best scientific efforts to prevent it. Scientists reliably tell us that the Earth will slowly begin to recover at a rate that will sustain the remaining population, and that in the far distant future there will in all likelihood be centuries with patterns of human flourishing and suffering that resemble our past. Finally, it becomes clear that hopes of finding other intelligent life in the universe and other habitable environments are futile. Scientists confirm that the speed of light and the distance between Earth and other possible sources of life preempt any rational hope of extraterrestrial solutions. What we can be sure of is that after a number of cycles of human flourishing and suffering, there will be a cataclysmic end to the Earth and all its history. We and all our relationships and accomplishments will be destroyed without a trace, as if we had never existed.

Now assume that you have at your disposal a bomb, call it the clean solution, the detonation of which could end it all very painlessly and instantly for everyone. Would you now have reasons for not detonating the bomb or employing some other clean solution were it available, and what would those reasons be? If you would not employ the clean solution now under these assumptions, at what point in such a cycle of developments would you use it, if at all, and why or why not? The primary concern here is how those of us who are secular nontheists would answer these questions and what the answers tell us about our values and our sense of tragedy. Would it be a greater tragedy to end it all now than to wait for a later point in the development of history on the pessimistic assumptions?

A secular version of the problem of evil is the problem of pessimism, which takes the form of a positive comparative judgment that A is better than B. Given the facts of human suffering, says pessimism, it would have been better had human life as a whole never evolved. Understanding why the pessimist thinks this sharply distinguishes nihilism from pessimism. Nihilism worries that life might just be too dull to endure, and even if it is, that is no ground for tragedy. The good might prevail over the bad, but when it does, the victory is worth no great celebration, and when the bad prevails over the good, the loss is nothing about which to grieve. At worst, life is, for the nihilist, merely pathetic. Pessimism, on the other hand, recognizes that there are many things in life that in themselves are worthy of robust and passionate commitment. If these things prevail over the bad, there is great cause for joy, but if the bad prevails over them, there are grounds for despair. At worst, life is, for the pessimist, tragic. If pessimism is warranted, then, the tragedy of the human condition is that evil prevails over good, where the good is of robust value.

Can the gloom of pessimism be a reasoned response to the human condition?

One attempt to meet the pessimist's challenge is to provide a successful argument from the impersonal point of view that pessimism is irrational; another is to argue that practical reason does not proceed at the most basic level from the impersonal point of view. I will argue for the latter and that there are grounds for personal optimism, but first I will suggest that impersonal pessimism is a very serious threat.

The first task is to clarify what it is to take the impersonal point of view. Some have identified the impersonal point of view with the view from nowhere[1] or with the point of view of the universe.[2] The idea is that there is a point of view that we are capable of taking that does not involve any of our wants, desires, or sentiments, but that somehow allows us to make value judgments. That we can ask what we ought to do or what ought to be the case, no matter what we want or desire and no matter what our sentiments are, is supposed to yield evidence that there is such an evaluative point of view. We recognize that there might well be sadists who want very much, even after full consideration of the facts, to impose as much pain as possible on others without any anticipation of regret. Still we find ourselves insisting that the sadist

[1] See Thomas Nagel, *The View from Nowhere* (New York: Oxford University Press, 1986).
[2] See Henry Sidgwick, *The Methods of Ethics* (London: Macmillan, 1907).

ought not to act sadistically, no matter what he wants or desires. Feeling as strongly as we do about this, we insist that it must make sense that there is available even to the sadist an evaluative point of view that is independent of his own wants, desires, and sentiments and that he should take that point of view and act in accordance with it.

Yet, despite the fact that we sometimes talk this way about our moral convictions, it is difficult to make sense of an evaluative point of view of the sort in question. The reason that our insistence on such a point of view does not make sense (no matter how much we pound the table about horrible immorality) is that there is no possible psychology that lacked the affective and conative dimensions of wants, desires, and sentiments that would include a sense that there are things that matter. Practical reason deals in things that matter, and the challenge for constructing a conception of the impersonal point of view is the challenge of constructing an account of a psychology that includes a sense of things that matter in an impersonal way. It is utterly mysterious how things could matter for a being who had only a cognitive psychology but no affective or conative psychology. The insistence on wants, desires, and sentiments is just an insistence that the psychology of a practical reasoner must include an affective and conative dimension along with whatever cognitive dimensions are required. Valuing something is always some form of caring about something, and caring about something is always more than simply believing and knowing about something. The reason the universe has no point of view is because it is not the kind of thing that cares in any way about anything. The ultimate point of view any of us can therefore take as a practical reasoner is the point of view of what we can ultimately care about.

So if there is an impersonal point of view it will have to be a function of our valuing and therefore of our myriad ways of caring. One possibility is that rather than being the point of view from nowhere, it is the point of view from everywhere. The thought is that the impersonal point of view is that point of view of caring that we all share. Whether there is such a point of view is itself a hotly debated topic in moral philosophy, and one might think that until that issue is settled no progress can be made on other fronts. But this is a mistake. First, it does not follow from there being a common form of caring that the impersonal point of view is the best way to think of it. Suppose, for example, that the only common form of caring that we share is that we all love our families. This would not mean that we share an impersonal point of view. Just the opposite. Familial love is one of the most personal forms of caring. Second, there is a way of framing the issue of the impersonal point of view that is neutral about whether it is common to all humans.

We can say that the impersonal point of view is that point of view one takes that is uninfluenced by one's personal wants, needs, and sentiments. This is possible because there are forms of caring that are not, in an important sense, personal. When I am concerned about the suffering of a complete stranger, the concern is impersonal in the sense that it is not a special concern owing to my personal involvement with the stranger. The same can be true of other forms of caring as well. Because of my sense of respect, I can care about the dignity of a complete stranger, and because of my sense of excellence, I can care about the esteem conferred on various achievements even when I have no personal connection to those involved. The impersonal point of view, then, is best thought of as a function of forms of caring that are impersonal and independent of our special personal relations and connections.

It is important, however, to bear in mind two different kinds of contexts in which the impersonal point of view can be taken. The first is a transcendent context, and the second an immanent one. A transcendent context is a context in which a practical reasoner stands outside what is being judged and in which what he does will bring certain things of value into play. Think of designing a game. If the rules of the game are designed in one way, playing will be lighthearted and hilarious; if in another, serious but challenging. The crucial thing about transcendent contexts is that they raise the issue of what kinds of values to bring about. Immanent contexts, on the other hand, are those in which values are already in play and the task of the practical reasoner is to set priorities among them. Government labor negotiators are often faced with immanent contexts: given what labor and management want and given that the larger society is affected by the outcome, their task is to determine the best way to accommodate all the values that are already in play.

The response to impersonal pessimism might turn on whether it takes a transcendent or an immanent form. The transcendent form is the one presented by Schopenhauer in the quote at the beginning of the chapter. The transcendent pessimist isolates the suffering of the world from all other values to which it might or might not be related and carefully weighs it on one side of a ledger. He then isolates all positive values and weighs them on the other side of the ledger. He then views the world, its suffering, and its other values from the outside and wonders if it would have been better had life never evolved. Wouldn't it have been better, says the transcendent pessimist, had the natural variables been such that instead of producing the kind of life there is on Earth they had resulted only in the kind of biologically austere state of the moon? So construed, the issue of pessimism is very much like the problem of evil in theism. The transcendent pessimist takes the issue to be what it would be right or good to do if we were faced with the godlike task of creating two possible worlds: one with the suffering of this world and its other values, the other without the suffering and without the other values.

One very interesting thing to note here is that if one version of the evidential problem of evil is a decisive objection to traditional theism, then transcendent pessimism is a decisive objection to at least some forms of impersonal secular optimism.[3] Traditional theism must argue that barring the suffering for which human agents are responsible, this is the best of all possible worlds and that the remaining suffering is outweighed by greater good. That this is the best of all possible worlds is not enough. What is required is that the best of all possible worlds contains a net balance of good over bad. Otherwise the whole of creation, if we think of it as the product of design, was a tragic mistake. That so construed it was a tragic mistake is strongly suggested, for example, by the evidence regarding the age of the dinosaurs. The dinosaurs dominated the earth for 150 million years, and scientists say that they seldom died from old age but either as prey or from the ravages of disease. Their period in history, then, was one of unremitting suffering with little compensation in terms of good. It thus seems to many from the evidence of the past that not only is this not the best of all possible worlds, it has not even been a world in which there has

3 The evidential form of the problem of evil recognizes that it is logically possible that evil exists and that there is an omnipotent, omniscient, wholly good God, but it asserts that the evidence regarding the actual suffering of human and nonhuman animals provides evidence against there being such a God.

been a net balance of good over bad. If, then, the suffering of the past made it wrong for God to have made possible the good of the past because of a net loss in goodness, how can we justify continuing our history if our future projects such a loss? Transcendent pessimism, therefore, is to some forms of secular moral theory what this version of the evidential problem of evil is to traditional theism. Yet many secular moral philosophers seem to think (i) that the evidential problem of evil refutes traditional theism's view that this world contains a balance of good over bad, (ii) that taking the moral point of view is taking a God's-eye point of view of consequences, and (iii) that what we should be doing is maximizing the balance of good over bad. How can all these beliefs common to secular consequentialism be rational? Secularism has its own problem of evil to contend with, and not just any response will do.

The secular consequentialist might respond that there is a crucial difference between the perspectives of traditional theism and impersonal consequentialism on suffering. The difference is that traditional theism takes a retrospective point of view but impersonal consequentialism takes a prospective point of view. The question is whether this makes any difference in whether it is rational from the impersonal point of view to be an optimist or a pessimist. Is there any real distinction between looking back over the history of suffering and human values and weighing them up and looking forward to a projected history on such calculations that would make any real difference?

The answer might turn on what appears in the columns of the ledger. According to hedonistic utilitarianism, the negative column will list suffering in each and every instance of its occurrence, and the positive column will list happiness in each and every instance of its occurrence. No occurrence of either will be discounted or overlooked. What reason is there to think that so measured the past included a surplus of suffering but the future promises a surplus of happiness?

It is a natural thing in some sense to think of the world in terms of what one perceives in one's immediate surroundings, in terms of what one is used to in one's everyday dealings. Most of us in the developed countries (20 percent of the world's population) think of history as a kind of progressive, though gradual, reduction of misery. The less we see of suffering, the less we think it is there, and our faith in moral progress is sustained by our ignorance. But if the trajectory of moral progress is gauged by the reduction of human and animal suffering, such faith is anything but clearly justified.

It is true that (counting only humans) world life expectancy is increasing, but this does not mean that there is less suffering in the world. The fact is that in absolute numbers there are more people suffering in the world today than ever before, and there are more people suffering under primitive conditions now than ever before. According to a report from the World Health Organization, three billion of the world's six billion people now suffer from malnutrition.[4] The total population of the world in 1950 was 2.52 billion, which means that if the numbers regarding malnutrition are accurate, the number of people now suffering from malnutrition alone is greater than the total world population of only fifty years ago.[5] If this trend continues, there will be as many people suffering from malnutrition alone by the middle of the next century as there are now people on Earth. And even on the most optimistic estimates, the total number of people suffering in this way will increase significantly. Currently, more than eleven million children die each year of pneumonia, diarrhea, measles, malaria, and malnutrition before the age of five.[6] Discounting all other forms of suffering, that toll for the last decade of the twentieth century itself would have been 37 percent of the world population in any year between the beginning of the Christian era and 1000 A.D. What seems clear is that the more material conditions improve for some, the larger the number of those who suffer as a result. Why? Because poverty does not diminish the number of hungry mouths to feed but multiplies them.

Consider also that as material conditions improve, populations decrease but demand on the environment increases. The good news is that the rate of population growth in the United States has gone down; the bad news is that the United States uses far more of the world's natural resources than any other country. Is this due to something peculiar to United States citizens? If the technological balance suddenly shifted away from the United States to Europe or China, would there be less

4 See David and Marcia Pimentel, "Ten Billion Mouths to Feed," *World Population Awareness, News Digest,* April 4, 2000 <http://www.overpopulation.org>.

5 See Population Division of the Department of Economic and Social Affairs of the United Nations Secretariat, *The World at Six Billion* (ESA/P/WP.154), 12 October 1999.

6 See World Health Organization Press, Press Release WHO/64, pp. 1–2.

grounds for worry? European and Chinese virtue notwithstanding, I doubt it. People, including Europeans, Chinese, Canadians, and everyone else, are inclined to use their technological advantages to improve their lives. So what if we became complete technological egalitarians? Would this result in progress? The evidence suggests that the population would decrease but that the environment might very well be destroyed. Moreover, the destruction of the environment would probably accelerate faster than the rate of the population growth would decrease. But the more slowly we distribute technology to underdeveloped countries, the more people starve.

These observations do not prove (and are not intended to prove) beyond any doubt that transcendent pessimism is warranted, but they are intended to challenge the naive optimism both of contemporary moral philosophers and of the educated public. Anyone who has actually reflected on the historical facts regarding the suffering of human and nonhuman animals and who has studied the effects of demography on the environment and the prospects for the future can hardly avoid taking seriously the probability that the next century will include more suffering than ever before. The problem is compounded by the fact that the leisure produced by improved material conditions brings its own form of suffering to the privileged. The psychological suffering of modernity is the reward for having overcome the physical sources of discomfort. Criminologists can tell us how much crime in advanced countries is due to poverty and how much is due to boredom. As Schopenhauer was all too ready to show us, nature is not kind. It seems to have designed us to live a life of frustrated dreams. Dreams unfulfilled bring the frustration of desire; and dreams fulfilled, the frustration of boredom. All too often, freedom from material constraints on our dreams is just another word for nothing left to do. Though some may be able to handle such freedom and turn it to good purpose, the evidence suggests that many, perhaps most, cannot.

Then there are the bacterial and viral infections. Consider retrospectively how much human and animal misery has been the result of such infections prior to the development of antibiotics. Reflections on the bubonic plague of the fourteenth century alone should give the theist pause. But then why think that something similar does not await humanity in the future? Overuse of antibiotics has resulted in bacterial and viral adaptations that threaten to put us back to where we were before antibiotics were discovered. Some speculate that we may be only a few decades away from such a reversal.[7] Even if they are wrong about the near future, what makes it reasonable to believe that research and development will always allow us to stay one step ahead of the deadliest virus? Contrary to what James said about pessimism being a religious disease, it seems to take a religious faith in the inevitability of human dominance to justify such optimism. If the competition for survival is between ourselves and the ordinary roach, the roach will win. Why? Because its powers of adaptation are better. And viruses are yet more adaptive than the roach.

In the light of this, it is puzzling how one can be a theistic humanist. If God could not have improved on the past, why think that we can improve on the future? Yet this seems to be just what some theistic optimists believe. To think that we could reverse things if only we would use our free will rightly to do the good is to presuppose a solution we are unwilling to implement. What is it?[8]

The truth is that in all probability we will exhaust the Earth long before the sun exhausts itself and the solar system of which we are a part. Lower organisms will view our tombstones with a sense of history even less informed than that of the average college graduate. To be envied are those who can believe that God will step in and save us from ourselves and the forces of nature. What seems right-headed about theistic interventionists is that they recognize that viewed impersonally, if there is no God to intervene in this process, there is little reason for optimism in the long run. If this is right, then transcendent secular optimism in a utilitarian form is even more puzzling than the theistic version.

Of course, we might change what is listed in the columns of the ledger in our book of calculations. What if human suffering is weighed off, not against human happiness, but against human dignity? Imagine

7 For an interesting discussion, see Stuart B. Levy, "The Challenge of Antibiotic Resistance," *Scientific American*, March 1998, pp. 46–53.

8 Of course, to say that we do not have a solution to providing a net balance of good over bad does not mean that everything we do in this regard is a matter of indifference. On any reasonable estimate of the future of the planet, and on almost any set of values anyone is likely to have that gives any of us reasons to continue with life, we have conclusive reasons for being more aggressive than we are in preserving and protecting the environment.

retrospectively from the God's-eye point of view whether all the suffering of both human and nonhuman animals that predated and accompanied human dignity was worth the emergence of human dignity. Then imagine prospectively from the God's-eye point of view whether all the suffering of both human and nonhuman animals that will accompany human dignity in the future will be worth the continuance of human life.

One possible response is that happiness and dignity are incomparable in the literal sense that they cannot be compared. If so, and if practical reason tracks comparability, then we simply cannot make a rational judgment about the future or the past in this regard. Most moral philosophers who think that the evidential form of the problem of evil is decisive against traditional theism are hardly ignorant of Kantian claims about human dignity and its worth. What Kantians believe is one of the secular legacies of Christianity, that human dignity is strictly superior in its worth to the worth of human and animal happiness. If this is true, then there is no amount of happiness that can provide a reason for violating human dignity. Does it follow from this that the production and maintenance of human dignity is worth any amount of suffering? Would God have been justified in bringing about any amount of human and nonhuman animal suffering in order to create humans and their dignity? If so, it is hard to see how the evidential form of the problem of evil for theism could even get off the ground. Why? Because on this conception of the value of human dignity, nothing could count as evidence that enough is enough when it comes to the costs of human dignity.

I doubt seriously that anyone can really believe this upon reflection. What if there were a literal hell, an everlasting fire and all of that? And what if the cost of the earthly life of a single human came to the fact that all nonhuman animals would have to spend an eternity in a literal hell suffering miserably? Would the cost of human dignity then be too high? If so, then the worth of human dignity is not strictly superior to the worth of happiness and the avoidance of suffering. Does this not show that a platitudinous morality dangerously engenders indifference to things of great importance?

The theistic optimist has the resources to respond that human dignity will live on in eternity and that this makes all the difference. Even Kant thought so, which is why both the existence of God and the immortality of the soul are according to him postulates of practical reason.[9] One problem with this move is that it is inconsistent with the claim about the strict superiority of dignity over happiness. If human dignity must last forever to be superior to some quantity of happiness or suffering avoided, then there is some quantity of dignity that is not superior to some quantity of happiness or suffering avoided. How could this be any clearer? Secular Kantians, however, do not have the resources of traditional theism. What, then, are we to think of their comparative judgments about the relative worth of dignity and happiness or suffering? From the transcendent perspective, what are the scales the secular Kantian employs to judge from the evidence regarding the history of suffering and dignity that traditional theism is unwarranted but that the continuance of human history with its dignity and suffering is a good thing? In other words, what is the covering value for the comparison? This is not a rhetorical question, so platitudes regarding human dignity will not suffice as a response.

What the Kantian should say is that practical reason does not proceed from a transcendent context but from an immanent one. Our respect for human dignity does not rationally compel us to produce humans but to respect humans once they exist.[10] Respect, then, is the recognition of a value that is already in play, which reveals that respect for human dignity emerges only in immanent contexts. Taking this view, the secular Kantian could deny that the goal of producing human dignity justifies the suffering that has attended its production and could maintain that the evidential form of the problem of evil is decisive against traditional theism. At the same time, he could maintain that we must be impersonally optimistic about the future because respect for human dignity renders the future worthy of pursuit as long as dignity lasts. So the ultimate claim here is that secular Kantian moral theory allows us a response to impersonal pessimism that does not require a defense of traditional theism. It does this by rejecting

9 See Immanuel Kant, *Critique of Practical Reason*, translated by Lewis White Beck (Indianapolis: Bobbs-Merrill, 1956), 126–36.

10 This is the view, I believe, of several contemporary Kantians. See Barbara Herman, *The Practice of Moral Judgment* (Cambridge, Massachusetts: Harvard University Press, 1993); Thomas Hill, Jr., *Dignity and Practical Reason in Kant's Moral Theory*, (Ithaca, New York: Cornell University Press, 1992); and Christine Korsgaard, *Creating the Kingdom of Ends* (Cambridge: Cambridge University Press, 1996).

the impersonal point of view as arising from a transcendent context and by insisting that the value that supports optimism is the value of human dignity, which is a value already in play.

Is immanent, impersonal optimism of this sort compelling?

Consider a question asked by William James:

> . . . if the hypothesis were offered us of a world in which Messrs. Fourier's and Bellamy's and Morris's utopias should all be outdone, and millions kept permanently happy on the one simple condition that a certain lost soul on the far-off edge of things should lead a life of lonely torture, what except a specifical and independent sort of emotion can it be which would make us immediately feel, even though an impulse arose within us to clutch at the happiness so offered, how hideous a thing would be its enjoyment when deliberately accepted as the fruit of such a bargain?[11]

The point pressed here applies most to those who think that there is some quantity of happiness that can justify the production of such suffering. One might also take the point to be that when suffering and happiness are compared, the avoidance of suffering is far more important, so important that very large amounts of happiness cannot compensate for even small amounts of torture. Finally, one might take the comparison to be not about happiness and suffering but about happiness and dignity. On this view, what is so repulsive about such a utopia is that it comes at the cost of human dignity. It is the fact that a human being rather than another animal is suffering that blocks the endorsement of utopia for the many at the cost of a lone sufferer.

But what if we change the utopia from a utilitarian one to a Kantian one, from the society of satisfied desire to the Kingdom of Ends of autonomous wills – and the lone sufferer from a single human to large numbers of several species of animals? How much difference would this make? Do we really believe that from the impersonal perspective the production of the Kingdom of Ends in which mutual respect for free and autonomous choice was perfectly exemplified would be worth any amount of suffering of lower animals? Of course the comparison is unrealistic, but the reason it is unrealistic is not because it exaggerates the amount of animal suffering that accompanies the maintenance of human civilization. Surely the actual amount of such suffering is and

[11] William James, *Essays in Pragmatism*, edited by Alburey Castell (New York: Hafner, 1968), 68.

will continue to be enormous. Rather, the comparison is unrealistic because there will never be such a utopia. Those who think so simply have not been paying attention to history. How anyone can have utopian hopes and expectations in regard to the future and yet believe that traditional theists are naive about suffering has got to be one of the mysteries of the intellectual world. It is just hard to see how faith in utopian conceptions of moral progress is based on anything like evidence, and it is easy to see the dangers of utopian aspirations. So if we are to justify continuing with human civilization, we will have to do it without projecting utopia, whether Kantian, utilitarian, or Marxist, as the final destination. Immanent Kantian optimism cannot plausibly project utopia as the benefit that will justify the costs in terms of animal suffering of the probable autonomous choices of humans who now and will exist. The real comparison, then, is between the amount of suffering, both human and nonhuman, that will in all probability attend the lifestyles of human choice that fall woefully short of the Kingdom of Ends. Moreover, the comparison really is not like the one suggested by James's question. Rather than the many benefitting while the few suffer, the actual likely result of continued respect for human choice is that the few will benefit while the many suffer.

So viewed impersonally from where we are now in history, it is hard to see how the value of human dignity has the status to rescue us from pessimism and to redeem the future. Nor is it clear how to distinguish those secular Kantian optimists from traditional theists who think that God was justified in creating the world with its actual probabilities. If traditional theists are naive about how much animal suffering preceded the evolution of human beings, immanent secular Kantians are naive about how much suffering will likely attend the future of human history.

Are other possibilities more promising?

One possibility might combine what has come to be known as virtue ethics with consequentialism and wed our Classical Greek heritage to the aspirations of the Enlightenment. According to the so-called virtue solution to the problem of evil, if we think carefully about the evidence and the relative value of virtue and of avoiding suffering, we can see how God as traditionally conceived could have created the actual world. Could secular consequentialists deny the theistic version of this argument but employ a secular version to combat impersonal pessimism, claiming that the virtue promoted in the future will leave us with a net balance of good over suffering that did not exist in the past?

In order to do this, the form of virtue ethics would have to be consequentialist but allow that virtue has intrinsic value, and it would have to argue that there is something about the intrinsic value of virtue and the future that makes it rational to believe that though the past did not include a net balance of good over suffering, the future probably does. In this way, it could refute the theist's appeal to the virtue solution to the problem of evil but employ its own virtue solution against secular impersonal pessimism.

According to Thomas Hurka, there is a form of consequentialism that can afford virtue intrinsic value.[12] The recursive account, as he calls it, asserts that virtues are attitudes toward intrinsic generic goods. A virtue is a loving attitude toward intrinsic goods, like pleasure, knowledge, and achievement, and a hating attitude toward intrinsic evils, like suffering, failure, and false belief. The recursive account affords these attitudes themselves intrinsic value, thereby accommodating the intrinsic value of virtue within a consequentialist framework. He argues against the virtue solution to the problem of evil by claiming that the value of an attitude toward an intrinsic good is less than the value of the generic good. Similarly, the intrinsic value of avoiding a generic evil is greater than the intrinsic value of the attitude of hating that evil: suffering may be good in rendering compassion possible, but the negative value of intense suffering is greater than the virtue of the compassion it generates.

Assume for the sake of argument that Hurka's recursive account refutes the virtue solution to the problem of evil. Can it support secular optimism? This turns out to be a very complicated issue, and we will come back to it later when the discussion of perfectionism is taken up in later chapters. But, for now, I will simply suggest that this kind of account does not clearly recommend optimism. In order to do so, it must put an enormous premium on the intrinsic values of achievement and knowledge and paint a very rosy picture of future gains in both. But though both knowledge and achievement have been increasing,

[12] See Thomas Hurka, *Virtue, Vice, and Value* (New York: Oxford University Press, 2001), 156–61, 170–1.

so have failure and ignorance.[13] Just as there is more suffering than ever before, there is more failure and ignorance than ever before. Nor does it appear that the love of excellence is on the increase. In fact, it seems to be in a precipitous decline. Similarly, the love of knowledge seems to be anything but on the rise. There is not only the ignorance that comes with poverty, but also the cultural disregard for truth even within our universities. If self-deception is a form of ignorance and false belief, it can hardly be maintained that there is reason to believe that people now have more self-knowledge than ever before. Indeed, the complexities of the modern condition seem actually to have made the problem proliferate. And there is the additional fact that people actually seem to enjoy false belief. How else could they take such delight in things like professional wrestling?

Where are we then? No doubt there are other kinds of attempts that secular impersonal moral theory might make to meet the pessimist challenge, but meet it it must, and so far secular moral philosophers simply persist in ignoring the problem. Are they naive, or do they have reasons for thinking that the evidence from the impersonal point of view so clearly supports optimism that there is no need to address the issue? I cannot see how the latter view could be remotely plausible. The truth is that much of analytic moral philosophy simply ignores the intellectual tradition of the nineteenth century, as though an intellectual reaction to the Enlightenment tradition that took the problem of pessimism seriously never occurred or was so misinformed as to be inconsequential.[14] If the latter were true, there would be a clear, unequivocal response to the problem of pessimism; but there is not. It is hard, then, not to take the silence of academic philosophy as anything but embarrassingly naive about the trajectory of intellectual history. And this is especially embarrassing at the dawn of the twenty-first century. It is the business of philosophy in the best sense to ask and try to answer the hard questions, and if academic philosophy is to be relevant, it cannot avoid this and other pressing problems any longer.

[13] Hurka includes not ignorance but false belief as the evil that stands opposite of knowledge. For a more thorough discussion of this issue, see my "The Virtues, Perfectionist Goods, and Pessimism," in *Virtue Ethics: Old and New*, edited by Steven Gardiner (Ithaca, New York: Cornell University Press, 2005), 193–210.

[14] For a good antidote to this trend, see Susan Neiman, *Evil: An Alternative History of Philosophy* (Princeton, New Jersey: Princeton University Press, 2002).

What, then, if having addressed the issue, impersonal moral theory fails to give us grounds for optimism? Could we avoid pessimism? The only way, I believe, would be to see that practical reason does not proceed from the impersonal point of view and that it does not project indefinitely into the future. That none of us will seriously entertain ending the history of sentient life on Earth at this point in history should tell us a great deal about practical reason and our values. While we might in the light of the previous observations admit that the existence of human and animal suffering is itself a tragedy, it would be a greater tragedy still to end it all. How can we account for this tragic sense, the sense that something important would be lost with such a termination? This sense reflects one of the most important comparative evaluative judgments any person, philosopher or not, can ever make, and any developed answer to the question must yield a view of the human condition.

It is by shifting emphasis to the personal point of view that we can begin to make sense of the human condition and the tragic sense that it would be even more tragic to give up on life. For those who have a modicum of good luck, the problems that confront practical reason arise in the first place in the context of an ongoing meaningful life. The relevant comparison, then, is between the disvalue of prospective human and animal suffering and whatever the values are that give a person's life meaning from his or her own point of view. It is the values that give meaning to a person's life that give her a reason to go on, and it is only in terms of these values that a person can be optimistic or pessimistic.[15]

What is it that gives meaning to life for most of us? What is it that we care about that might give us reasons for living and for taking some joy and passion in life, even in the clear knowledge of the facts about suffering and the prospects for the future? If we cannot answer this question from the personal point of view, then it seems we are just propelled into the future by habit or weakness of will.

For most of us, it is our loved ones – our spouses, our parents, our children, our friends, and our neighbors – and their well-being and good fortune and sharing life with them that are the most central

[15] I have argued for this extensively elsewhere. See my *Agent Centered Morality* (Berkeley: University of California Press, 1999).

elements in terms of which we find life alluring. This is an aspect of our social nature. We are the sorts of creatures for whom a life without love is devastatingly lonely. It is not that we love in order to avoid loneliness; rather, we are prone to loneliness in the absence of intimacy because we are loving creatures. If we think of suffering as an affliction of feeling, as an overall state of feeling bad to a significant degree, and of happiness as an overall state of feeling good, consider how much of the good feeling of happiness we are willing to forgo for the sake of our loved ones, and how much suffering we are willing to endure for their sake.[16] This should tell us that for a loving person, the meaning of her life from her own point of view is far more determined by how well things are going for her loved ones than by how she feels, either good or bad. Indeed, one of the noble things about love is that unless suffering is completely unbearable, it factors very little into our practical deliberations when it comes to the central well-being of our loved ones. Viewed from this perspective, much of the suffering in a loving person's life is taken as a matter of course. Comparatively, then, the overall meaning of suffering in a loving person's life is relatively insignificant when compared with the meaning and direction provided by her loving commitments. To be sure, we should not overstate this. If a person suffers enough, even love can fade, wither, or simply die from fatigue. But outside very austere and extreme conditions, love does not so much as blink in the face of a good bit of suffering, let alone does it take a pessimistic view of life.

It is also important to keep in mind that love involves a form of suffering. So much so that love could be described as a form of suffering itself. Granted, it is more than that, but part of what it is to love others is to suffer their ill fortune. Yet, knowing this, we continue to find our lives most meaningful in terms of our loved ones. Viewed in this way, the meaning of what love adds to what we take life to be about can be gauged by how little significance we give to considerations of such suffering in our practical deliberations. Rather than taking such suffering to be grounds for pessimism, we look with suspicion on those

[16] This way of making out the distinction between happiness and suffering is defended by Jamie Mayerfeld in his book *Suffering and Moral Responsibility* (London: Oxford University Press, 1999). Mayerfeld is one of the few contemporary moral theorists who to my knowledge actually take the problem of pessimism seriously.

who go on and on about it. We take them to be gauging the meaning of their lives by ignoble values. In fact, we often think it a tragedy that a person cannot love in a way that does not hesitate in the face of some significant suffering.

So how do things stand when we compare the meaning of our own suffering and the meaning of our loved ones in the overall meaning of our lives? We cannot say that the value of our loved ones is strictly superior to the value of the avoidance of our own suffering, but we can say that it is vastly superior. This is just part of what it is to be a loving person.

Consider also the comparative value of pursuing excellence at something, on the one hand, and the value of the avoidance of one's own suffering, on the other. The truth (rather than the romantic rhetoric) about the pursuit of excellence is that it is often nothing short of brutal in its demands. Of course, it is not always that, but to pursue excellence is to take the chance that one is not up to the challenge. For this reason, we do not expect to see the fainthearted or those whose deliberations are highly sensitive to their own suffering engaged in such pursuits. One of the admirable things about Freud was his refusal to take pain medication because he thought it would interfere with the concentration required for his work.[17] Had his own suffering factored into the meaning of his own life from his own point of view in a significant way, he could not have thought it rational to go on as he did. The reason he was not infected with pessimism was due not to how his working (or not working) might make him feel but to the meaning it had in his practical deliberations. His willingness to suffer showed how much more important the quality of his work was to the meaning of his life from his own point of view than how he felt.

Consider also the comparative worth of the love of knowledge and the value of the avoidance of one's own suffering. By the love of knowledge, I do not mean the abstract collective knowledge of humanity but one's having knowledge rather than ignorance. Of course, some knowledge is relatively trivial. Few of us would undergo any suffering at all to learn how many names are in the local phone book. Curiosity about matters of that sort are not enough even to kill a cat, but the price

[17] See Ernest Jones, *The Life and Work of Sigmund Freud*, vol. 3 (New York: Basic Books, 1957).

of the passion to know has dealt those who possess it a large share of pain and disappointment. People have literally worked themselves to death in its pursuit. Because dissatisfaction with one's own ignorance grows proportionately with the increase in one's knowledge, the love of knowledge, too, is a form of suffering. In the absence of the most austere conditions, the will to know pushes hedonic considerations, especially considerations of one's own suffering and discontentment, far into the background. This is just what it is like to have a deeply inquiring mind and a love of knowledge.

What can be said about knowledge can also be said about the pursuit of art and the love of beauty. The value of creative activity is at least as important to most of us as the value of knowledge, and no less demanding. Acquiring the fundamental skills that went into Michelangelo's work in the Sistine Chapel was no less tedious than acquiring the mathematical skills that went into Einstein's discovery of relativity. So whether you want to play the "Moonlight Sonata" or understand the principles of thermodynamics and how to apply them, there will be hours and hours of work to do in preparation. Those who think that in order to justify the effort the work must on balance be fun reveal a kind of soul in which a certain kind of love does not reside. And for every scientist and philosopher who has endured the disappointment and frustration of misleading lines of inquiry, there is an artist broken by an aesthetic vision beyond the reach of her skills and dedication. Yet we toil away at the vision, thinking little of how we feel, good or bad. Or at least the artists among us do. To live well seems to be this: to be caught up in something besides our feelings, even some very bad feelings, so that we do not care about them in a way that distorts the meaning of our lives. One form of tragedy was Beethoven's deafness and how being deaf made him feel; another would have been his taking his feelings as a reason to give up. The value of creating great music was so important to him that he would not be deterred by the disappointment of knowing that he would never be able to hear it.

In all these cases, the value that we actually place on personal goods – our loved ones, excellence, knowledge, art and beauty – shows that when compared to the value of the avoidance of our own individual suffering, these personal goods are vastly but not strictly superior to the value of how we feel. To be too attuned to how one feels in this sense is to be cut off from some of the goods that make life most meaningful, even if not the most pleasant or pain free. This says something very deep about the nature of our valuing and our tragic sense. To value how we feel, to care about our feelings to a certain degree and in a certain way, is itself a great tragedy. It is the tragedy of missing out on certain nonhedonic values.

So far, however, I have considered only the comparative value of one's own suffering and these other values. What about the comparative value of these other values and the suffering of others? For this question to reflect the issue at hand, we have to care (and care very deeply) about the suffering of others, not just our own. Moreover, we have to know about the suffering involved and live in the light of it; we cannot simply ignore it by immersing ourselves in personal goods or hide it with talk about the value of personal love, the commitment to excellence, and the pursuit of knowledge and art. To talk about the value of personal love, the commitment to excellence, and the pursuit of knowledge and art in cultivated ignorance of suffering is to convert such talk into platitudes.

As a way of focusing attention on the awareness of suffering in the comparative judgments to follow, return to the pessimistic assumptions we made at the outset regarding the prospects for humanity's future. You have at your disposal the bomb or some other version of the clean solution by which you can end it all for everyone both instantly and painlessly. Would you now have reasons for not employing it, and what would those reasons be? Could you be a secular personal optimist, even with your concern for the suffering of others? If you would not employ the clean solution now under these assumptions, at what point in such a cycle of developments would you and for what reasons? Would it be a greater tragedy to end it all now than to wait for a later point in the development of history on the pessimistic assumptions?

Different people will have different answers to these questions, even after careful reflection. For myself, I can only say that I would have reasons not to detonate the bomb, as long as I thought that there were reasonable prospects for my loved ones to live a meaningful life from their own points of view, that there were excellences left to aim for, that there were important things yet to learn and accomplish, that there was some beauty yet to be experienced in life, and that there was something significant left for me to do, short of detonating the bomb, to help some other people with their suffering. Moreover, I believe I could live my life with some passion and joy, though it would also be filled with a great deal of sadness. None of this makes any sense from the impersonal point of view. Some will say that it makes no sense at all, or that it merely reflects the attitude of someone indifferent to the plight of others. I can only say that it makes all the sense in the world to me, and that I live with a keen awareness that there is and will continue to be great suffering in the world. My life and the lives of my loved ones come at a cost, namely, that there are others who could take our place among the relatively privileged. This will always be so for others, until there is no one left.

So Jesus was right that we will always have the poor and the suffering with us. But what instruction should we take from this fact? Those of us who are fortunate should either take steps toward "detonating the bomb" or do what we can for those who are suffering, consistent with taking some delight in what gives our lives their central meaning. If we do neither, then we seem to waste the opportunity for what makes life worth living only to prolong the agony of others. So which should it be? The choice will result in the most profound tragedy, no matter which option we take. For those who have no hope for divine intervention, the choice will reflect a comparative judgment of which is the greater of two impending tragedies. Those who choose the apocalyptic solution believe that the tragedy of suffering is greater than the personal tragedy, the missed opportunity to live a life focused on the goods of love, of excellence, of knowledge, and of art and beauty. Those who reject the apocalyptic solution see the greater tragedy in forgoing a meaningful personal life even at the cost of relieving the suffering of the many.

What might a person who takes this latter view of the tragic alternatives be like? He might very well be a romantic realist. A romantic realist is a person who has impersonal values but who, with his Romantic predecessors, sees the ultimate significance of life in personal terms. He is also very aesthetically inclined. That the opportunity for beauty and creativity be missed is very nearly unthinkable to him. It is crucial that he live his life in a way that radiates beauty, even in an ugly world. Moreover, he has the capacity for horror and for living his life in the light of the facts, which means that his aesthetic capacities are tempered by other human concerns. He will not think with Nietzsche that the highest art humanity can produce can justify any cost in terms of suffering. He does not romanticize art and the aesthetic point of view in that way. Nor will he engage in any other pernicious fantasy, whether religious or secular. Still, if he loses a sense that life cannot be lived beautifully even in the awareness of a significant amount of tragedy, he will not find life worth living. Consequently, he will not harden himself against sympathy and respect for others. But neither will he let these concerns crowd his caring in a way that eclipses his awareness of the beauty of life. He will therefore have a very developed sense of tragic beauty, not of the sentimental sort that recoils from the awareness of horror and suffering, but one that courageously affirms life while remaining sensitive to the plight of others.

A person who takes this attitude will care very deeply about the suffering of others and will act on that concern, but he will not allow the suffering of others to eclipse his view of what makes his life worth living. It is a person of this sort, a person whose outlook on life is primarily personal and positive, who can sustain optimism that is not naive. Naive optimism blinds itself to the suffering, but the personal optimism of the romantic realist is dominated by joy even in the sorrowful recognition of suffering. For persons of this sort, not only is it true that they value these personal goods as vastly but not strictly superior to avoiding their own suffering, they also value them as vastly but not strictly superior to avoiding the suffering of others. To endorse life in the face of this is to realize that there is no escaping tragedy but that some forms of it can be avoided by those who have the courage to give themselves to the sources of value that are, with enough good luck, available.

Also, to be perfectly and brutally clear: the romantic realist is fully aware that romantic realism is a view for the fortunate. He is fully aware that his struggle for a meaningful life comes at a tragic cost to others and that were it not for enough good luck, the apocalyptic option would be his alternative of choice. He does not kid himself that his privileged position is somehow justified in terms of what is best for the least advantaged. This, he knows, is false. He is a realist, after all, a person not given to moral sentimentalities and pernicious fantasy. He knows that he is like other animals, a predator: he must eat to survive. And as he eats, and loves, and works, and creates, others starve and die. But, like the lion, he preys only as necessity requires, and it is this that he expects from others. Life is hard, but it can be beautiful, and this is one of the things that consoles him.

Finally, if we return to the thought experiment at the beginning of the chapter, it is important to point out that the temporal horizons of practical reason are never extended in the way that the thought experiment suggests. We do not extend the scope of our deliberations into eternity, nor do we extend them so far back into history as to outstrip our capacity for making sense of our lives from where we are now, from where we are now in our personal lives. We would not have the slightest idea of how to do such a thing. Why? Because the meaning of the future is framed by the meaning of the present, and there is nothing about the meaning of the present that extends so indefinitely into the future as to allow for certain kinds of calculations. None of us can any more calculate what it would be rational for future generations to do if they were to undergo a radical change in cultural values than Achilles could have anticipated how to cast a rational vote in a contemporary United States presidential election. What this should tell us is that the ultimate grounds for pessimism or optimism are first and foremost to be found in our personal values, the values that give us reasons for living from our own points of view. Which attitude we take will be a function both of luck and of character. We will need enough good luck to be given an adequate chance at a good life, and having the chance, we will need the courage to seize the day. If we have both, then life can be better than death.

5

Monism

An Epitaph

So there is no need for things which involve struggle.

Epicurus, from *The Principle Doctrines* by Diogenes Laertius

Nature has placed mankind under the governance of two sovereign masters, pain and pleasure. It is for them alone to point out what we ought to do, as well as to determine what we shall do. On the one hand the standard of right and wrong, on the other the chain of causes and effects, are fastened to their throne. They govern us in all we do, in all we say, in all we think: every effort we can make to throw off our subjection, will serve but to demonstrate and confirm it. In words a man may pretend to abjure their empire: but in reality he will remain subject to it all the while.

Jeremy Bentham, *The Principles of Morals and Legislation*

It is better to be a human being dissatisfied than a pig satisfied; better to be Socrates dissatisfied than a fool satisfied.

John Stuart Mill, *Utilitarianism*

Some things die hard. Rasputin and his zeal, a parent's love for a child, bigotry, first loves, addictions, and simple-minded solutions to complex problems – all come to mind. Others die easily enough but decay slowly, spoiling the environment in which they reluctantly dissolve. Rotting human corpses piled high at the gates of medieval cities during the bubonic plague are vivid examples. Ideas that have outlived their time are like both: they die hard yet linger like the animus of an old feud.

Discredited moral theories are like this, reinforcing the lesson that it is best to bury deep the dead or burn the bodies. When we turn from the dark views about value, nihilism, and pessimism to more positive, optimistic views, we find none more optimistic or pernicious than monism in its several varieties.

Almost everyone who has thought deeply about monistic theories of value now believes that they fail. Yet they remain discussed well beyond their relevance, while the more important work of understanding the conflicts among our values creeps along. What is needed is not another attempt to preserve the tradition, but a summary epitaph of why monism in its various forms arose historically, what contributions it has made to our understanding of our values, and why it died. But die it did, and it is time to burn the body and move on. Why? Because the body is diseased, infecting us with a severe inability to recognize the real tragedy of the human condition. Its most crucial flaw is the tragedy that it conceals and by concealing does nothing to diminish.

So I will not pretend here that any monistic theory has a claim to being taken seriously any longer as a guide to our lives. What we learn most from these theories are their mistakes and the mistakes of the views they replaced. Nor do we need to study every version of monism ever devised before we can get on with dealing with the plurality of our values. Rather, it is enough to learn some central lessons from some prominent monistic theories so that we are never tempted to think so simplistically again.

What, then, is monism? What are some of its central forms? Why did they arise? And what mistakes did they make that we should not repeat, particularly regarding the issue of tragic loss?

A monistic theory of value is one that says that all intrinsic value is reducible to one thing. The Epicureans claimed that it is tranquility; some Peripatetics of the Aristotelian school that it is the development and perfection of human capacities; the Stoics that it is virtue; Jeremy Bentham that it is intense pleasure; John Stuart Mill that it is pleasure both quantitatively and qualitatively measured; and some recent thinkers that it is "utility," the value that "economic man" allegedly seeks to maximize. Despite the differences, the essence of all monism is the claim that value is one and not many.

Secular versions of monism have usually emerged as alternatives to religious and other traditional conceptual schemes that appeal to authority to settle practical matters. This was as true in the classical world of Epicurus as in Bentham's world of the eighteenth-century Enlightenment. A consideration of hedonism will prove the point.

EPICURUS

In the world of ancient Greece, hedonism found its greatest exponent in Epicurus. It is important, then, to gain some historical perspective on how Epicureanism arose and what it opposed. Within the wider perspective of Greek intellectual history, it was one of many largely secular views that were in competition with the Greek religious tradition. Just as there was a breakdown in the authority of religion in the modern world that began with the Protestant Reformation, the influence of Galileo, and the success of the scientific method that culminated in a shift to secular thinking about morality, something similar occurred in the ancient world. The big difference between the two is that the influences that brought about the secular shift in the ancient world were more literary than scientific.

Consequently, appreciating the intellectual development of ancient Greece requires an understanding of the evolution of its literary history, one crucial theme of which is the struggle with the gods. Whether it was Homer, or Aeschylus, or Sophocles, or Euripides, one important task of the dramatist was to come to grips with a view of the relationship between the gods, the heroes, and the ordinary mortals. As that tradition developed with a recasting by different dramatists of the stock of Greek characters – Hector, Achilles, Odysseus, Agamemnon, Helen, Oedipus, Antigone, Hecuba, Iphigeneia, Electra, Zeus, Apollo, Prometheus, and the rest of the cast – an increasingly secular view emerged, with Euripides openly criticizing much of the religious tradition that had preceded him. Perhaps the pinnacle of the shift to a secular perspective in the ancient world came with Plato's dialogue *Euthyphro.* If the Protestant Reformation and Galileo's telescope were the gateways to secularism in the modern world, it can plausibly be argued that Euripides' plays and Plato's dialogues were the gateways to secularism in the ancient world. Once Socrates asked Euthyphro whether the gods loved the good because it was good or the good was good because the gods loved it, reason had opened a door that could not then be closed.

The problem of polytheism was the problem of conflict among values. If appeal to the gods was to settle issues regarding values, and if there were many gods with conflicts among them regarding their values, then religion directed lives in conflicting ways. The solution was to simplify: monotheism was one such way, and secularism another.

Although Plato himself never succeeded in liberating himself entirely from an otherworldly perspective, Aristotle and the thinkers who succeeded him in the Hellenistic era and the later Roman period made great strides. Though there are other dimensions to that intellectual development, one salient feature is its largely (though not entirely) secular bent. Nowhere is this more explicit than in Epicurus and his hedonistic version of monism.

Understanding the context in which the various competing moral views were considered is important. Instead of asking, Do the gods command that we do x or live in way y?, the question of what to do and how to live was posed within a conception of practical reason that dominated the ancient philosophical world. The question was, What is the best way to live?, and there was a widely shared conceptual scheme in which competing answers to that question were debated.[1] The best life was one that would satisfy certain criteria, none of which had to do with the commands of the gods.

The two most fundamental criteria were best articulated by Aristotle, who claimed that the best life must be both self-sufficient and final.[2] By self-sufficient, he meant that the best way to live is the way that is inclusive of all the goods that make for a good life. The crucial question regarding a way of life and the test for its self-sufficiency is this: can anything be added to or subtracted from that way of life to make it better? If the answer is yes, then that way of life is not self-sufficient. The thought is that as long as there is an alternative way of life that includes more of the kinds of things that are recognized as important from the perspective of those living it, then it is rational for them to take steps to improve their way of living so that it includes and recognizes these things. By finality, Aristotle meant that the best life must be such that it is chosen for itself and not for something

[1] Julia Annas, *The Morality of Happiness* (New York: Oxford University Press, 1993).

[2] Aristotle, *Nicomachean Ethics*, translated by Martin Ostwald (Indianapolis: Bobbs-Merrill, 1962), 14–19.

else.[3] The best life, then, is not lived in preparation for another life, as some religions would have us view our current lives. Together, these criteria open an inquiry of a completely secular nature into how to act and live. Practical reason is liberated from the authority-based conceptual scheme of religion, and the question of the religious life is subordinated to the criteria of finality and self-sufficiency. Religion is either eliminated or rationalized. Either way, secularism prevails. Of course, there was still talk about the gods by some, but the talk was largely a fifth wheel in the conceptual scheme, much as it often is today.

Epicurus's version of hedonistic monism was presented as an alternative to both the authority of religion and other competing secular views, especially Aristotle's. The best life, according to Epicurus, is the life of pleasure, because pleasure is the only thing that is good in itself.[4] Doggedly opposed to the religion of his day, Epicurus maintained that if we reflect on what could improve the life of pleasure, we will find that there is nothing. The test of self-sufficiency in the sense already mentioned is that if nothing can be added to or subtracted from a life to make it better, then it is self-sufficient. So what could be added to or subtracted from a life of pleasure to make it better? Epicurus thought that reflection would reveal that anything that caused anxiety, especially religious beliefs about an afterlife, made life less good than it could be and that this showed that pleasure understood in a certain way is the sole intrinsic good of life.[5] As will become clear, this contrasts sharply with the views that assume that more is always better and that the good life is such that it can always be improved.

The way Epicurus would have us understand pleasure is in terms of tranquility rather than as an intensely felt affective state, such as the intense pleasure of passionate sex. In this regard, his view of pleasure was much different from the modern conception advocated by Bentham. Pleasure understood as tranquility is an equilibrium state rather than something that can be charted on an ever-ascending scale. Think of the difference between the graph of a normal

[3] Aristotle, *Nicomachean Ethics*, 14–15.

[4] Epicurus, *The Epicurus Reader*, edited and translated by Brad Inwood (Indianapolis: Hackett, 1994), 60–2.

[5] He actually thought that anxiety depended on false belief, but it is hard to show how that is always the case. See my discussion in *Dignity and Vulnerability*.

electrocardiogram and a graph that would reveal a bullish stock market. For Epicurus, a graph that accurately reflects the life of pleasure looks much more like a normal electrocardiogram than one charting a bullish market. In this sense, pleasure as tranquility is not something that is subject to certain kinds of maximization strategies, and this distinguishes Epicurean hedonism from the modern variety that eventually led to the maximization strategies of contemporary decision theory. The emphasis on the life of tranquility is on reaching a certain state and maintaining it, rather than on being on the lookout for ever-greener pastures. One should therefore give oneself only to those experiences that maintain the tranquil life. Any particular good thing is measured by its conduciveness to such tranquility. Moreover, the tranquil life is chosen for itself rather than for something to which it can lead.

As the best life, the life of tranquility is ahistorical in the sense that it is lived for the moment, or at most for the short term. *Carpe diem* is the motto. The past and the future matter only to the degree to which they bear on the present. We should not be committed to things in the past in a way that disrupts our tranquility. The same applies to the future. To be committed to things in this way creates anxiety, and a life without anxiety is better than one with it. Moreover, more of a life with tranquility is not necessarily a good thing. To want a longer life of tranquility, to have the desire to extend one's tranquility indefinitely into the future, is a source of anxiety and is therefore irrational. It is also irrational because death is not a loss of tranquility. Losses can occur only to experiencing subjects, and dead people are not experiencing subjects. Death is nothing to us, because death is the end of our existence. Religious fears of the afterlife are thus one form of anxiety that is avoided by guiding one's life by the value of tranquility.

The essential thrust of Epicurean monism is that the good life is a life without conflict. The strategy for satisfying the self-sufficiency criterion is an eliminativist one: simplification by elimination. Eliminate the sources of conflict in your life, and tranquility is the result. Conflict and tranquility are incompatible with each other; so conflict, and whatever generates it, is incompatible with the good, and is therefore bad. The criterion of self-sufficiency requires that, if possible, conflict be subtracted from one's life in a way that leaves it worth living for itself. The point is to direct your life by caring about a value that by its intrinsic properties does not generate conflict, and Epicurus believed that pleasure understood as tranquility is the only thing that fits this description. So understood, Epicurean hedonism was a secular alternative to both monotheism and polytheism, as well as to other pluralistic views of value, such as Aristotle's. All these opposing views introduce conflicts among values into the lives of people and prevent them from living the best life. The solution is simplification by elimination: eliminate concern for anything that generates conflict and care only about what is left, which, for Epicurus, was tranquility. He even went so far sometimes as to define pleasure as the absence of pain, which can only be seen as a philosophically desperate attempt to find a value so devoid of conflict that the aims of his monism could be secure.

No doubt there is good advice to be found here, especially for those of us who live modern, hectic lives. We would all do well to detach ourselves from many of the sources of our anxiety, thereby improving our lives, not to mention the lives of those around us. There is no need worrying about the afterlife in the sense that there is something there that is utterly terrible to be feared. Nor is there something so grand there as to be anxiously anticipated. When you're dead, you're dead, and that is not like anything at all, good or bad. And it is a tragic fact about much religion that it keeps so much of humanity in a state of torment over this issue, a clear case of the bad prevailing over the good. If we learn nothing else from Epicureanism, it should be this: religion that teaches eternal damnation is evil (and so is religion that teaches eternal reward for bypassing the good things of an earthly life). That religion keeps the suicide rate down is true, but its means are suspect, especially considering how the thought of eternal damnation plays a role in deterring some from the relief of their suffering because it would be a cardinal sin to implement its remedy. Nor should we spend our time thinking that if we could just win the lottery, all our troubles would be over. Studies consistently show that improvements in income do not correlate with significant improvements in subjective well-being; sometimes, just the opposite.[6] Given a certain stability in some of the central things in our lives, we would all do well to clean

[6] See *Culture and Subjective Well Being*, edited by Ed Diener and Eunkook M. Suh (Cambridge, Massachusetts: MIT Press, 2003); and Tim Kasser, *The High Price of Materialism* (Cambridge, Massachusetts: MIT Press, 2003).

out a good bit of rubbish by simply not caring a whit about what a lot of people are fussing about. Many lives are wasted on anxieties about things that should not matter when some rather good things are present or easily within reach. Whether this is tragic or pathetic is sometimes hard to say.

It is one thing, however, to say that we should not care about some things or that we should not care about them as much as we sometimes do. But it is quite another to say that we should care only about one thing. Any plausible secular view about value will give the advice of the previous paragraph. So there is nothing special about Epicureanism or any other version of monism in regard to this advice. Epicureanism makes the much stronger claim that the elimination of conflict that results in the life of tranquility does not come at the loss of other good things. If it does, then the life of tranquility fails the criterion of self-sufficiency in the sense that something good is missing from that way of life. This is precisely what Aristotle thought.

Prior to the advent of Epicureanism, Aristotle had taught that the good life includes deep attachment to certain external goods – friends and family and community, for example. To the extent to which the existence and well-being of these good things are subject to conditions of risk, the best life will include a certain amount of anxiety and conflict. The contrast between the two views can be put in the form of an argument. Epicurus seemed to argue the following: (i) if something disrupts tranquility, then it is not a good that is to be included in the best life; (ii) deep attachment to externals causes anxiety and conflict and disrupts tranquility; therefore, (iii) deep attachment to externals is not a good that is to be included in the best life. Aristotle, on the other hand, reasoned in just the opposite fashion: (i) if deep attachment to externals is a part of the best life, then the best life will include some anxiety and conflict; (ii) deep attachment to externals is a part of the best life; therefore, (iii) the best life will include some anxiety and conflict.

Both arguments are clearly designed to satisfy the criterion of self-sufficiency, understood as the requirement that the best life should not leave any good thing out. On the one hand, Epicurus thought that although we are deeply attached to externals, when we learn how caring deeply about them causes anxiety and conflict, we will see that subtracting this kind of concern from our lives makes life better. Thus, on his view, the life without anxiety and conflict passes the self-sufficiency test. Aristotle, on the other hand, thought that life without such deep commitment would not be worth living, even if the life of deep commitment includes a certain amount of anxiety and conflict. His view of the self-sufficiency test requires a life with some anxiety and conflict, and therefore pleasure, even understood as tranquility, is not the only good.

Of course, the argument did not end there. The Epicureans appealed to another self-sufficiency test, which I will call the vulnerability test, as a criterion for whether a life was the best life. To meet this criterion, not only must the best life be self-sufficient in the sense that it is inclusive of the goods of life, and not only must it be final in the sense that it is chosen for itself and not for something else, it must also be self-sufficient in the sense that it is the life that is least vulnerable to the forces of chance. The idea is that the best life is one that is under the full control of the person living it, and one that is vulnerable to the forces of chance is not.[7] Aristotle himself had seemed to endorse this criterion at one point when observing that the gods live the best life and that their lives do not depend at all on chance.[8] Again, the strategy is eliminativist: vulnerability decreases the control one has over one's life; therefore, eliminate concern for values that generate conflict. The Epicureans thereby used the vulnerability test against Aristotle by employing it to defend the view that the tranquil life is superior to the life with deep commitments to externals, the former life avoiding the vulnerability of the latter. In fact, the vulnerability test seems to be the bulwark in the defense of Epicurean monism, the argument being that the life given to tranquility is the life most under our control and most invulnerable to the forces of chance, the one immune to conflict.

This is a very telling dispute. What it reveals is that the dispute between Aristotle and the Epicurean monists turns on the recognition of tragedy. If you accept the vulnerability test as a criterion for practical decisions about how to live and what to do, you will be searching for a way to live that precludes the possibility of tragedy. The whole appeal of the life of tranquility and complete self-control seems to be that it

[7] Epicurus, *The Epicurus Reader*, 30.
[8] Aristotle, *Nicomachean Ethics*, 291–5.

eliminates the kind of conflict that can give birth to tragedy. Nothing, even one's own future, is worth caring enough about to generate anxiety, let alone grief, horror, and despair. But if you are like Aristotle, you have a sense of tragedy because of what you think is important in life. You think that friends, and family, and community, and other things over which you have limited control are central to what life is about, more central than your control over life. Your sense of what is important together with the self-sufficiency test will lead you to reject both the vulnerability test and any theory that depends on it for success. In short, Aristotle's conception of tragedy was that even if we have a full view of the best life and exercise all the control we can in regard to its pursuit, bad luck might still prevent us from living the best life, the one that is self-sufficient and final.

Though it is part of my argument that Aristotle's view is too optimistic to account for the full force of tragedy, Nussbaum is right that Aristotle recognizes that we are not invulnerable to tragic loss. By contrast, the Epicurean view is such that we can never experience tragedy in virtue of aiming at the best life. It is by aiming at the kinds of things that can bring conflict and tragedy in their wake that we fail to live a good life, let alone the best life. We should eliminate concern for things that generate conflict and aim at something that is invulnerable to loss. Once again, the problem for which monism is a solution is the problem of conflict-generating values, and the strategy is eliminativist. What monotheists sought in heaven, Epicureans sought on Earth: a kind of value that would make life immune to sorrow.

If the best life is open to loss, then the vulnerability test cannot be a fundamental test of practical reason, because it assumes that ultimate value is such that if it were fully realized, there would be no occasion for sorrow. Assuming, therefore, that Aristotle was right, that the things that make a good life good for most of us do make us vulnerable to loss, the classical model of practical reason proceeds with two criteria for testing whether an action is a component of the best life: the criteria of self-sufficiency and finality. If we accept our tragic sense as showing us something deep and important about our values, we should reject the vulnerability test as a criterion for deciding how to act and live. But it is hard to imagine making a practical choice that leaves out of consideration anything that might be importantly affected by our actions (self-sufficiency). It is also hard to see how the ultimate justification for a way of life could be other than the fact that it just does preserve all of what is found to be important in life in a way that makes it worthy of choice for itself and not for something to which it leads (finality).

The dispute between Epicurus and Aristotle, then, is instructive in two crucial regards. The first involves the classical form of practical reason, and the second, our tragic sense. I take the form of practical reason on the classical tradition to be one guided by the criteria of finality and self-sufficiency. As applied to decisions about whether to do x or y, the most fundamental issue is how doing x or y reflects and expresses a way of life that duly recognizes what a person believes is intrinsically good. Living well is a matter of constructing a way of life around things that are valued for themselves. The classical conception of practical reason is therefore essentially an expressivist conception.[9] By this, I mean (in part) that it is about more than the means to ends. Of course, there is much in practical reasoning, even on the classical view, that is about taking the best means to intrinsically valued ends. But sometimes we are faced with a more basic task, the task of ordering our ends. On the classical conception of practical reason, the criteria of self-sufficiency and finality allow us to order our ends in a way that expresses an integrated picture of what the best life is about. On this view, a rational person lives in a way that clearly expresses the value of her life. To accomplish this, she must act in a way that expresses an integrated view of the things she values intrinsically, and in order to do this, she must act in a way that expresses priority relations among her ends. She will therefore be very careful when she is constructing her way of life not to exclude from her deliberations some ends that she values. Moreover, she will be careful to see to it that her actions express the kind of value any particular end has for her. If an end is of minor value, she will be careful to see to it that her pattern of behavior and reasoning reflect this fact. On the other hand, if an end is of enormous value, she will be careful that her life with its pattern of behavior expresses this fact as well. And if there are different kinds of ends that express different kinds of value, she will be concerned that her life and its patterns of behavior express these differences in kind. These are all considerations of self-sufficiency. Finally, it will be crucial

9 Elizabeth Anderson, *Value in Ethics and Economics* (Cambridge, Massachusetts: Harvard University Press, 1993), 17–43.

to her that her life and its patterns of behavior reflect the fact that her life is chosen just for the fact that it expresses what the best life is about, namely, that it accommodates all the things that she thinks are intrinsically important in the way that she thinks them important. In this sense, there is a deep connection between the classical conception of practical reason and Romanticism. The Romantics would have us live in such a way that our lives are works of art. The classical thinkers would agree.

Now to the second point about tragedy. What would make you believe that when others are in serious danger, composure rather than anxiety is always the best expression of what you think life is about? What would make you think that calmness in such circumstances is the ultimate expression of wisdom? Of course, you might think that calmness is called for in order to act most effectively to deal with the danger. But this is not the Epicurean point. Calmness, on the Epicurean view, is an indication of the value of what is at stake. On what assumptions is that sort of calmness a reflection of wisdom? What view of intrinsic value must you have to think that poise and serenity in such circumstances are qualities of the most expressive actions and that acting in fear, grief, and horror expresses betrayal of what is most important? Would it not be either because you believe that nothing can harm those you value or because you believe that they are not important in their own right? You might believe both, if you are a hedonist of the Epicurean sort. By reflecting on the criterion of self-sufficiency you find that there is only one thing of intrinsic value and that when properly understood the life of pleasure without conflict leaves no room for anxiety. You will be very concerned, then, that your life does not express a tragic sense. Indeed, to do so would be to betray what your life is about, and that, given the expressivist function of practical reason, would be irrational.

If, however, you do value others and you do believe that they can be harmed, you will not see a life of complete composure, poise, and tranquility as expressive of what your life is about. Rather, you will see a life guided by value that is inherently devoid of conflict-generating properties as expressing a betrayal of what you think is most important. You will see it as excluding consideration of goods that it ought to include and as an expression of the intrinsic value of a life you think is not worthy of choice. Moreover, you will want to live in a way that makes it clear that you reject such a life and its priorities; otherwise, your life will not express what it is about. To express what your life is about, it must express the tragic dimensions of life. To do this, it must express the fact that life is about some things external to us that are not entirely within our control. For this to be the case, life cannot just be about tranquility or any value that is inherently invulnerable to generating conflict. That there is such a value is a pernicious fantasy.

In this context, it is crucial to note that when practical reason is understood to have an expressive function, as it was in the Greek world, the expression or repression of emotion becomes paramount. Both the Epicureans and the Stoics had an expressivist conception of practical reason, and they thought that the best life would repress and subordinate the emotions in a significant way. To live the life of a good Epicurean or Stoic was not just to live a life uncontrolled by the emotions but to live a life that actually expressed a certain attitude toward the emotions.[10] So too for Aristotle. It was important to him that the best life for humans express and make explicit the appropriate emotional engagement with valued externals. A person who is practically rational will reason differently about his emotional life than one who is irrational. For Aristotle, this meant that the rational person's actions will express courage in the face of fear but not foolhardiness.[11] For the Epicureans and the Stoics, the best person, the most rational person, the person with true knowledge of value, will have extirpated his fear, and this will be expressed in his behavior and way of life.[12] All these ancient schools of thought were expressivist, and, as such, they all required a certain transparency of practical reason. Unless their lives – their behavior and their reasoning about their actions – made transparent their emotional engagement or lack of emotional engagement with the world, then their lives did not express what their lives were about. We can add, then, to self-sufficiency and finality the transparency criterion as the third criterion employed by the classical conception of practical reason. In its Epicurean form, the transparency

[10] Martha C. Nussbaum, *Upheavals of Thought* (Cambridge: Cambridge University Press, 2001).

[11] Aristotle, *Nicomachean Ethics*, 70–2.

[12] Martha C. Nussbaum, *The Therapy of Desire: Theory and Practice in Hellenistic Ethics* (Princeton, New Jersey: Princeton University Press, 1994), 102–39, 280–315.

criterion is met by an emotional repertoire that expresses no sense of conflict, and this, on their view, is because of the nature of ultimate value: it is inherently free of conflict-generating properties, which is to say that if fully realized it would present no occasion for sorrow. In its Aristotelian form, and in any form that duly recognizes a tragic dimension to life, practical reasoning about how to live must express the tragic emotions of sadness, grief, and horror, along with the positive emotions. Not only must life with its conflicts be properly thought and felt, it must also be properly expressed.

Whatever we learn from Epicureanism, then, it cannot be that we should guide our lives by a value that is invulnerable to conflict. And once that lesson is learned, we can keep the advice about avoiding anxiety based on false religious beliefs and other superstitions. We can also take to heart the challenge to reduce the rubbish in our lives by caring less about things that do not really matter. But it is well past time to burn the body of Epicurus's thought that says that we should care only about one thing. In this regard, his monism no more resolves the conflicts among our values than the religious views he sought to supplant. And, in Nietzsche's terms, it is hard not to see Epicureanism as a form of decadence, a flight from the will to live for the things we value most.

If there is then to be a hedonistic basis for thought, feeling, and expression in regard to our values and our tragic sense, it will have to be found in some hedonistic alternative to Epicureanism. With this in mind, it is time to turn to Bentham's quantitative hedonism. The lessons to be learned from rejecting Bentham's hedonism are different than those learned from rejecting the Epicurean version.

BENTHAM

Bentham published *The Principles of Morals and Legislation*, the work that sets out his theory of value, in 1789, and he died in 1832. He entered Oxford University at the age of twelve, subsequently studied law, which he never practiced, and spent the remainder of his life working for legal reform in a society in which privilege and religion kept the majority of people living truncated, often miserable lives. Anyone familiar with Victor Hugo's *Les Miserables* or Charles Dickens's *A Tale of Two Cities* should have an idea of the effects of what Bentham saw himself as trying to correct. Most simply, what he wanted to do was to turn a society in which the greatest good for the fewest number was the status quo into a society in which the greatest good for the greatest number prevailed. Given that way of looking at the choice, it is hard to disagree with Bentham.

The sources of the status quo were aristocratic privilege and asceticism, both of which had their foundation in established religion. Two examples of legal reforms that were eventually made (due in no small part to the influence of Bentham's work) illustrate the point regarding aristocratic privilege. In 1828, four years before Bentham's death, the Test Acts, acts that prevented Protestants who were not members of the Church of England from attending universities, working in government jobs, or holding positions in the professions, were repealed. Prior to this, Protestants, who were not a part of the privileged Anglican aristocracy, were cut off from the primary sources of social well-being, and many of them were left to languish in poverty. Shortly afterward, in the 1830s, Earl Grey's reforms changed an electoral system in which the only voters who were allowed to elect members of the House of Commons were those who owned large tracts of land that had been created in medieval times under the influence of the church. Here, again, aristocratic privilege buttressed by religious tradition served to cut off the majority from the political means of relief.

Asceticism worked in another way to preserve the status quo, and here it is the religion of the majority that is the culprit. It is one thing for the High Church of the aristocracy to tell the miserable majority that they should be satisfied with their plight, and quite another for them to be told this by the populist religion of evangelical Protestantism itself. Though John Wesley (1703–1791), who laid the foundations for the Methodist Church, was educated at Oxford into the Anglican ministry, his sentiments and teachings were anything but religiously aristocratic. He even worked for reforms to improve education for the poor and for the abolition of slavery in the British colonies. But the fact remains that his gospel was largely that of Calvinism and the asceticism that went along with it. Indeed, Calvinism was very much in the air that the less fortunate had to breathe during the British Enlightenment. On the one hand, Calvinism reinforced trends of the Enlightenment by teaching the work ethic and the visibility of the elect. But on the other, it taught that it is not the rewards one reaps here on Earth that matter, but those that come in the life hereafter. Here we must be willing to live the austere life and forsake the life of pleasure and comfort for the sake of more spiritual values. The result was a message that reinforced passivity to privilege, eventually making the spiritual message of evangelicalism palatable even to the Anglican Church.[13] Low Church is fine, as long as it keeps the rabble in their place.

Bentham's thought is best understood in the context of his tendency to see the ideas of his day as being either favorable to the status quo or opposed to it, whether those advocating those views were aware of it or not. Just as the spirituality of the impoverished Protestant believer did not see his asceticism as reinforcing aristocratic privilege, neither did the advocates of natural law, or natural rights, or moral intuitionism. Nevertheless, Bentham tended to see all his competitors as either willing or unwilling supporters of the status quo. What was needed from his point of view was a foundation for morals and legislation that would reverse the moral equation and that would be based on science rather than religion.

Bentham, then, did not want us, as Epicurus did, to eliminate the things we care about over which we have little or no control. To the contrary, he wanted us to take control of our circumstances and create an environment in which the greatest number can live in the best possible way. Where Epicurus had advocated an introspective solution to the problem of conflict, Bentham advocated political action backed by rigorous science, and he thought that there could be a science of how we could do this. What is common to both is that they thought that the key to dealing with conflict is to simplify value to a matter of one thing.

But how did they differ?

Not only did Bentham have a different conception of pleasure than Epicurus, he also employed a different strategy for addressing conflict, as well as a different notion of what practical reason is like. It is important to see all three points. Where Epicurus's conception of pleasure was equable, Bentham's was cumulative. Where Epicurus's strategy for addressing conflict was eliminativist, Bentham's was reductionist. And where Epicurus's conception of practical reason was expressivist, Bentham's was mathematical.

[13] Wesley is memorialized in Westminister Abbey.

Bentham was a quantitative hedonist, meaning that he thought that the only positive value is pleasure and that the terms in which pleasure (or pain) can be measured are all quantitative in nature. No qualitative categories apply. Bentham was an Enlightenment thinker of a distinctively British sort. He saw himself as the Newton of legislation, trying to stem the tide of aristocratic privilege and religious superstition. He wanted to quantify morals and legislation in a way analogous to the way in which Newton had quantified physics. He wanted a science of morality and legislation that was empirical and subject to empirical testing. So he saw himself, as did other British Enlightenment thinkers, as constructing a view of reason that was distinguished not only from religious authority but also from the a priori methods of the continental Enlightenment tradition. He thought, as did Locke and Hume and other British thinkers, that recourse to a priori truths or innate ideas was little more than a disguised appeal to authority that sealed off progress from the benefits of experience. If human reason is really to be autonomous, it must tie itself to induction. That is what the British Enlightenment was most fundamentally about.[14] What he sought in a theory of value was one that provided the basis for rigor, for measurement, for experimentation, for some public means of verifying normative claims, and above all for reducing and eliminating conflict. Just as physics should be based on a self-correcting method that is empirically and publicly testable, so should morals and legislation. The result of such a method would be the systemizing of legislation analogous to the Newtonian systemizing of physical nature. And it would be based on a single value that excludes nothing good. All this he thought he had found in his version of hedonism. Bentham was so confident of this that he once predicted that his Constitutional Code would be in force in all the nations of the world by the year 2825.[15]

How, then, does Bentham's hedonism anatomize and quantify morals and legislation in a way as to make a science of them? The answer: by reduction, by reducing all good things to one simple value and all bad things to one simple disvalue. Where Epicurean monism was strategically eliminativist, Benthamic monism was strategically

[14] Roy Porter, *The Creation of the Modern World: The British Enlightenment* (New York: Norton, 2000).

[15] John Dinwiddy, *Bentham* (Oxford: Oxford University Press, 1989), 122.

reductionist. Both, however, were essentially defined in terms of a search for value that was inherently conflict-free.

The foundation for morals and legislation must be in human happiness rather than in the divine right of kings, the will of God, or any other mysterious source. The latter, according to Bentham, are all "fictions" rather than science. Moreover, human happiness itself must also be understood in a way that avoids fictions and is scientifically quantifiable. The opening lines of *An Introduction to the Principles of Morals and Legislation* are stark but instructive:

> Nature has placed mankind under the governance of two sovereign masters, pain and pleasure. It is for them to point out what we ought to do, as well as to determine what we shall do. On the one hand the standard of right and wrong, on the other the chain of causes and effects, are fastened to their throne.[16]

If there is to be a moral science, a science of value analogous to the science of physics, it must have its foundation in something both simple and empirically observable. The study of human psychology provides both. By studying human psychology – the facts of what we care most deeply about – the legislator learns what we value as the greatest good and what we have reasons for doing. According to Bentham, the only thing we really care positively about can be reduced to one thing – obtaining pleasure – and the only thing we care negatively about can be reduced to one thing – avoiding pain. All else is illusion, fiction, and scientific rubbish. Just as physics is a matter of discovering the laws of nature governing quantifiable variables, so too are morals and legislation. The imperative is to quantify, quantify, quantify.

The question is how to quantify pleasure and pain. Again, the monistic strategy is reductionist: its object, the eradication of conflict. Just as all positive value is reduced to pleasure, all pleasure is reduced to one simple property of an affective state. So too for pain. Bentham thought that pleasure and pain were simple affective states or feelings with only one qualitative property each. Pleasantness, according to Bentham, is that simple qualitative property of a feeling in terms of which it is worthy to be pursued and obtained, and painfulness is that simple qualitative property of a feeling in terms of which it is worthy of

[16] Jeremy Bentham, *An Introduction to the Principles of Morals and Legislation* (New York: Hafner, 1948), 1.

avoidance. Moreover, the intrinsic property of pleasure that makes it worthy of pursuit is such that in itself it does not generate conflict with other things of value. It cannot, because of its simplicity. More good is always more of the same simple thing, and less good is always less of the same simple thing. For this reason, there cannot be any conflict between good and good. In this sense, positive intrinsic value is a unity because pleasure is a unity. The same is true in reverse of pain. Because of its simple avoidance-worthy property, pain is also a unity. Less pain is always better than more pain, but it is never good. It is always, even as a lesser evil, something worthy of avoidance. So conceived, Bentham thought of generic types of value in terms of their simple, intrinsic good-or-bad-making properties that can vary only in a limited number of purely quantitative ways. Just as physics is best studied by reducing the world to its smallest atomic parts, morals and legislation are best studied by reducing value to its basic parts. Pleasure and pain, then, are the basic atoms of the normative world. The value of reduction in physics is in the eradication of conflicting explanations, but the value of reduction in morals and legislation is in the eradication of conflict in action, policy, and feeling. Normative reductionism will be successful and conflicts in value will prove eradicable if all value can be quantified in terms of intensity, duration, propinquity, certainty, fecundity, purity, and extent.[17] Considering these categories is instructive of how deeply Bentham was committed to having us think of morality in a way analogous to the emerging physics of the Enlightenment, and it is a way of thinking that is decidedly foreign to poetic temperament and expression.

A consideration of four of the categories is sufficient for understanding the real thrust of the view. As to the first category: to the extent to which the intensity of a feeling or affective state is pleasurable, to that extent the more intense it is, the more pleasurable and thus the more valuable it is. If pleasure x is twice as intense (as a pleasure) as pleasure y, then, everything else being equal, pleasure x is twice as valuable as pleasure y. The reverse, of course, is true of pains. So too with duration. To the extent to which an affective state is pleasurable, to that extent the longer it lasts the better. If pleasure x is just as intense as pleasure y but lasts twice as long, then, everything else being equal,

[17] Ibid., 29–32.

pleasure x is twice as valuable as pleasure y. Note here the difference with Epicurus: tranquility is not measured in terms of intensity, and a life of pleasure, according to Epicurus, is not made better by longevity. For Bentham, pleasure is cumulative; for Epicurus, it is equable.

Intensity and duration are thus the primary quantitative categories of Bentham's calculus. Before addressing the categories of fecundity and extent, however, it is important to note a looming problem for Bentham's hedonism as a version of monism. For Bentham, pleasure is a unity because of its simplicity, and pain is a unity because of its simplicity. But is hedonic value a unity and a simplicity? We know how, on Bentham's view, to compare one pleasure to another pleasure, and one pain to another pain, but how are we to compare the relative worth of obtaining pleasure and avoiding pain? On his view, it is clear that a pleasure that is twice as intense or that lasts twice as long as another is twice as valuable. Similarly, it is clear that a pain that is twice as intense or that lasts twice as long as another is twice as disvaluable. But what is the comparative positive value of a particular pleasure and the negative value of a particular pain? Suppose that a particular pleasure measures +4 as a pleasure on the combined intensity and duration scale, that a particular pain measures –4 as a pain on such a combination, and that everything else is equal. Now, what if the cost of obtaining this particular pleasure is the occurrence of this particular pain? Do the numbers cancel out, or is the avoidance of pain more important than the gaining of pleasure?

The way Bentham instructed us to make the calculations assumes that –1 unit of pain is the negative equivalent of +1 unit of pleasure. They are inversely equivalent in the sense that –1 unit of pain cancels +1 unit of pleasure, making the overall hedonic value zero. The way of comparing pleasure to pain is reduced to the way of comparing pleasure to pleasure and pain to pain. But this reduction of hedonic measurement goes against the strongly and widely held belief that, everything else being equal, the avoidance of pain is more important than the gaining of pleasure. The problem is showing how Bentham's quantitative hedonism could allow for this. If +1 unit of pleasure and –1 unit of pain are inversely equivalent in terms of the quantitative categories, and if avoiding pain is more important than pursuing pleasure, then either (i) there are other quantitative categories than those employed by Bentham, or (ii) there is a qualitative difference between the pursuit of pleasure and the avoidance of pain, or (iii) there is some nonhedonic covering value that accounts for the difference. This is no small problem for his theory of value and his reductionistic ambition to anatomize and quantify human happiness as the basis for a science of morals and legislation. Indeed, it is unclear that hedonic value, even assuming the simplicity of pain and pleasure, is in the end monistic. If pleasure is one thing and pain another, and if avoiding units of pain is more important than acquiring units of pleasure, as the Newtonian analogue to physics would have it, what is it that they are both units of such that they are units of the same thing but measured differently? What is hedonic value, the scientific study of which shows this to be the case? I will come back to this later; for now, it is important to understand the role of two other categories in Bentham's calculus in their stark mathematical expression: fecundity and extent.

Fecundity is the mathematical likelihood that an affective state will be followed by an affective state of the same kind – that pleasure will beget pleasure and pain will beget pain. In calculating the fecundity of a pleasurable activity, Bentham would have us add each additional pleasurable occurrence to the first to get the net value of the tendency of that activity. A consideration of the pleasure of games is instructive. Take the simple game of tic-tac-toe. For a person of normal intelligence, the pleasure of playing this game is in the time it takes to learn that if both players play intelligently, no one can win. This is to say that playing the game gets old very quickly. The first time might result in a small payoff in intensity, but the second time would yield considerably less. Chess, however, works in just the opposite way. The game is difficult, which makes the first playing a bit pleasurable but also a bit frustrating. As one repeats the game and gains skill at playing it, the pleasure increases. This shows that the pleasure of playing chess is more fecund for most people than that of playing tic-tac-toe. A similar analysis is true of the relative worth of poetry over network television. It is not that there is some qualitative difference between the pleasures, but that one is more fecund than the other. To say that a source of pleasure is fecund, on Bentham's view, is to say that it repeatedly rewards in the currency of a simple affective property or feeling. This was Bentham's quantitative reduction of the concept of quality. It was his way of keeping value simple and free of inherently conflict-generating properties, as would be the case if some pleasures had some inherently pursuit-worthy properties and other pleasures had other such properties, which would make them qualitatively distinct values. It was also behind the claim attributed to him by John Stuart Mill that pushpin is as good as poetry, perhaps another way of Bentham's showing disdain for what he saw as aristocratic intellectual pretensions.

Finally, there is extent. Intensity, duration, and extent (along with propinquity, certainty, and purity) measure what we can call individual utility, the hedonic payoff for a single individual regarding some action or policy. Extent is the category that measures social utility, the hedonic payoff for a society as a whole rather than for an individual. The figure for extent is gained simply by adding all the individual utilities affected by an action or policy. In this way, the sum of utility is the sum of units of the same simple thing.

Such are the basics of Bentham's science of morals and legislation insofar as the theory of value is concerned. Just as Newton's laws were designed to take the mystery out of motion, Bentham's theory of value was designed to take the mystery out of human value. Everything, at least in theory, is properly quantified. There is no distinction between pleasures (or pains) in quality or tone, but only in intensity and duration. For this reason, there cannot be conflicts of certain sorts. Why? Because value is a unity, and this because it is simple. That value would be a unity free of inherently conflict-generating properties was a prized desideratum for Bentham. Without it, the unity Bentham sought to bring to legislation was threatened. As we will see, this raises the issue of whether Bentham's hedonism can account for our tragic sense. But the basic point here is that, for Bentham, the apparent plurality of value is really an illusion. The multiplicity of the things we seem to value are better seen rather as different *sources* of the same simple thing, namely, pleasure, than as distinct values themselves. Everything we hold dear is preserved within the bounds of science, and there is no need for religious superstition or appeal to something equally puzzling called the natural law. Moreover, this gives us a solid footing to undermine the status quo and to get on with the serious business of improving people's lives.

No doubt, there can be certain kinds of tragedies on Bentham's account. In fact, he wanted to point to the tragic situation of the poor and unfortunate, often the majority of the people of his day. When legislation (which was Bentham's major concern) was based on anything other than securing the sources of hedonic value, the promotion of pleasure and the avoidance of pain, the results were tragic, he thought, a tragic case of the bad prevailing over the good. Reconsider what he saw himself as combating. On the one hand was the asceticism of religion and the moralists, and on the other was the privilege of the aristocracy. Just as Newtonian science found its greatest foes in the church and Aristotelian science, human happiness, Bentham thought, found its greatest foes in religious asceticism and aristocratic privilege.[18]

What Bentham wanted his religious contemporaries to understand was that they had mistaken evil for good and that there is nothing to be said on behalf of asceticism as an ideal. Whether it is motivated by religious fear or by the moral vanity of Stoic self-indulgence and indifference to suffering, asceticism is a sickness that only cuts people off from what is good about life. To be cut off from life because religious belief or Stoic moralizing about virtue frowns on the enjoyment of pleasure is one of the great tragedies of ignorance and superstition. Bentham could only have thought that any serious suggestion that modern problems be solved by a return to Stoicism was a sign that the Enlightenment had failed miserably, and that to step back into a conceptual scheme of that sort, however revised, was to step back into darkness. The forces of ignorance not only prevent the progress of science and true belief, they also block the road to happiness and a life well lived. The tragedy of asceticism, then, is the tragedy of the irrational loss of pleasure and the irrational incurrence of pain because of ignorance, superstition, and fear – all the common enemies of the Enlightenment. The tragedy of aristocratic privilege is that the many suffer for the pleasure of the few, for no other reason than that the privileged control the law and its power. Here it is impossible not to notice that there is not all that much difference between Marie Antoinette's advice to the poor, let them eat cake, and religious and Stoic advice to the suffering, let them learn to love virtue and see that pain is a matter of indifference. In either case – asceticism or privilege – the tragedy is accounted for in terms of loss that is quantified in exactly the same way. The tragedy is that there is another way of arranging legislation that would have prevented the needless loss of pleasant and gratifying lives.

[18] About asceticism, see especially ibid., 9–10.

Which, then, seems more plausible from a secular perspective: Bentham's hedonism or aristocratic privilege and religious (and moral) asceticism? From that vantage point, Bentham's monism looks like the progressive view he took it to be. Better a monist than a defender of the tragic effects of privilege and asceticism.

So why should we reject it?

Historically, many reasons have been given, some of the most prominent of which have to do with justice. But I want to focus on the forms of tragedy that it conceals. We have seen some of the ways in which it recognizes tragedy as the bad prevailing over the good: the minority of aristocratic privilege and religious asceticism prevailing over the majority of the poor and unfortunate and their access to the sources of joy and pleasure. But what other forms of tragedy might there be?

Viewed in terms of his own theory, the Benthamic conception of tragedy must be expressed mathematically. The question is how to define a hedonic baseline or threshold in terms of which to measure hedonic loss as tragic loss. What level of hedonic value is the mark below which tragic loss begins? For Bentham, the baseline must be expressed in the numbers under the category of extent, and initially the most plausible candidate is hedonic zero. How on Bentham's calculus could you call a positive balance of pleasure over pain tragic? There seems no room for the thought. What would be tragic about it?

Perhaps the tragedy might be that things could have been better. Whether this is plausible depends on the case. Suppose I have just enough pleasure to have escaped a negative balance. I am dangling near the precipice of hedonic abyss. I am not at all miserable, but I am not far from it. Now suppose this is true for a whole population. Then it seems a tragedy if something much better is available. So we can add this kind of case to the Benthamic stock of tragic forms: first is the case of the bad prevailing over the good, where a negative hedonic balance prevails over a positive hedonic balance, and now we have the second case of the lesser good prevailing over the greater good, where both the lesser good and the greater good have a positive balance.

Can we say that anything less than the hedonic maximum is a tragic loss, a case of the lesser good prevailing over the greater good? Surely not. A world full of extremely ecstatic people with their sources of joy fully secured would not be tragic in any plausible sense just because there might be another world with one more person in it who is extremely but not quite as ecstatic as the people in the first world. There are many degrees of less-than-perfect lives that are not tragic lives, and whatever Benthamic conception of tragedy we construct from his theory must respect this fact. There is some point, therefore, at which lives are pleasant enough that their not being made more pleasant is not a tragic loss. To deny this is as silly as the views Bentham sought to replace. Yet there is nothing, absolutely nothing, about Bentham's calculus that tells us where to mark the baseline. Whatever consideration would make the baseline clear would be a consideration *imposed* on the numbers of Bentham's calculus. It would not be *revealed* by the numbers. The numbers, then, do not express the value at stake.

One possibility is that there are other values at work in defining the baseline, a point that it is Bentham's burden to address. It is, after all, part of Bentham's argument that the appearance of the plurality of values can be explained away by appealing to the apparent objects of value as different sources of one simple thing. Consequently, it is for him to show how that thesis can solve the problem with the tragic baseline. Otherwise, he is left with the ridiculous position that anything short of the maximum balance of pleasure over pain is a tragic case of the lesser good prevailing over the greater good. And that is a promiscuous and indulgent stock of tragic forms.

In other ways, his stock is woefully impoverished. Sometimes it fails to recognize cases in which, even considering hedonic value alone, the bad prevails over the good. I have in mind cases involving the relative value of pleasure attained versus the value of pain and suffering avoided. Despite appearances, Bentham's hedonism fails to distinguish adequately the relative importance of these two hedonic values. Indeed, it fails to provide a way of distinguishing pain from suffering. By so doing, his monism is blind to a conflict at the heart of human experience, and, when combined with his mathematical conception of practical reason, it conceals forms of tragedy that even any adequate account of hedonic value should reveal. Even worse, it allows, as will become clear, the very status quo principle, the greatest good for the fewest number, that Bentham so wanted to replace.

Imagine a hospital unit in which pain medication can be distributed in a way that relieves everyone's pain and allows each a significant degree of pleasure, or can be distributed in a way that allows some people to suffer excruciating pain but allows others to sustain a state of drug-induced euphoria without the consequences of addiction (the medical equivalent of aristocratic privilege). Suppose the mathematical expression of the value contained in each of these states of affairs on the Benthamic calculus is the same – say, +100 units of positive hedonic value, the excess balance of pleasure over pain. On Bentham's account, the hedonic states would be mathematically and morally equivalent and opaque to the results of the different distributions.

But it is hard to see how the second distribution does not involve a loss not incurred by the first. In order for the second distribution to be possible, where some suffer from a negative balance of pain over pleasure (assuming the number of people involved remains constant), some of the people in the first distribution, where everyone is living pleasantly, would have their well-being, which was already good to very good, increased. For them, therefore, there is a loss on the first distribution in comparison to the second. As we have already noted, however, a loss of this sort is not a tragic loss: there is a point at which the loss of excess pleasure is not a tragedy. Only the spoiled and the indulgent can think so. Now consider the fate of some of the others. In order to get the second distribution, some people who previously had, on the first distribution, a net balance of pleasure over pain would have, on the second distribution, a negative balance in this regard. They would go from living pleasantly to coping with excruciating pain. In regard to these people considered only as a group, this is clearly a Benthamic tragic loss, if anything is. Yet Bentham's calculus with its notion of extent is designed to be opaque to the distinction necessary to see the tragedy. Otherwise it could not yield the result that the two states are hedonically and morally equivalent, as Bentham's monism requires. According to his view of extent, there is no loss involved in the two distributions overall, and without loss, there is no tragedy. Surely, this is unacceptable. Something has gone wrong somewhere. And whatever has gone wrong has resulted in a moral mathematics that is opaque to one kind of tragedy that any moral view should be designed to express.[19]

[19] Note that in the example, Bentham's calculus allows the greatest good to be determined by the minority. But surely this is not the greater good.

The source of the problem, of course, is that Bentham, even considering pleasure and pain alone, does not give us a good way of comparing the importance of avoiding pain to the importance of promoting pleasure. If there is to be a hedonistic account of our tragic sense in the last case, it cannot appeal to some other nonhedonic value, such as fairness or the worth of persons, to account for the loss. It must appeal to hedonic considerations alone. There must be something about pain that makes pain something more to be avoided than there is about pleasure that makes it something to be pursued. It is only on the monistic assumption that pain is to be avoided to the same degree that pleasure is to be pursued that the notion of extent can work the way Bentham employs it in his calculus. But it is just this assumption that offends our tragic sense, even when restricted to hedonic considerations alone.

The crucial point is that a mere mathematical designation of a level of intensity of pain does not reflect its practical significance in our lives. For one thing, it says nothing about whether it is disabling and, if so, to what extent. It does not make transparent, as the expressivist conception of the classical tradition would, the meaning of pain as suffering. Bentham's theory, therefore, fails one of the three major criteria of the classical conception of practical reason: it does not make transparent an element of the meaning that pain has in the lives of the people affected. It does not capture the loss and thereby conceals the tragedy.

No one who thinks, as Bentham and other utilitarians do, that benevolence is the foundation of morality can afford to endorse a theory of value that makes tragedy invisible. Nor can anyone who thinks that benevolence plays any significant role in a life well lived. Moreover, there is also something very misleading about a theory that asserts that the only real problem with the view that benevolence is the foundation of morality is that it puts benevolence where fairness and justice should be, which is one of the traditional objections leveled against Bentham's utilitarianism. That this is misleading and that the issues of justice and tragedy are distinct should be evident upon reflection: even some just distributions are tragic. Indeed, some may be so tragic that it is, all things considered, better to avoid them. If so, then any theory that construes morality to be only about fairness does not allow us to raise this issue and in that way trivializes the relevance of tragedy.

The solution to Bentham's problem would have been for him to abandon his monistic account of hedonic value by accepting the fact that pleasure attained and pain avoided are distinct hedonic values, and that the latter is the more important hedonic good. This would have allowed him a more progressive basis for undermining the status quo of his day. Even if the pleasure obtained by aristocratic privilege was quantitatively higher than anything the minority could have achieved by changed social policy, the fact remained that the relief of their misery was more important than the preservation of hedonic luxury. So hedonic value is not one thing, and not to see that intense suffering avoided is better than intense pleasure obtained is to fail to see an important form of tragedy. It is to make the same error Bentham accused his opponents of making, namely, that of mistaking the good for the bad. In fact, the relief of suffering needed in his day did not require any form of monism at all, only the point that sometimes the relief of suffering is more important than any number of other values. With this understood, much of the motivation for Bentham's monism loses its practical foundation.

Yet there is another form of tragic loss that Bentham's quantitative monism conceals and fails to acknowledge that is associated with the thought of John Stuart Mill (1806–1873). The form of loss is this: sometimes what is lost in the lesser good when the greater good prevails is of enormous value but is nonetheless vastly inferior to what is gained in the greater good. The problem with Bentham's calculus is that it cannot recognize one good as being vastly superior to another and therefore is blind to some of the most significant cases of tragic loss that it is rational for us to regret. A consideration of Mill's views is important because Mill was a near-contemporary of Bentham and formulated his views in a nearly identical social context.

MILL

Where Epicurus and Bentham wanted simplification, Mill saw a need for complexity. Hedonism is not a theory that dies easily, and Mill was intent on repairing what he saw as deficiencies in Bentham's version of it by distinguishing among different kinds of pleasures. Most crucial to him was the contrast between what he called the intellectual and moral pleasures, on the one hand, and physical pleasures on the other.

In contrast to Bentham, Mill claimed that the former were qualitatively superior to the latter. Moreover, he thought that this was confirmed by empirical observation, which is to say that he believed that, contrary to Bentham, a proper science of morality would show that quality is a distinctive category in the measurement of value. Just as natural science should not sacrifice explanatory power for simplicity of hypothesis, the science of value should not sacrifice richness of value for the avoidance of conflict. Reductionism in either instance should be rejected when it conceals the loss of truth or goodness or when it distorts our tragic sense. The question here is whether even Mill's more sophisticated version of hedonism fails in the face of tragedy. I will argue that it does, but not before it strikes a fatal blow to Bentham's monism.

Following Pope's dictum that the proper study of mankind is man, both Bentham and Mill believed that the best study of human value is the study of the psychology of human valuing. Both firmly rejected superstition, religion, and a priori moralizing as legitimate sources of the knowledge of value. When we engage seriously in the study of human psychology as a source of knowledge about value, Mill thought, the empirical evidence shows that we value some things as vastly superior to others. That is, the evidence shows that we value some things, A, in relationship to other things, B, in a way that only great improvements in B or great diminishments in A could ever make B better than A and no changes in the value of A or B could ever make A and B equal. The crucial claim that Mill is making is that vast superiority is a datum that any adequate science of value must explain. Any science of value that ignores it is not truly scientific. If this is true, and if all positive values are forms of pleasure, then there are differences in kind among pleasures. In particular, as we will see, Mill thought this about the comparative value of the intellectual and moral pleasures in relation to physical pleasure. What he rightly thought is that there is no way on Bentham's calculus to account for this. So there must be something wrong with quantitative hedonism. He thought that Bentham's calculus needed a category of quality that made it possible for one kind of pleasure to be more valuable than another, even if the less valuable ranked higher in terms of all the relevant quantitative categories.

Mill believed that the empirical evidence that we make judgments of vast superiority among different kinds of pleasures was reflected in the value judgments of qualified judges. He proclaimed famously in his essay *Utilitarianism* that it is better to be a human being dissatisfied than a pig satisfied, and Socrates dissatisfied than a fool satisfied.[20] Reflection on these judgments, he thought, would reveal that human valuing reflects the value relation of vast superiority between the intellectual and moral pleasures and physical pleasures. Those who are qualified to evaluate the relative merits of the different kinds of pleasures must be experienced in pleasures of different kinds. Pigs and fools cannot judge that physical pleasures are better than intellectual and moral pleasures because they are experienced only in the former. They are therefore unqualified as judges. Human beings, however, can make such judgments (when they have the requisite experience), and their judgments must be authoritative. They know what physical pleasure is like, and they know what the pleasure of inquiry and the pleasure of poetry are like. They also know what the moral pleasures are like: the pleasures of society, of helping the needy, of developing character, and of maintaining dignity. They are therefore in a position to make a comparative judgment of the overall worth of the intellectual and moral pleasures in relation to the worth of physical pleasure that lower animals and inexperienced human beings are not.

What is there, then, about the judgments and lives of qualified judges that reflect judgments of vast superiority? If qualified judges do value intellectual and moral concerns as highly as Mill says, then why does this not just show that when we do the quantitative calculus, we see that intellectual and moral pleasures are more intense, last longer, are more pure and more fecund than physical pleasures?

Mill's answer is in terms of the sacrifice of contentment qualified judges are willing to incur to pursue a form of life that includes the intellectual and moral pleasures.[21] Qualified judges know that the life of intellectual inquiry and the life of concern for others will never be one of contentment. In fact, it will carry with it a great deal of dissatisfaction, a sense of loss, and thus a sense of regret. Yet, when given the opportunity and when they have the requisite knowledge, human beings do not opt for the life of contentment – the life of the pig

[20] John Stuart Mill, *Utilitarianism* (Indianapolis: Bobbs Merrill, 1957), 14.

[21] See George W. Harris, "Mill's Qualitative Hedonism," *The Southern Journal of Philosophy* (Winter 1984): 503–12.

and the fool. Rather, there is a vast difference between the portion of their lives that is dedicated to intellectual and moral concerns and the portion devoted to physical pleasure. It is only when the intellectual and moral life is extremely costly in terms of physical pain that qualified judges will prefer the life of physical pleasure. Mill thought that the only way to account for this in hedonic terms was to admit that some pleasures are valued by those qualified to make the judgment as vastly superior to others. And, for this reason, he thought that some pleasures are qualitatively superior to others. Qualitative hedonism is therefore his scientific explanation for the datum of vast superiority that is reflected in our informed choices.

What is right about Mill's analysis is that if these judgments are to be made sense of on a hedonistic model, then there simply is no way to account for them on Bentham's theory. Bentham's hedonism cannot allow that there is a value relation of vast superiority. Bentham could never allow that pleasure A could have a certain quantitative payoff, that pleasure B could have a slightly better quantitative payoff, and yet recognize that A is better than B. But Mill's claim is that the facts regarding well-informed, actual human choices show that we make not only judgments of this sort but also judgments according to which the expected quantitative payoffs for pleasures of kind B are significantly larger than for kind A, yet we prefer pleasures of kind A over kind B. This is exactly what a judgment of vast superiority is like. The empirical fact that well-informed human beings have a psychology in which such judgments have a significant place, Mill thought, falsifies Bentham's quantitative hedonism.

To be sure, Mill thought that if the intellectual and moral life were painful enough, the life of physical comfort would be preferable, that is, he thought that qualified judges would as a matter of fact sacrifice the moral and intellectual life if it came at too great a cost in terms of pain. But this only shows that strict superiority (the view that A is better than B no matter what improvements or diminishments occur in A or B) is not the relation that holds between these different kinds of pleasures. Moreover, it reinforces the claim that vast superiority obtains. Those who enjoy philosophy, science, art, athletic achievement, and human society know full well that a life dedicated to these things is a life with a great deal of frustration, in addition to whatever intense pleasure it contains. They also know that the intensity of physical pleasure obtained and of physical and psychological pain avoided can be much greater if life is lived in another way.

Now, thinking of yourself as a qualified judge, imagine how much intense pleasure you would have to forgo to be an accomplished writer, scientist, musician, philosopher, social leader, or, for that matter, simply an intellectually and morally honest person. Imagine that you are faced with a decision of pursuing one of the following ways of life. The first is a life dedicated solely to achieving and maintaining intense physical pleasure: live hard and die young, that sort of thing. The likelihood is that a life dedicated solely to gaining as much intense physical pleasure as possible would be short, even if successful on its own terms. Now consider a second way of life in which if you adopt that way of life, your intellectual and moral sensibilities will be dulled, as will your capacities for very intense physical pleasure. What will be gained is a way of life containing pleasure of a fairly low level of intensity and very little pain, sustained over a long life span. This is the life of contentment – the life of the fool, the pig, the couch potato. The ways of achieving it are myriad. The third way of life is one in which you can cultivate your intellectual and moral sensibilities to a significant degree, but this will bring with it a significant amount of intellectual and moral dissatisfaction, as well as significantly less physical satisfaction than you could have had by pursuing another way of life. Finally, imagine a fourth way of life in which you can pursue intellectual and moral matters but only at the cost of excruciating physical and psychological pain over a long period of time.

Mill believed that the life of pain can be so bad that even the pleasures of the intellectual and moral life can be eclipsed by the value of avoiding it. For this reason, the fourth way of life is the one most to be avoided, which shows that Mill did not believe that the intellectual and moral life was strictly superior to the life of physical pleasure. But that qualified judges do, as a matter of fact, judge that the intellectual and moral life is vastly superior to either of the other two ways of life was for Mill confirmed by the empirical facts. When given the opportunity and provided with enough experience, the large majority of people do choose to pursue a life in which the intellectual and moral sensibilities are cultivated, even in the full awareness of the kind of dissatisfaction that comes with the realization that intellectual issues are never fully resolved, that the more one knows the more one is painfully aware of one's ignorance, that creative activity most often fails (and even when it does succeed, the bar is continually raised until failure is the result), and that the more we care for others, the more pain we are likely to bring into our lives. That such a choice could not be explained quantitatively, Mill thought, is obvious upon reflection. What is obvious is that one has to choose between two distinct positive hedonic values. Hedonic value, then, is inherently vulnerable to conflict – good conflicts with good – something neither Epicurus nor Bentham wanted to admit.

Interestingly, if the actual facts of human valuing are taken into account, there is not that much difference between Epicurus and Bentham regarding the kind of life that would be best hedonically. Over the course of a life, it is probably better quantitatively to go for pleasures that sustain an even keel than constantly to seek the most intense pleasures available. Even given Bentham's categories, the life of contentment is probably the best one to have as a target if you are measuring quantitatively. This makes the practical difference between contentment and tranquility hard to discern. Moreover, if this is true, it is hard to justify from a quantitative perspective attaching yourself deeply to intellectual and moral concerns. To do so would invite the kind of misery the Epicureans warned against. Bentham's hedonism, then, faces a dilemma: if quality is left out of consideration, moral and intellectual concerns seem best avoided. This would suggest that the Epicureans could gain a foothold in Bentham's calculus by arguing that Bentham would do better to submit to Epicurean psychological therapy aimed at dulling his attachment to others than to dedicate his life to revising England's legal code. Faced with such results, Mill thought it better to endorse the concept of quality and interpret our judgments of vast superiority as having a rational foundation in hedonism properly understood.

What, then, are we to say about qualitative hedonism and its implications for a tragic sense? What account can we give of a tragic sense on Mill's hedonistic assumptions? Can there be loss, and can there be loss of a tragic sort? What did Mill see as tragic about his time?

Like Bentham, Mill had no use for asceticism of either the religious or the Stoic sort. To dedicate oneself to a vindictive and austere God or to a sense of moral virtue unrelated to human happiness was for Mill, as it was for Bentham, the result of ignorance, superstition, or a sense of self-loathing and disgust for humanity. No enlightened person could take these views seriously. Rather, an enlightened person could only think of people whose lives were governed by such attitudes as the tragic victims of an unenlightened mind. And like Bentham, Mill was only too aware that the depth of this tragedy was measured by its extent. The history of asceticism was a tragic history of wasted lives.

As to the aristocracy, Mill had a different view than Bentham. Neither thought that the history of aristocracy was a history of wasted lives, at least for those enjoying its privileges. In this regard, aristocracy had something to say for itself that asceticism did not. Someone, at least, truly benefits from the aristocratic way of life, even if many suffer as a result. But Bentham's calculus was blind to any qualitative difference in the things that were made possible by the aristocratic way of life. Had the poor been relieved of their oppressive working conditions and thus given more time for pushpin, perhaps they would have been just as happy as the aristocracy. And if they were, nothing would be lost from Bentham's perspective. Mill, however, thought that the most you can hope for from a life of pleasure measured quantitatively is a life of contentment. What the aristocracy had access to by virtue of its way of life was the intellectual and moral pleasures, yet the intellectual and moral life brought discontentment where the successful life of physical pleasure brought the bliss of ignorance. Since Mill thought that human beings, when competent to judge, value the intellectual and moral life as vastly superior to the life of physical pleasure and contentment, he could see the life of contentment only as a loss, and a tragic one. Unlike Bentham's baseline for measuring tragic loss, Mill's starts with a way of life that includes values that are vastly superior to other values and defines tragic loss as the sacrifice of values of a vastly superior kind to values of a vastly inferior kind. This is a sense of tragedy distinct from one available only on the quantitative view of hedonism and one that strikes at the very heart of the human condition.

What Mill wanted to do (as did Marx in a different way) was to bring the highest pleasures of the aristocracy to the masses. He wanted to free the poor from oppressive labor so that they could engage in creative activity, to provide them with access to education so that they could taste the pleasures of inquiry and the fruits of knowledge, to free everyone from the intrusive arm of the government in their private lives so that they could experiment in living in ways that would liberate them sexually and morally, and to challenge views on gender in a way that would free women from the life of mere contentment to one of true happiness. The emphasis throughout is on freeing people from either a life of suffering or a life of contentment to pursue a life of meaning defined in terms of higher values. Indeed, apart from the life of excruciating pain, Mill thought the life of contentment was one of the most tragic forms of life human beings could be forced to endure. For the majority of people throughout history to be forced to live like fools or pigs, however content, because of the way the state's institutions are ordered was for Mill a story of wasted lives not visible on the quantitative measure of tragic history. To be sure, in the past the majority have lived lives not of contentment but of misery, and this does add to the tragedy of it, to the loss of high value in a dangerous or indifferent world. But imagine what Mill would have thought of so many contemporary lives. At least in the developed nations, there has never been greater access to education, greater personal freedom, or greater sexual equality than today. Yet both contentment with ignorance and indifference to character seem widespread. Perhaps this is a tragedy of wasted lives not imagined even by Mill. That so many people would live like fools and pigs in the midst of such prosperity is perhaps a version of the tyranny of the majority, where the emphasis is not on the injustice but rather on the tragedy of it.[22]

What is clear is that Mill had a much more robust tragic sense than Bentham. It recognized two forms of loss not recognized by Bentham, both involving the recognition of different kinds of value, even within a hedonistic perspective. The first is where the bad prevails over the good, where the higher goods of life are needlessly sacrificed for the lower goods of life. For Mill, the tragedy wrought by aristocratic privilege would not have been remedied by the majority leaving their poverty only to enter a life of mindless contentment. That is trading one tragedy for another. And notice that this is not the view of an ascetic. The second is where the greater good prevails over the lesser good but at a huge cost in physical and mental suffering. The goods of the intellectual and moral life come at a high cost. That is one kind of tragedy, but it is not as tragic as subordinating the higher goods to the lower goods where they retain their superiority. None of

[22] This is one kind of case in which what is being allowed is just but tragic.

these thoughts is available to Bentham or to any theory that does not recognize a difference in kind among values.

Of course, there is the additional fact that hedonism of any variety is false. When we reflect on what pain can distract us from, we can see, as Bishop Butler did so many years ago, that pleasure and pain are not the only things we care about.[23] Indeed, as Butler and others have pointed out, there is a paradox about hedonism. It seems that in order to pursue pleasure in any effective way, we must first care intrinsically about something else. There is, as the critics of hedonism have pointed out, a difference between the object of desire and the result of satisfying a desire.[24] Hedonists like Bentham would have us believe that the object of desire is pleasure. Often it may very well be that the satisfaction of our desires is pleasant, but it does not follow that the pleasure of satisfying desire is the object of our desires. In fact, people who seem to care only about pleasure have a hard time living pleasant lives. The desire for pleasure is actually a very sophisticated second-order desire that presupposes nonhedonic primary desires. Hunger is the name of a primary desire, the desire for food. The desire to satisfy hunger is a distinct, secondary desire, one that the gourmet cultivates. One, then, can learn to cultivate the pursuit of pleasure by cultivating certain desires and then satisfying them. Sexual desire can often be treated in this way. But other desires and modes of caring do not seem to allow themselves this sort of treatment. Consider sympathy and love. To have sympathy for someone is to care about that person's well-being. Among other things, it is to care about that person not experiencing needless pain. Yet to cultivate the need for sympathy in order to satisfy it seems to go against the nature of sympathy as a form of caring and desiring in the first place. So too with love. To love a child as a parent does is, among other things, to take some delight in being the one who comforts the child in times of trouble. Yet it seems completely foreign to parental love to cultivate trouble in order to experience the pleasure of comforting the child. Love is not about itself in the way that hunger can be.

[23] Joseph Butler, *Five Sermons* (Indianapolis: Hackett, 1983).

[24] C. D. Broad, "Remarks on Psychological Hedonism," in *Readings in Ethical Theory*, Wilfred Sellars and John Hospers (New York: Appleton-Century-Crofts, 1970), 686–9.

Moreover, the desires and ways of caring that are like love and sympathy are myriad. And pain can be so intense that it can render us incapable of focusing on what we care about when we care in these ways. This means that we cannot define the baseline for loss in purely hedonic terms. Avoiding pain not only can prevent us from realizing pleasure, which is itself a distinct consideration of value, it can also prevent us from realizing the nonhedonic goods to which our lives are most primarily attached. When it does, the loss is sometimes, certainly not always, of a tragic degree. What we should conclude from these observations, then, is that even hedonic value is pluralistic, but more pluralistic is the nature of our desires and ways of caring. To account for the kinds of loss to which we are subject, Bentham's monism is clearly inadequate. His passion for simplicity – for reducing the value of one thing to the value of another – was the source of his pernicious fantasy, and no one was more aware of this than John Stuart Mill.

Yet some of the remarks about hedonism that derive from the nature of desires and ways of caring that apply against Bentham also apply against Mill. For example, though the satisfaction of your desire for knowledge may be pleasant, it does not follow that your desire for knowledge is for the pleasure of inquiry and the products of its success. Indeed, it seems that Mill has given us good empirical reasons for thinking that we do not desire knowledge or engage in inquiry just for whatever pleasure is involved. Why? Because the pain of inquiry and the probability of failure make it implausible that the result will be a net balance of good feeling attained over bad feeling avoided, however good and bad feeling are defined. The value added, then, to the value of inquiry must be more than whatever pleasantness it promises, and that value must be nonhedonic in type. Moreover, the same point applies to other goods like personal relationships and achievement. The intrinsic properties of personal relationships, knowledge, and achievement that make them intrinsically worthy of choice are not those that result in a preponderance of good feeling. That this is true is further revealed by the fact that we would not choose to live our lives in a virtual reality in which we seemed to have personal relationships, knowledge, and achievement but really did not.[25] If we were hedonists

[25] For the famous experience machine example, see Robert Nozick, *Anarchy, State, and Utopia* (New York: Basic Books, 1974), 142–5.

in any sense, we would have no reason for refusing to substitute a virtual reality that was pleasant for a real one that is considerably less pleasant, and we do not have to be either religious, aristocratically privileged, or infected with asceticism to have these values.

Some of the reasons for rejecting hedonism, then, are perfectionist in nature. To recur to Pope, the proper study of "mankind" shows that we value perfecting our human capacities as well as obtaining positive affective states. Suffering is (sometimes) one kind of tragedy; mediocrity is (sometimes) another. The tragic loss of excellence in thought, in action, and in human relationships is sometimes measured by the suffering we would have ourselves and others endure to avoid it. Any science of value that denies this is falsified by the facts. It cannot, then, be a form of enlightenment to believe it.

We should not, however, take these observations to justify a shift from one monistic project to another, from monistic hedonism to monistic perfectionism. There are many reasons for this, but one alone will do. It is a corollary to the claim just made: the tragedy of suffering endured is sometimes measured by the loss of excellence in thought, in action, and in human relationships we would have ourselves and others tolerate to avoid it. The avoidance of suffering is not a perfectionist good, but it is sometimes the greater good, even compared to our highest perfectionist values. And nothing said about perfectionism and suffering by Nietzsche can change this fact. It cannot, then, be a higher form of spirituality to believe it.

DECISION THEORY

Finally, modern economic theory might be thought to provide one last haven for the monistic instinct that is supposedly honored by having some scientific basis. I want to say briefly why this is a mistake without engaging in a lengthy technical discussion of decision theory or the history of economics as a science.

Suppose we had an economic theory that was as reliable in its ability to predict the informed choices of people in the market as physics is in predicting the behavior of physical objects at the macro or nonsubatomic level. To have such a theory, we would need a theory of rational choice, which decision theory labors to produce. Imagine that we have it. What we would have is a means of measuring how much any particular person values one thing in comparison to another. Moreover, we would have a means of measuring how much one person values something in comparison to how much another person values that thing. We might then think that our knowledge includes a knowledge of the one thing that people value in terms of which the differences in strengths of valuing can be explained. But reflection should reveal why this is not true.

Knowing how strongly someone values something is not the same as knowing the way in which it is valued or the kind of value it has. Reflection on how the notion of risk might play a role in determining strength of valuing should illustrate the point. Game theory, a branch of decision theory, employs the notion of risk in roughly the following way: if you want to know how much someone values something, find out how much he or she is willing to risk for it. There are problems involved in how to devise a method for measuring risk in a precise way, but suppose they could be solved. Suppose we had a way to know that you are willing to risk far more for something than I am. It seems very plausible to say that unless there is something different about our situations or unless one of us is uninformed or something of that sort, then you value what is at risk more than I do. The idea, of course, is derived from an economic model tied to market economies: what people are willing to risk their resources for in the right kind of market is the ultimate indicator of what they value most. But the idea need not be restricted to the economic arena and the market. Suppose we are forced into playing poker with the things we cherish most in life: when the bidding begins in earnest, we will find a way of determining who values what and how much. Now suppose we could do this with perfect mathematical accuracy and predictive success. We might decide to give a name to the results and say that what we are measuring is "utility." However, if what we think we have discovered in the notion of utility is the ultimate kind of value or way of caring that underlies all rational choice, we are making a huge mistake.

To understand this point, suppose you and I are forced by the circumstances of life into playing a zero-sum game in which everything we each hold dear is at stake. As the game progresses, we are both forced to protect what we cherish most, sacrificing the lesser good for the greater good in our scale of "preferences." Now suppose that what you care about most is expressed in your sympathy for lower animals and that what I care about most is expressed in my love for my family, but that you care more about what you care about most than I do. On the assumptions just made, we can determine how much more you care about lower animals than I do about my family. But notice that we will not have determined that there is one form of caring that underlies both of our strategies for winning the zero-sum game. My love, which is one form of caring and valuing, does not match the strength of your sympathy, which is another form of caring and valuing, in the contest of values. To say that the risk situation measures one thing called "utility" is therefore deeply misleading in just the same way that Bentham's hedonism was misleading. It is opaque to the kind of value that is at risk for you versus the kind of value that is at risk for me. Should I lose the game, the loss can only be understood as a loss of the goods of love. Should you lose the game, the loss is a loss in the well-being of lower animals. (The point is magnified when we reflect on how the same conflict might occur within one's own values.) On the view that "utility" measures one thing, there is only the loss in "utility." The distinction that is necessary to make transparent what values are in conflict is obscured, and the tragedy for the loser is distorted by the myth of monism.

Understood as a science of predicting market behavior, economics would have no need for a theory of value if it could deliver on the project just outlined. It could predict market behavior without solving the philosophical problem about whether value is one or many. That such an enterprise is important no one should deny. But what we should be acutely sensitive to is that when we take "utility" to refer to a value being measured and assign mathematical functions to it for purposes of comparison, we have left economics behind and blinded ourselves to the nuances of value that make tragedy visible. We can make tragedy visible only by describing the choices in the "games" we have to play in terms of the multiple forms of caring that are at the heart of human life. To do this, we need to describe the narratives of how people reason in risk situations in terms of the classical criteria of finality and self-sufficiency in such a way that what people do in zero sum games makes transparent what their lives are about. When we know *that,* we will know something about the nature of their values, their gains, and their losses. The language of utility functions can never accomplish this, whatever else it accomplishes in predicting market behavior or any other kind of behavior.

To the credit of economists, at least the best of them, they know all this. It is only some philosophers strongly influenced by the monistic tradition that continue to talk as though the science of decision theory has somehow reduced value to one thing. Nothing about decision theory, game theory, or economic theory lends a scintilla of evidence to support such a view. Just the opposite. It is one thing to understand human valuing from the perspective of predicting market or other forms of human behavior. It is an altogether different thing to understand human valuing in a way that makes transparent the experience of loss. This is something that the notion of utility can never provide.

Having then reviewed some of the most important forms of monism, how should the final epitaph for monism be read? Perhaps the best way to get some perspective on the monistic tradition is by putting it in the context of the larger Enlightenment, Romantic, and Classical traditions. Enlightenment thinkers want us to live a life based on true belief, freed from the shackles of ignorance and superstition. Romantics want us to live a life that is properly and passionately felt as well as thought. And Classical thinkers want us to live a life in which our patterns of behavior and reasons for action make transparent by their expression what our lives are about. No form of monism can satisfy all of these demands or any one of them taken separately. That monism conceals in all its versions one form or another of tragic loss condemns it as a failure in the court of all these great traditions. It should fare no better in ours, and its epitaph should be read for the pernicious fantasy it is. We should not, however, think that this is an epitaph for secularism, for secularism need not rest on such an infirm foundation.

6

Moralism and the Inconstancy of Value

In the kingdom of ends everything has either a price or a dignity. If it has a price, something else can be put in its place as an equivalent; if it is exalted above all price and so admits of no equivalent, then it has a dignity.

Immanuel Kant, *Groundwork of the Metaphysics of Morals*

Were it not for the loss of value involved, it would be wonderful if the view that value is one and not many were true. What would be so wonderful about it is that if we could just stay alert to averting one form of loss, where the bad prevails over the good, our ethical task would be complete. We could then view the world in a fairy tale sort of way in which the only real conflict in life is that between good and evil. The only real difficulty would be in figuring out how to win the battle against evil. Much of our everyday rhetoric suggests that we do think this way, and, unfortunately, that rhetoric is encouraged by monistic theories of value. But if nihilism is to be rejected because it is superficial, all versions of monism are to be rejected because they are naive and simpleminded. It is time we put them behind us and thought more maturely about value. It is time we recognized that tragedy takes the form not only of evil prevailing over the good, but also of good conflicting with good. This means recognizing and living in the light of the fact that values are plural and conflicting, that good conflicts with good in such a way that some goods are sometimes sacrificed for greater goods but that the loss of the lesser good is tragic nonetheless. The question, then, becomes which form of pluralism to accept. Which form of pluralism can allow us to see the tragedy involved not only when the bad prevails over the good but also when the greater good prevails over the lesser good? This is the question that the next three chapters is dedicated to answering. Chapter 9 will deal with tragedy that involves incomparable loss.

Supreme value pluralism is a pluralistic tradition with a long and storied history. It recognizes that values are plural and conflicting, that sometimes we must choose between the greater good and the lesser good, where the value contained in the lesser good is not contained in the greater good, and that in some of these cases, though certainly not in all of them, the result is tragic loss. What it recommends as a solution is what I will call the consolation of supreme value, which is one form of the consolation of reason for tragic choice. Any time we are faced with a tragic choice between the greater good and the lesser good, where the greater good contains the supreme value and the lesser good does not, we are, according to this view, to be consoled by our comparative judgment that what is lost in the lesser good is strictly inferior to the greater good, no matter how good the lesser good is. Supreme value pluralism, then, is committed to a view of value that says that there is a kind of value that is strictly superior to all other values. If we think of A as the supreme value and B as any other kind of value, supreme value pluralism asserts that A is strictly superior to B just in case A is better than B no matter what improvements are made in B and no matter what diminishments are made in A, or, put another way, no matter what the extent and degree of A and no matter what the extent and degree of B and all other values combined. Moreover, supreme value pluralism asserts that there is such a value and that it is always rationally accessible to us, that it is always possible to make the comparative judgment that the lesser good is worth sacrificing for the supreme value. I will argue that this is a form of pernicious fantasy distinct from the fantasy of monism, but that it is destructive and delusory nonetheless. Where monism denies the existence of plural values in order to avoid the recognition of some important forms of tragedy, supreme value pluralism elevates the status of some value to the point of casting a shadow in which other values cannot be seen in their fullness and appreciated for what they are. In that way, other values are tragically lost to our vision.

Supreme value pluralism can succeed only if there is something of value that has the qualities of overridingness and purity. To have these qualities in a way that supports its strict superiority to all other values, the supreme value must satisfy two conditions: (i) its qualities must be such that they outweigh the qualities of all other values, no matter what their extent or degree and no matter what the context, and (ii) the intrinsic qualities of the supreme value cannot themselves lead to a change in the nature of the supreme value.

If the first condition is not satisfied, then there is some context in which the degree or extent of some other value outweighs the supreme value, in which case the tragic loss of supreme value would be the loss of a lesser good. But, according to supreme value pluralism, such a loss is never rational just because it is never possible. The consolation of supreme value as the solution to coping with tragic loss would be undermined.

If the second condition is not satisfied, then the supreme value contains the bad within its own intrinsic qualities, thereby undermining its claim to superiority no matter what the context. Supreme value pluralism consoles us not by having us believe that good can never conflict with good, but with the thought that there is a kind of good that does not conflict with itself and that this value is strictly superior to all other values. For this reason, the supreme value must be pure. If it is not, then even the highest value can conflict with itself in ways that lead to tragic loss, again undermining the consolation of reason that supreme value pluralism was supposed to provide.

The problem, however, is that there is no plausible set of qualities that satisfies either of these conditions. The leading candidates for the supreme value fail to provide grounds for our judging that there is a value that is always overriding. Moreover, there are good reasons for thinking that all values of any high degree of importance are impure in two senses: (i) no important kind of value is such that it does not itself generate conflict in its own terms, and (ii) the intrinsic qualities of the things we value most make a metamorphosis from good to bad possible. Value is plural, conflicting, impure, and inconstant in its priorities. If so, it is a serious mistake to seek solace from tragedy in this form of the consolation of reason. To do so is to seek relief in a philosophical opiate that clouds our ability to recognize the real value of things.

Consider first the inconstancy of value.

A particular value is inconstant if there is some context in which some other value is superior to it, and value itself is inconstant if there is no value that always has priority over other values regardless of context. Since the concern here is to make sense of value from a secular, naturalistic perspective, otherworldly religious values are set aside. What kind of value, then, could possibly be constantly superior to all other values? Historically, the most prominent answer has been moral value.

On the view that supreme value is moral value, the consolation for tragic loss in cases where the greater good prevails over the lesser good but where the lesser good contains value not contained in the greater good is that moral value is constantly superior to all other values in a way that should provide us with solace. Moreover, moral solace of this sort has been offered from various quarters from antiquity to the present, with two leading candidates for what the supreme moral value is: virtue and the dignity of persons.

The ancient Stoics claimed that virtue is both necessary and sufficient for a life worth living and that it is the only thing of intrinsic value. So stated, ancient Stoicism is a version of monism. Since I have already given good reasons for rejecting any version of monism, I will consider here a view that is slightly more plausible than ancient Stoicism but that has a family resemblance to it. I will call it modern Stoicism.[1] It asserts that there are many different things of intrinsic value but that only virtue has categorical value. Since everything else has, on this view, noncategorical value, virtue is strictly superior to all other values, which makes modern Stoicism a form of supreme value pluralism.

To understand modern Stoicism, then, it is necessary to understand the concepts of categorical qualities and categorical value. First,

[1] Lawrence Becker refers to his version of Stoicism as the new Stoicism, and Martha Nussbaum refers to hers as neo-Stoicism. Becker's version attempts to preserve some of the controversial theses of original Stoicism that Nussbaum's version denies. What I am calling modern Stoicism is a version that is less revisionary than Nussbaum's and more like Becker's. It preserves the central Stoic claim that virtue is both necessary and sufficient for happiness. The revision is that it elevates the value of externals to a status greater than what the ancient Stoics called preferred indifferents. This is, in effect, what Becker does. I give here an account of how that might be understood. See Lawrence C. Becker, *A New Stoicism* (Princeton, New Jersey: Princeton University Press, 1998); and Martha C. Nussbaum, *Upheavals of Thought* (Cambridge: Cambridge University Press, 2001).

consider the concept of categorical qualities. Categorical qualities are central to the integrity of a thing in the sense that they are the qualities necessary for a thing to be what it is.[2] Take them away and the thing loses its integrity as the sort of thing it is. For example, take away hydrogen molecules from this liquid and it ceases to be water. Similarly with other things: change at some point turns wine into vinegar, people into corpses, molten lava into stone, and a coherent functional psychology into a dysfunctional one. In all these cases, the qualities of a thing have changed in a way that leads to a change in what it is. Moreover, the point applies no matter whether the thing is a natural kind or a social construction.

Now consider the concept of categorical values.

Categorical values are objects of what Bernard Williams has called categorical desires, and these in turn are categorical qualities of a coherent functional psychology.[3] As they function within the psychology of a person, categorical desires are the basis for the fundamental unity of personality and the integrity of the psychology as a whole. They are also at the heart of a person's character as being one kind of character versus another or no coherent character at all. When categorical desire is significantly frustrated, the wholeness of personality is fragmented, integrity in that sense is lost, and the psychology becomes dysfunctional to varying degrees. Just as hydrogen molecules are categorical to a liquid being water, some things are categorical to the meaning of a person's life from his or her own point of view. These are a person's categorical values. Take them away and the person's psychology is shattered by depression, by malaise, by self-destructiveness, by loss of the will to live, and the like. The sign, then, that a value is categorical within a psychology is how the frustration of categorical desire affects the integrity of a person's psychology. Frustration of categorical desire brings integral stress to a person's psychology, threatening integral breakdown in the form of psychological dysfunction of various sorts: severe depression, loss of fundamental control, pervasive denial and self-deception, loss of the will to live, and other dysfunctional

[2] See George W. Harris, *Dignity and Vulnerability: Strength and Quality of Character* (Berkeley: University of California Press, 1997), 7–11.

[3] See Bernard Williams, *Moral Luck* (Cambridge: Cambridge University Press, 1981), 11; George W. Harris, *Agent Centered Morality: An Aristotelian Alternative to Kantian Internalism* (Berkeley: University of California Press, 1999), 88–107.

states. The central thought is this: if you want to know what is central to a psychology, a set of values, or a character, see what it will take to break them down under stress. The concepts of categorical desire and categorical value are employed to isolate those components of a psychology that are most central to its functioning.

Noncategorical values are the objects of noncategorical desires. They play a role in a person's psychology, but their frustration does not undermine the integrity of a person's psychology and does not constitute integral stress. They vary in their importance to a person from being matters of minor importance to being very important, but they never carry such importance that their loss would undermine the very meaning of a person's life from his or her own point of view. The contrast, then, between categorical and noncategorical values is a contrast between the functional roles different values play in an overall psychology.

Modern Stoicism, as a form of pluralism as I am construing it here, asserts that many things are of noncategorical value but that only one thing has categorical value to a person of good character, and that is virtue. It does not deny that other things are of intrinsic value, even significant value, but that value is always less than categorical. This means that if things other than moral virtue matter to you so much that losing them would shatter your life, would cause you to become dysfunctional or to lose the will to live, then you have your priorities out of order. You categorically desire things that are worthy only of noncategorical desire. This form of Stoicism does not, as ancient Stoicism does, require a person of good character to extirpate her emotions but to manage them in a way that keeps their influence compartmentalized so that the overall functioning of her psychology is not threatened by them.[4] Modern Stoicism denies, in effect, the ancient Stoic argument called "the argument from excess" that the emotions should be extirpated because they invariably lead to the excesses of vice.[5] What I take both ancient and modern Stoicism to assert is that a person of the best sort of character is one whose categorical desire for virtue and virtue alone is always under his or her own control. Otherwise, virtue could not be both necessary and sufficient for happiness.

4 See Becker, *A New Stoicism*, 44, 47, 102, 103, 110, 128–32, 145.

5 See Harris, *Dignity and Vulnerability: Strength and Quality of Character*, 107–23.

What can tragic loss be like on this view?

One form is simply the loss of the greater good of moral virtue to bad character. Shakespeare's Macbeth might be seen through a modern Stoic's eyes as an example: blind ambition destroying the virtue of a good man. On this view, the subsequent psychological fallout from Macbeth's betrayal and murder of Duncan was the result of a war between different elements of a psychology made possible only where the benefits of status had been elevated in a way that would compete with but not extinguish Macbeth's concern for his own virtue within his values. Being a person of virtue should have meant more to him, and a person of good character would have had his desire for virtue under control. Had he not come to value categorically what was only of noncategorical value, he would not have been moved to disloyalty, and had he been able to extinguish his desire for virtue, he would not have been tortured in the aftermath. That this is tragedy of an extreme sort, no one would deny. Moreover, the lesson here is always worth repeating. Good people value things other than virtue, and it takes character development and maintenance to keep one's priorities in check so that one's character can be preserved, which is certainly one of life's greatest goods.

The problem is that this is not a very convincing account of Macbeth's tragedy. Sure, he should have had better character, even though there is evidence that he had a good deal of real character. But what would have prevented his disloyalty would have been more love for Duncan. Had his love for Duncan been categorical and his love for the benefits of status noncategorical, the tragedy would have been averted. Love, however, is a categorical desire for another person; it is not a categorical desire for one's own virtue. Certainly, Macbeth failed in virtue, but this was because he lacked the virtue of caring categorically about something other than virtue. The modern Stoic's interpretation of Macbeth's tragedy obscures one's vision of the real values at stake, as well as one's vision of the nature of virtue itself. The categorical desire for the virtue of loyalty makes no sense apart from the categorical commitment to those one loves, who are not themselves elements in one's virtue. So even the modern Stoic analysis of bad prevailing over good fails.

But what would be a case for modern Stoicism in which the greater good prevails over the lesser good but the result is nonetheless tragic because of the loss of value contained in the lesser good that is not contained in the greater good? For modern Stoicism, this form of tragedy would have to be a case of a noncategorical good not being contained in the categorical good of virtue. Note that if our virtue is always under our control and immune to integral stress, as ancient Stoics clearly maintained and I assume modern Stoics do as well, then the first form of tragedy is always avoidable and the second takes a form such that it is something with which a person of good character can always cope: the loss of a noncategorical good is not essential to the basic functioning of a person's psychology, a person's integrity, or the meaning of a person's life from his or her own point of view. Yet, according to modern Stoicism, the loss is supposed to be tragic. This is the modern Stoic's recognition of and solution to the problem of tragedy. It denies that the loss of categorical value is ever necessary, or even possible, for the best sort of person. What is tragically lost is always of noncategorical value.

Clear examples are hard to imagine. What examples would have to display is the loss of an important value rather than a trivial one, but not one important enough to be an object of categorical desire. Suppose, not due to any wrongdoing but owing entirely to the circumstances, I have to choose between two of my three children – which two will live and which one will die. Such a choice is for any loving parent a tragic one. But it is not a choice between a categorical good and a noncategorical good. It is a choice among categorical goods. Moreover, it is not a choice that finds consolation in the fact that the supreme value of virtue compensates for the loss of a good that is not a good of virtue. We might think that in some circumstances choice of this sort would be possible for a virtuous person (in others it might not be), but we would still think of the tragedy involved as a conflict among categorical goods. A steady diet of such choices would choke the life out of any loving parent, either by destroying her capacity to love or by causing a complete emotional breakdown. This is what happens when categorical values conflict. It is an unfriendly fact of the human condition that the legacies of Hellenistic ethics refuse to accept.

What makes things so difficult for any version of supreme value pluralism is that it has to confine its account of tragedy to conflicts between the categorical value of the supreme value and the noncategorical value of all other values. It requires of any moral agent that in cases where choice involves a conflict between the supreme value and any other value, the other values not mean so much to him as to be crucial to the functioning of his psychology and to the meaning of life from his own point of view. But this problem is particularly acute for modern Stoicism, where the supreme value (the consoling value) is moral virtue. On what account of moral virtue is this remotely plausible?

Recall the previous discussion of Hurka's recursive account of the virtues and his refutation of the "virtue solution" to the problem of evil. Compassion is a virtue, but the compassionate person is one who hates the evil of suffering. This being the case, the compassionate person will not consider an occasion for compassion as important as the prevention of suffering involved. The truly compassionate person has a categorical desire that suffering not exist. She does not console herself with the thought that the suffering makes possible the greater good of her virtue.

If the virtue solution to the theistic problem of evil does not work, and if it does not work for the secular problem of pessimism, then there is no reason at all to think that it will work for the problem of tragedy either, and for the same reason. The value of virtue is less than the values to which it normally attaches. Loyalty to friends and family is a virtue and has intrinsic value, but it is not as intrinsically valuable to a loyal person as his friends and family are. By elevating virtue to the status of supreme value, modern Stoicism casts a shadow in which both the value of other things and the value of virtue itself are obscured from vision, and the nature of tragedy is distorted. More crucially, the distortion of tragedy brought about by the desire to avoid facing it causes us to miss the nature of our real values. This is what makes any philosophical opiate, which is what an overly moralized view of life always is, so pernicious. Many find the religious appeal to virtue as redeeming the horrors of life repugnant. It is repugnant, they think, because it seems to be a flight from reality for the sake of a comfortable feeling of religious security against tragic suffering. Why should people find alluring in modern Stoicism what they find so repugnant in some forms of religion?

Concealed in the shadow of virtue as supreme value are the value of the avoidance of extreme pain and suffering; the value of intimacy; the value of sexual passion; the value of curiosity, of play, of fancy; and other values. It is not that new or modern Stoicism, unlike its ancient predecessor, cannot make a place for these things but that it cannot make a proper place for them. It denies that some threshold level of these goods is of categorical value to human beings of minimal psychological health. It denies that the categorical value of virtue itself is constrained by the categorical value of these things in the way that the categorical value of these things is constrained by the categorical value of virtue. The evidence for these claims is that if these other values are either eliminated from the lives of normal people or are significantly scarce, the results are the tragic consequences of human despair in life's having any personal meaning at all. This is just the kind of creatures we are. To the extent to which new or modern Stoicism is predicated on claims about human psychology regarding the emotions, there is far more evidence that human beings cannot maintain minimal psychological health without intimacy, physical health, meaningful work and play, community with others, and the like than there is that they can do so without virtue. These observations confirm that overly moralized views about the central values of life are pernicious indeed. Moralism is a disease of the human spirit; it is not a source of its liberation. There is no way of dressing moralism up that will change this fact.

The point is no less valid for Kantian moralism than for Stoic or religious moralism. Kantian moralism maintains that human dignity is the sole supreme value. All other values live within its shadows as their supreme regulator.[6] The basic idea is the following.

What is most important about human beings is that we are agents rather than mere subjects, choosers of our own fate rather than mere products of our environment. Lower animals differ from us in the sense that lower animals are ruled by their pathological nature – by their appetites, desires, sentiments, and passions. For this reason they are not agents but mere subjects. We, on the other hand, are capable of regulating our pathological animal nature by an aspect of our wills that is governed by respect for ourselves and others as autonomous, self-determining agents of our own fate. This is what gives us our dignity: our status as autonomous, self-determining agents.

To value the dignity of others is to respect their autonomy, their power to construct the meaning of their lives as they see fit (as long as

[6] See Harris, *Agent Centered Morality*, 52–87.

they show an equal concern for the autonomy of others to construct the meaning of their lives as they see fit). In this regard, we have duties to others not to interfere with their choices through coercion, manipulation, or deceit. This requires that respect for the dignity of others obligates us to deal with them openly, truthfully, honestly, noncoercively, and with tolerance for their differences. The dignity of others also requires us to take on certain goals and ends as guidelines for our behavior. Not only must we not interfere with the legitimate choices of others, we also must actually promote the conditions under which it is possible for others to act as masters of their own fate. Three conditions are prominent: the conditions under which it is possible for others to pursue their own happiness, the conditions under which it is possible for others to develop their own character, and the conditions under which it is possible for others to cultivate their talents. Though we cannot make other people happy, develop their character, or cultivate their talents, we can assist them when through no fault of their own and through the circumstances of luck, they are unable without assistance to pursue their own happiness, develop their own character, or cultivate their own talents. When we act on our desires, sentiments, and passions where they have not been regulated by these concerns, we put a price on dignity by giving way to our animal nature and placing higher value on our own pathological ends than on what is most valuable about ourselves and others, namely, the fact that we are rational self-determining agents, whose dignity consists in just this fact.

To value one's own dignity (as opposed to the dignity of others) is to have respect for one's own autonomy, one's own power to construct the meaning of one's own life as one sees fit within the boundaries of respect for the equal autonomy of others. I respect my own dignity when I insist that others respect my autonomy and my right to direct my life in accordance with my own vision of what makes it meaningful. I have duties to myself not to allow myself to be used as a mere means by others in the pursuit of their desires. Their dealing with me must be open, truthful, honest, noncoercive, and tolerant of my differences. My valuing my own dignity also requires that I have duties to myself never to undermine my own rational agency. This requires that suicide, that failure to promote my own happiness within the boundaries of the rights of others, that refusal to develop my own character, and that negligence in cultivating my own talents are wrongs against my own agency and, as such, are violations of my own dignity. When I construct the meaning of my life just out of my desires, appetites, sentiments, and passions, without subordinating these concerns to the fact that I am a self-determining agent, I am treating myself without respect and without regard for what gives me my dignity.

On the Kantian view, it is the fact that we are capable of regulating our pathological desires by the ideal of respect for ourselves as agents rather than as mere subjects that gives us our dignity. And it is dignity, so construed, that is the supreme value, the value that has no price. We have, then, on the Kantian view a conception of dignity where dignity is the supreme regulative ideal.

The question is: what view of tragedy is implied by the Kantian notion of dignity as the supreme regulative ideal? What are the implications for tragedy as (i) the bad prevailing over the good and as (ii) the greater good prevailing over the lesser good when the lesser good contains value not contained in the greater good?

With regard to tragedy as the bad prevailing over the good, there are many things to be said for the Kantian view, and it is a mistake to underestimate them. The essence of all of them is the loss of some aspect of agency in exchange for something of less importance: self-respect for selfish desire, responsibility for excessive security, or the need for discipline for the life of lust and leisure.

Examples abound.

The African slave trade,[7] the Taliban's treatment of women, and the rape of Nanking[8] are tragedies of coercion. These and many others like them are the most obvious examples and are easy to understand. Dignity ravaged is their essence; humiliation, their intended psychological effect. But humiliation is not the only source of coercion that threatens the tragic loss of dignity. Paternalism is another. The instinct to protect others from the harm of their own choices is a strong human predilection. History is full of forms of government whose central design was to protect against harm at all costs. The result has been miserable failure, and the loss in human dignity incalculable. It is easy to take the view that totalitarian instincts are always borne of malicious intent, but they

7 See Hugh Thomas, *The Slave Trade* (New York: Simon & Schuster, 1997).

8 See Iris Chang, *The Rape of Nanking: The Forgotten Holocaust of World War II* (New York: Basic Books, 1997).

are not. They are sometimes born of good intentions, especially the intent to protect against harm. If you start with an ethic that says "first, do no harm," whether that ethic is religious, secular, humanist, or feminist, you have the seeds of the totalitarian instinct. Dignity, which brings with it the capacity to make huge mistakes with your life, will be shelved for something thought to be better, namely, security. Dignity cannot exist in complete security. So to have dignity, you must give up some security. Kant himself did not fully understand this, because he thought that God was completely secure but nonetheless an agent with dignity. Nevertheless, he thought that one of the great wrongs that can be done to a human being is to protect her against her own informed choices. Moreover, he believed that it is a violation of someone's dignity to interfere with her informed choices even if it is guaranteed that the result of interfering would be good for her. To be unable to make our own mistakes and live with them is to lose a central part of ourselves. Totalitarian governments and well-meaning but overbearing parents have effected a great deal of tragedy by valuing security over the responsibilities of agency. Though they did not intend to humiliate their citizens and children, the result was the same. There is no way to understand the tragedy involved without recognizing that respect for dignity as the capacity to construct the meaning of one's own life from one's own point of view is at least sometimes far more important than the loss of security.

Some security, however, is necessary for dignity, and one of the great tragedies of history has been how people have been reduced to living as less than agents or as seriously truncated agents because the means necessary for exercising control over their lives were denied them. When the Taliban denied education to Afghan women and required that they appear in public only when accompanied by a man, they were forcing women to surrender the control of their lives to others. They were requiring women to surrender their agency. When poverty sets the task of life as mere survival, it renders the pursuit of happiness as a goal impossible. When the drug trade enslaves the unsuspecting and naive to the habits of addiction, it renders the development of character beyond the reach of those afflicted. And when unemployment and lack of opportunity reduce people to a life of idleness, the cultivation of talent is rendered impossible. What we must do to avoid as much of this tragedy as possible is assist people in ways such that the conditions under which they can take responsibility for the direction of their lives actually obtain. If they then squander their lives, this too will be a tragedy, but not the tragedy of never having the chance to live a life of dignity.

Less visible but no less tragic are the tragedies of manipulation and deceit. Sexual harassment by men in authority can reach tragic dimensions, as can the use by women of gender profiling to create an environment in the workplace that shields incompetence from criticism in order to advance a career. Both are horrible. Both ruin people's lives. And both are anything but rare. Myriad, then, are the methods of manipulation, and the evil is one employed by men and women alike. But I will leave it to Kantians to tell their own story of tragedy in its detail. What should be clear is that our agency, our capacity to direct our lives, to construct meaning for our lives from our own points of view, and to take responsibility for our lives, is of categorical value to us. When it is lost or undermined in significant ways, the result is tragic. This much is right about the Kantian view: our agency is often more valuable than other things we value. Whether, however, it is strictly superior to other values in a way that establishes that dignity is a value that is constant and overriding, a value without price, is another matter.

It can be shown that we do not believe that human dignity is a value that is constant and overriding if it can be shown that we sometimes value other things over it in at least some contexts when adequately informed of all that is at stake. This will be the case if human agency is sometimes the lesser good. An excellent illustration involves cruelty to and mistreatment of animals. Consider the issue both individually and globally.

Suppose that through my neglect my horse starves to death. Is this tragic? I think so. Horses are magnificent animals. Moreover, it is more tragic the more trivial my reasons for the neglect. On the Kantian view, the more tragic loss when autonomy and other goods are involved is always the loss of autonomy. But that is not what is lost here. What is lost here is the horse, not its being my riding companion but its life and the avoidance of its suffering. Horses are not autonomous agents, but sometimes their lives and the avoidance of their suffering is the greater good than the autonomous choices of human agents. Globally, the point is even more pressing. Just how much suffering can we impose on lower animals in order to accommodate lifestyles constructed by human agents without regard for their impact on lower animals? That the answer is that there is some such limit just in terms of our concern for lower animals shows conclusively that we do not think that respect for human choice is limited only by respect for human choice, as the Kantian conception of dignity as the supreme regulative ideal maintains.[9] Indeed, the value we place on control of our own destinies is regulated by an ideal in which concern for lower animals puts some restriction on what we can do with our agency and our lives. This could not be the case on a conception of dignity as the supreme regulative ideal. Sometimes autonomy is the lesser good.

The same is true of the value of personal relations and other values. Though we want some control over the direction of our lives, and in this sense value being agents, we also value being subjects and having good things happen to us. Moreover, we would give up a good bit of our autonomy for these things. Suppose you could be granted any wish. If you held the view of dignity as the supreme regulative ideal, you would wish that nothing would happen to you that you did not choose. But, surely, that would be among the worst forms of life. Love comes at inconvenient times and places and with inconvenient people and commitments. Moreover, it seldom comes with perfect honesty, openness, tolerance, and without some degree of coercion, manipulation, and deceit. Denying this seems to me among the worst forms of moralism. Anyone who has ever had a decent marriage or friendship knows that the concern for too much control over the direction of a relationship bears the seeds of its destruction. Moreover, the best marriages and friendships are not those in which the parties choose not to exercise control over the relationship but those in which the parties just value the relationships more than they do control. A certain degree of autonomy is the lesser good for them.

What we find upon reflection is that if we endorse a regulative ideal, it is not one in which dignity as autonomy regulates our other values but is unregulated by them. Rather, it is a regulative ideal in which the value of a certain vague degree of control over our lives regulates

9 Of course, Kant thought that we have an indirect duty to lower animals not to harm or mistreat them, but the story of indirection is just implausible. What we care about is the animals themselves, not just their use or relationship to us.

the value we place on other things, and the value we place on other things, such as on lower animals and on being subjects and having good things happen to us, regulates the value we place on being in control of our lives. This kind of mutual regulative effect of our values on each other within our psychology shows that we do not accept the view of dignity as the supreme regulative ideal.

Though we value not being humiliated, we do not see every degree of lack of control as humiliating. This has led Daniel Statman to distinguish two concepts of dignity: the Kantian one that focuses on autonomy and morality and another that focuses on what he calls dignity as nonhumiliation.[10] If our concept of human dignity were identified with autonomy, then any loss of autonomy would be a loss of dignity, but there are losses of autonomy that are not humiliating. So there is a concept of dignity that is not strictly tied to the notion of autonomy. Might this notion of dignity as nonhumiliation be constant and overriding where dignity as autonomy is not?

Statman believes that one of the virtues of dignity as nonhumiliation is that it makes no claim to being constant and overriding. It is one of many important human values, which in some contexts is overriding and in some contexts is not. Notice that people who value their relationships more than they do control over their lives do not feel humiliated by this fact. Perhaps if the degree of control were reduced past a certain point, they would. If so, then dignity as some degree of autonomy and dignity as nonhumiliation would overlap, as I suspect it does. Also, notice that those who show responsible concern for lower animals as a regulative restriction on how they can construct their lives do not feel humiliated by this restriction on their autonomy, despite the fact that it is accepted on behalf of nonrational animals. On the other hand, that they would feel humiliated by being treated as mere subjects like pigs or pets to be affectionately patronized shows something else. It shows that their self-respect does indeed turn on seeing themselves as having some degree of control over their lives and that they are not mere subjects, on some interpretation of what it means to be an agent.

[10] See Daniel Statman, "Humiliation, Dignity, and Self-Respect," *Philosophical Psychology* 13, no. 4 (2000): 523–9.

There is, then, a relationship between dignity as autonomy and dignity as nonhumiliation. We value having some control over our lives in terms of their direction and meaning. In this regard, we find it humiliating when we are thought of as being mere subjects in regard to our fate. On the other hand, we value being subjects and having good things happen to us that we do not control. In this regard, we do not find it humiliating when we have some threshold level of control over our lives and these good things happen to us. This means that our normative notion of dignity is that of a value regulated by our other values as well as that of a value that regulates the place of other values within our psychology.

Even so regulated, however, the value of dignity is not supreme. If there are worse things than loss of autonomy, there are worse things than being humiliated. I can be humiliated in a variety of ways. One way is to suffer a blow to my self-respect. I may, for example, be humiliated by my own poor preparation for teaching a class, even if my students do not notice. Another is to suffer a loss of respect by those I respect. My peers may have reasonable but false beliefs about me that I rightly find humiliating. That they falsely but rationally believe that I have done something gravely wrong might be an example. Still another is to be forced, manipulated, or deceived into doing things I find intolerable by those for whom I have no respect. Life in the concentration camps was replete with examples. Still, there are worse things, which means that in some cases we endure humiliation for the sake of something we regard as the greater good or the lesser evil in the context.

I remember feeling humiliated before a class during the early infancy of my first daughter. Lost sleep and primary care during much of the day left me little time to prepare. As a result, I had to teach without much preparation and on the reserves of past teaching experience. The bad days were not up to my standards, and I felt humiliated on those days, even though I concealed it from the class. Still, there was no doubt in my mind that caring for my daughter in that context made the humiliation bearable, though it certainly was stressful. It might be objected that it is one thing to be humiliated as a teacher but another as a person, and that I did not feel humiliated as a person by sacrificing the quality of my teaching to the greater good of my daughter's welfare. Therefore, the example, according to the objection, does not illustrate that there are worse things than being humiliated as a person.

But are there not things worse than a loss of self-respect as nonhumiliation? I agree that examples are extreme, but that there are examples shows that dignity as nonhumiliation is not strictly superior to all other values. I would not only teach classes poorly and write trash in order to save my family, I would also do much more self-degrading things if necessary. That I would not find this humiliating even in the full knowledge of why I was doing it is, I believe, utterly implausible. The same, I believe, is true for those who endured the humiliation of the concentration camps in order to bear witness later. It is not that they managed to avoid humiliation by concentrating on a higher purpose, though there may have been some of this, but that they bore the humiliation, the loss of dignity, because of something they valued more. If so, they valued dignity as the lesser good. Good people are like that. Their sense of dignity is derived from other things that they value, and they are able to endure humiliation for the sake of those other things.

What this suggests is that the value of dignity is recursive in the way that Hurka believes that the value of virtue is. This is a very important point, one crucial to understanding the place of dignity in our values. Recall that for Hurka the value of compassion as a virtue is less than the value of suffering relieved, and so too for other virtues. How much less valuable is hard to say, but that it is less intrinsically valuable seems clear: no compassionate person values compassion as much as the relief of suffering. What about dignity, where dignity is tied to agency and autonomy? If dignity is like virtue, there is a recursive relationship between the value of an agent and the values pursued by an agent, as there is between virtue and the goods to which virtue is attached. If the recursive value of autonomy as an additional value is either less than or equal to the values pursued by an agent, then the conception of dignity as the supreme regulative ideal cannot be correct.

Interestingly, Kant gave a recursive account of the value of a good will, but he does not do so for the value of agency and autonomy. The good will is made good by its good motive, which is to say that the intrinsic value of a good will is proportionate to the purity of its motive. Since, for Kant, such a motive does not come in degrees, the value of a good will is equal to the value of its motive. This is clearly one type of recursive account. What he and contemporary Kantians deny, however, is a recursive account of the value of the worth of persons. Persons are valuable and worthy of respect on Kant's view just because they are agents, regardless of what kind of agents they are. I cannot see any plausibility to this view, even if rejecting it requires us to reject the notion of the equal worth of persons, which I believe we should. Unlike Kant, I do not see any dignity in the autonomous pursuit of evil. If Hitler did what he did, and was who he was, through autonomous choice rather than through sickness or pathology, he was intrinsically worse than if he were compelled to do what he did and be who he was. Consider, in this regard, the following two claims as corollaries: (1) if A does the good autonomously and B does the good pathologically, then A is better than B, and (2) if C does evil autonomously and D does evil pathologically, then C is worse than D. But then what about the comparison between B and C? What is behind the thought that an autonomous Hitler would have any dignity that a pathological Mother Theresa would lack? What this suggests is that the value of autonomy is no better than the kind of meaningful life in which it is exercised. Even if dignity requires some degree of autonomy, autonomy does not guarantee dignity. And if the recursive relationship between agency – control over one's own destiny – and dignity is the one I have suggested, then the conception of dignity as the supreme regulative ideal has to be untrue to our deepest values.

Consider how this is illustrated when we try to analyze tragedy in Kantian terms in the case of the greater good of dignity prevailing over the lesser good of other things when the lesser good contains significant value not contained in dignity. Remember that any version of pluralism must allow that there are tragedies of this sort. And clearly, there are cases of this sort. Sometimes we may maintain our dignity only at great cost. Sometimes the only expression available to us over which we have control regarding the meaning of our lives is defiance. In the face of humiliation and restricted control, we sometimes have only the refusal of a bended knee to express the meaning of our lives. The costs might be enormous in other things. But to really make sense of such a case as being a case of tragedy, these other things have to be the objects of categorical desire. Otherwise, the stakes are not high enough to reach to the level of tragedy. Kantians cannot treat these other things as of noncategorical value, as modern Stoics do, and expect to succeed.

The notion of defiance and sacrifice at stake testifies to a recursive account of dignity. It is control in regard to things otherwise worthy of choice to which dignity is attached.

Consider the desire to die with dignity. What I have in mind is a request for assisted suicide because of hopelessly bad health. What kind of value judgment is it that a person is making when in the light of full knowledge he chooses to request help in ending his life because it is bereft of any of its meaning and only the capacity for choice is left? Is he not judging that the preservation of autonomy and rational agency is not the greater good when it comes at the cost of any meaningful life? How could the preservation of life in such a case include a greater good than obtaining relief from a meaningless life? Is he not judging that dignity can only be preserved with other values? If so, he cannot believe either that dignity and autonomy are identical or that dignity is the supreme value regulating other values. He has to believe that dignity itself is regulated by other values. Of course, there are those who do not believe this. They believe that suicide is always wrong. But such people invariably have recourse either to religious values that refuse to recognize the depth of tragedy or to ideas that are the secular residue of religious perspectives, as contemporary Kantianism is. When the body loses its vigor, the mind its energy, and the heart its passion, the power of choice can nonetheless remain, but there is nothing for it to serve, even morality. We can live with dignity or die with dignity, but we cannot live for dignity. No amount of moralizing against suicide can change this. Such moralizing is just a refusal to accept a certain form of tragic loss, and it flies in the face of reality. To lie in one's waste, to feel the decay of one's body, to be constantly bathed in one's own urine, and to see the hopeless waiting in the eyes of loved ones for one's own death is not the lesser of two tragedies. By far the lesser tragedy, the one that has the dignity in it, is the one that puts an end to a life that has lost its quality. But this story is not available on the notion of dignity as the supreme regulative ideal. Why? Because dignity can only be had in the context of a meaningful life, either in the midst of such a life or in death as an expression of what life was about.

It might be objected that the dignity found in making our own mistakes through bad choices undermines the claim that dignity is tied recursively to the quality of a meaningful life. If through my own best efforts I ruin my life, there is still some dignity in it. So how can it be that dignity is tied recursively to the quality of a meaningful life? The answer, I believe, takes the same recursive form that Kant employs in his account of the good will. My dignity consists in my best effort at living a meaningful life of good quality. To the extent to which I autonomously aim at a bad life, I lack dignity, and to the extent to which I aim at an inferior life, I have dignity inferior to others who aim at something better. Also, if I feel compelled to leave it to you either to ruin your life or to make something of it, it is not because I think you have dignity no matter what you choose but because I think that the only way you can have dignity is to take control of your life and make something good of it. This makes sense only on a recursive account of the value of dignity.

Nor will it do to object that the suicide example shows that dignity is the supreme value because the person in the example refuses to live without dignity. It will not do for two reasons: first, we have already seen that there are worse things than either humiliation or the loss of autonomy, and second, what the example shows is that the person in the example cannot see any dignity in a life without other values, and that is what is decisive against the notion of dignity as the supreme regulative ideal. What is hard to envision is a greater good that contains dignity but no other goods. If we cannot envision this, then it is hard to see how supreme value pluralism of this variety can deliver on an account of tragedy that treats dignity as strictly superior to all other goods. Not only is supreme value pluralism a fantasy in the sense that it is incoherent when taking this form, but it is also pernicious in deflating the value of things of great worth.

Some tragedy is avoidable only if we keep our values in perspective. When we inflate some values, we deflate others. In some cases, this amounts to arrogance, and nowhere is this more evident than in the doctrine of dignity as the supreme regulative ideal. In the first instance, it arrogantly elevates the value of human beings over that of other animals. One does not have to endorse what I believe is the rather strange view that human beings should value lower animals and themselves equally to see the arrogance of the doctrine in question. The doctrine of dignity as the supreme regulative ideal asserts that human beings are not only superior but strictly superior to lower animals. This is arrogance that casts a shadow over the suffering of lower animals, as well as other aspects of their existence, and it is this arrogance that is a pernicious fantasy.

In the second instance, the doctrine of dignity as the supreme regulative ideal seems anything but arrogant in denying that dignity comes in degrees. If dignity comes whole cloth or not at all, then everyone is of equal worth. Everyone has dignity, and none more than others. Egalitarianism is secured. So where is the arrogance? Ironically, egalitarianism of this sort is the worst form of arrogance. Though it ensures that no one thinks himself better than another, it also ensures that no one can recognize that someone else is a better person in his fundamental worth. This is humility bought at the price of arrogance. I cannot see how to endorse a conceptual scheme that does not allow me to recognize some people as better than me. If I have any moral knowledge at all, it is this: there are people who are better than me. As a consequence, they deserve better treatment than me and more recognition than me. I cannot conceal their goodness in the shadow of my alleged dignity. To do so is both arrogant and tragic. For the same reasons, I cannot endorse a conceptual scheme that does not allow me to recognize my superiority as a person to some other people. I will not live in the shadow of the alleged dignity of Charles Manson, Adolf Hitler, or, for that matter, even of Jerry Springer. My own sense of dignity and worth will not allow it.

Whatever version of egalitarianism we endorse, it cannot be the Kantian one of dignity as the supreme regulative ideal. That everyone should have a chance at a life of dignity is one thing; that everyone has equal dignity and worth is quite another. Perhaps the greatest tragedy of our current conceptual scheme in this regard is how it conceals the true worth of so many superior people – and all so that inferior people do not have to face their inferiority. Let me be clear: no one is better or worse than another because of race, or gender, or class, or things of this sort. But respectful, sympathetic, and loving people are better than people who are not. Moreover, honest people are better than liars, courageous people better than cowards, just people better than the unjust, and loyal people better than traitors. To deny this is to perpetrate one of the greatest tragedies of our age. It is to fail to recognize true dignity where it exists.

Finally, what can be said against modern Stoicism and the Kantian doctrine of dignity as the supreme regulative ideal can be said against any form of supreme value pluralism. The primary problem is this: the plurality of values in conflict include multiple categorical values. None is strictly superior to the others, regardless of extent and degree. Moreover, if we insist on feeding our increasing appetite for these moralizing doctrines, we will add to tragedy something that we could otherwise avoid. To moralize is to create a false sense of superiority that tragically eclipses our appreciation of other values. When Victorians moralized chastity, they cut off people from the joys of passion; when homophobes moralize heterosexuality, they limit the range of human experience; and when patriarchs moralize masculine virtues and feminists moralize those they think feminine, they do violence to difference. Moreover, there are myriad other ways in which the moralizing instinct can wreck havoc with important values in tragic ways. What it is absolutely crucial to understand is that human value cannot be expressed moralistically or within a conceptual scheme in which some value is held to be strictly superior to all other human concerns. Moralism is not a form of enlightenment, and it is ironic that it has been romanticized as such. What is concealed in the dark shadows of Stoic virtue and Kantian dignity proves the point.

To think and feel maturely about tragic loss is to give up not only the simpleminded view that value is one and not many but also the view that there is some supreme value that is always the greater good. It is just not so, and it is too late in history to keep this kind of hope alive. The cost in values obscured by value inflated is just too great.

7

Moralism and the Impurity of Value

Even worthless ground, given a gentle push
from heaven, will harvest well, while fertile soil,
starved of what it needs, bears badly.
But human nature never seems to change;
evil stays itself, evil to the end,
and goodness good, its nature uncorrupted
by any shock or blow, always the same,
enduring excellence.
Is it in our blood
or something we acquire? But goodness can be taught,
and any man who knows what goodness is
knows evil too, because he judges
from the good.
But all this is the rambling nothing
of despair.

Euripides, *Hecuba*

The dangers of moralism run deep and in more than one direction. The direction just surveyed is one fed by a current of arrogance: elevate virtue and dignity the way the Stoics and Kantians do and things of great importance will fade from view, sucked into the turgid waters of the moralizing mind. Pulling in another direction is a different current of moralism: the passion for purity. Perhaps the most passionate and intelligent moralizer in intellectual history, Immanuel Kant, argued that the foundation for morality must involve a value that is unqualifiedly good.[1] He went on to assert that such a value could not in itself ever lead a well-motivated person to do the wrong thing. If a well-motivated person ever does the wrong thing, it must be traceable to something independent of what is good about that person. The same point could be made in terms of virtue, Stoic or otherwise. Purity of virtue would ensure that nothing wrong done by a good person will be traceable to that person's virtues, but only to lack of knowledge, skill, resources, or something of that sort. Moreover, if virtue is what allows the Stoic sage to be happy even on the rack, it is because its purity secures immunity to evil. There can be no doubt, then, that the doctrine of the purity of value is one with a long and influential tradition. Its most central thesis is that a fail-safe guard against vulnerability to evil is a value pure and overriding.

The consolation of moralism for certain forms of tragedy is that what is good about us transcends the vicissitudes of fate. If we are good and tragic events occur as result of our best efforts, we can be consoled by reason in the knowledge that the bad did not issue from what is good about us and that what is of supreme value is immune to misfortune. On the other hand, if even moral goodness itself, however understood, is impure, then the kind of moralism that comes with supreme value pluralism is just another pernicious fantasy. It conceals things about ourselves that we should know and that by knowing would allow us to avoid tragedies that flow from fantasies of inflated worth. If this is true, then the cost of the passion for purity is too high.

The issue of purity is the issue of whether any candidate for the supreme value has basic properties that make a metamorphosis from good to bad possible. A pure value would not, in terms of its own basic properties (properties that make it what it is), allow such a transition. If it did, then there would be some contexts in which the supreme value itself leads to evil and would in that sense be divided against itself. But if any alleged supreme value is impure, then its own basic properties are such that under some set of circumstances metamorphosis of some sort does indeed occur.

[1] See Immanuel Kant, *Groundwork of the Metaphysic of Morals*, translated by H. J. Paton (New York: Harper Torchbooks, 1964), 61.

In another book, *Dignity and Vulnerability*,[2] I have argued that what is good about us leads under some circumstances of stress to what I called benign integral breakdown. In such cases, vulnerability indicates what is good about us, rather than some flaw or deficiency in us. The idea is something like the following. Litmus paper has certain basic properties that make it suitable for testing whether a solution is alkaline or acidic. Exposed in an alkaline solution, it turns blue, and in an acidic solution, it turns red. Of course, litmus paper is valued not as an intrinsic good but as an instrumental one, an instrument for testing whether a solution is alkaline or acidic. But suppose that for some odd reason you valued litmus paper intrinsically for its basic properties. You would then value it regardless of whether it turned blue or red in a solution. Why? Because the same basic properties have different modal expressions under different environmental conditions. Blueness is the modal expression of litmus properties under exposure to an alkaline solution, and redness is the modal expression of litmus properties under exposure to an acidic solution. The basic properties under one modal expression – litmus-as-blueness – are the very same basic properties under another modal expression – litmus-as-redness. Consequently, if it is the basic properties of litmus that you value intrinsically, you will value those properties under any of their modal expressions. The same is true of anything that is valued intrinsically for its basic properties, including what is good about people.

Love is a good example. If being a loving person can itself be something that is intrinsically good, then the basic properties that make a person loving are intrinsically valuable under any of their modal expressions. Consider one such modal expression: joy at the good fortune of a loved one. Any loving person is such that barring extenuating circumstances, the good fortune of a loved one evokes joy. If you never take delight in the good fortune of another person, this is conclusive evidence that you do not love that person. So one modal expression of lovingness is lovingness-as-joy. Now consider another modal expression of lovingness: grief at the loss of a loved one. Again, any loving person is such that barring extenuating circumstances, the loss of a loved one evokes grief. To be sure, there are sometimes extenuating

[2] See George W. Harris, *Dignity and Vulnerability: Strength and Quality of Character* (Berkeley: University of California Press, 1997).

circumstances. Sometimes the loss comes as a relief from an extended period of extreme suffering or at the end of a long and meaningful life that has run its course, in either case resulting in a lesser form of sorrow than grief. But barring extenuating circumstances and substitute expressions like denial, self-deception, and anger, the absence of grief at the loss of another is a sure sign that you do not love the person. Another modal expression, then, of lovingness is lovingness-as-grief. The crucial thing is that the basic properties that underwrite the modal expression of lovingness-as-joy are the very same basic properties that underwrite the modal expression of lovingness-as-grief. Consequently, if lovingness is something that is intrinsically good about people, then sometimes what is good about people makes them vulnerable to the effects of grief that are often devastating. If we were hedonists, we would value lovingness only under its pleasant modal expressions rather than for itself. I have argued that a similar analysis applies to all forms of human caring – love, sympathy, respect, and any other form of human concern – that are a part of what we value intrinsically about people.[3] Goodness without vulnerability is impossible because the modal expressions of vulnerability that are a function of the basic properties of goodness are the very same properties that we value intrinsically under more auspicious conditions.

Of course, nothing said here about the intrinsic value of lovingness implies that lovingness, or any other quality, is a kind of simple quality that exists in isolation from other qualities and as such is intrinsically good. The kind of lovingness that we think is intrinsically good is love that has been shaped in its qualities by other kinds of concerns, including respect. Kantians are right about this. However, nothing that is true about this fact changes anything that is said here about the central claim that qualities that are valued intrinsically are intrinsically valued under any of their modal expressions. Reflection on the joy and grief of a loving and respectful person should confirm this: joy and grief are modal expressions of the qualities of a respectfully loving person under different environmental conditions. The pertinent thought is this: you cannot be a respectfully loving person without vulnerability.

The issue of the impurity of value is a special case of the vulnerability thesis. Are the basic properties of goodness such that it is those very

[3] See ibid.

properties that make us vulnerable to becoming evil? If the answer is yes, then under some conditions good people undergo an evil metamorphosis because of the very properties that make them good. Given what I have said, it would seem that what we should say about the metamorphosis is that what appears to be evil is good because it is the modal expression of what is good about us. But I think it more plausible to say that while vulnerability to such metamorphosis is a modal expression of what is good about us, the basic properties we possess after the metamorphosis are the expression of a fundamentally different character and therefore not an expression of what is good about us. That is why the metamorphosis is from good to evil. The occurrence of metamorphosis, then, marks a restriction on how modal expressions of intrinsically good properties can be expressions of what is good about a person. The claim is that short of metamorphosis any modal expression of intrinsically good properties is an expression of what is good about us. This leaves intact the claim that lovingness-as-grief is a modal expression of love and therefore of what is good, but if love can turn to sadism, then the love has died and something bad and no longer good has taken its place.

Moral purists, of the Kantian, Stoic, or any other sort, must maintain that metamorphosis from good to evil is impossible.[4] To be more precise, their claim is a causal one: where V is the pure value, if A has V, then V cannot cause or play any causal role in A becoming E, where E is evil. For Stoics, this means that virtue cannot cause vice, and for Kant, that dignity cannot causally undermine dignity. The same kind of point applies to most Christian and other religious views. Godliness cannot lead to Godlessness, and lovingness cannot lead to lovelessness. On the other hand, if value is not pure in this sense and such metamorphosis is possible, then virtue can cause vice, dignity can undermine dignity, and love can cause hatred, indifference, and rage.

The difficulty is in knowing how to settle the issue. Can it be settled through a kind of conceptual analysis that is the stock-in-trade of many philosophers, or must it turn on what we can learn through empirical investigation? Of course, one way to settle the issue through conceptual analysis is to stubbornly insist that if something can lead to what is bad,

4 They would also have to claim that metamorphosis from good to neutral or indifferent is impossible.

it just is not good to begin with. If we take this route, I think we will find ourselves saying some very strange things about qualities we cherish most in people. My own inclination, then, is to say that ultimately the answer must come through empirical investigation about cherished human qualities and that we do not at present know enough to provide a conclusive answer, though the evidence points strongly in a certain direction. What we need to know about our own psychology and the conditions under which its basic properties function is what we know about litmus paper and the conditions under which its basic properties function. And, of course, what the basic properties of our psychology are is itself a burgeoning area of intellectual inquiry. What I say here, then, is admittedly speculative but not entirely so. I begin with some analysis of what we might be inclined to say with our current level of knowledge about some literary cases and then proceed to comment about some clinical cases and about some of what we know about neuropsychology.

The reason I proceed in this way is that I believe that narratival explanation is ineliminable from both value theory and psychology. Until we can tell the right kind of story about our lives, we have no real understanding about what our values are and the roles they play in our decisions and feelings. As to psychology and narrative, psychology and neurology without narrative is in a very important sense meaningless. It does not explain the relevant data, namely, what our lives are about from our own points of view. Patterns of depression, for example, have to be described narratively in order for certain kinds of neurological explanations to be explanations of the data in question. Thus the most robustly explanatory neurological explanations map onto narratival explanations that illuminate our understanding of ourselves and our behavior from our own points of view. Suppose I believe that I am happy when I am in fact manic. What levels of explanation are needed to make me understand my mistake? I need a narrative that makes better sense of the nature of my behavior than the one I've been telling myself, and I need an explanation of the neurological developments that underwrite the better narrative. When I have both, I have a robust psychological explanation. Something is left out of the explanation if there is only a neurological account, just as there is something left out of the explanation if there is only a narrative of depressive living. Psychological explanation converges both elements. On the other hand, literary analysis without historical, clinical, and neurological data is insufficiently testable. We need knowledge of the actual facts of the world to restrict our imagination in constructing a conceptual scheme with which to direct our lives and our thinking. This makes consideration of clinical cases crucially important. Finally, while meaning cannot simply be read off of neurological facts (linguistic reductionism in this sense is false), any meaning our narratives have for us is facilitated by our neurology. Consequently, if metamorphosis from good to evil of the sort we are considering is possible, there must be some neurological explanation for its possibility. Similarly, if it is impossible, there must be some neurological explanation for what makes it so.

Those who reject such modest scientific constraints on conceptual analysis cannot do so in the name of freeing human thought from scientific bondage but can only embarrass themselves in any meaningful narrative of intellectual history. The Socratic imperative of self-knowledge is not advanced by scientific ignorance, and we know for a fact that human psychology is a function of human neurology. To refuse to accept this fact about our place in nature in the name of human transcendence is not only nonsense, it is a colossal failure to take the problem of tragedy seriously. It is a failure to understand how unfriendly and chancy the natural world can be. Like the Homeric gods, neurological variables are quirky and indifferent to our fate, which is just one more reason to move tragic concepts to the center of our ethical thought.

With this in mind, the issue here is what happens when apparently good people turn bad.

Consider Hecuba, the tragic figure in one of Euripides' plays.[5] Before the fall of Troy to the Greeks, we find Hecuba, according to all the evidence, a woman of high character: a loving wife and mother and a noble queen. Wife of Priam, king of the Trojans, and mother of Hector, the great Trojan hero, she has four other children: Cassandra, who was loved by Apollo; Paris, who was later responsible for Achilles' death; Polydorus, who was too young to participate in the war; and Polyxena, who was a beautiful and coveted princess. But then comes

[5] See Euripides, *Hecuba*, translated by William Arrowsmith, in *The Complete Greek Tragedies*, edited by David Greene and Richmond Lattimore, vol. III, *Euripides* (Chicago: University of Chicago Press, 1992), 499–599.

the change in fortune characteristic of Greek drama. Hector is brutally slain by Achilles; Paris and Priam are killed; Troy falls to the enemy; Cassandra is given to Agamemnon as a concubine; and Hecuba and Polyxena are taken captive. At this point only Polydorus is spared, having been sent away earlier because of his youth to the safekeeping of Polymester, the king of Thrace. The play opens, then, with a husband and two sons dead at the hands of the Greeks, with one daughter a concubine of the enemy's supreme commander, with the sole surviving son facing an uncertain fate, and with Hecuba and her youngest daughter awaiting a life of slavery.

What we find at this point is exactly what we would expect to find in a good person: a wife and mother grieving the loss of her husband and two sons and anxious about the fate of her remaining children. There is no hint of exceptional bitterness, hatred, or evil intent; rather, there is only grief and anxiety. Then comes the awful news that the Greeks have voted to sacrifice Polyxena as a tribute to the fallen Achilles. The messengers inform Hecuba of how Agamemnon had tried to prevail against the majority (until he was accused of caring more for Cassandra's love than for the honor of Achilles) and of how Odysseus eventually carried the Greeks to their final verdict regarding the sacrifice of Polyxena. When she reveals to Polyxena her fate, her daughter's only concern is for her mother rather than for herself. Death, she says, is far preferable to a life of enslavement to the Greeks. Hecuba's response is grief, anxiety, and a fading sense that life is worth living at all, none of which is a sign of anything bad about her.

Then come the betrayals that play a crucial role in Hecuba's metamorphosis to the "bitch of Cynossema." What is crucial to note about these betrayals is that they systematically undermine the moral order of Hecuba's world. The first is the betrayal of Odysseus, who arrives himself with the final verdict and to escort Polyxena to the sacrifice. Desperate to save her daughter, Hecuba appeals, ironically, to the loyalty and honor of Odysseus. She had saved him before when he had tried in disguise to penetrate Trojan defenses. Through her own actions, his life had been spared, despite the fact that he was Greek and she a Trojan. Yet he had led the campaign for her daughter's sacrifice. He responds to her appeal to his honor with the cruelest form of betrayal. He insists not only that honor requires the death of a royal Trojan but also that Hecuba cannot herself be substituted for her daughter. Why?

Because strict reciprocity requires Odysseus to spare Hecuba's life, not her daughter's. He thereby condemns her to a fate worse than her own death. He even refuses to let her die with her daughter, further denying her any honorable means of dealing with her loss. He then leads Polyxena off to her death. Such is the honor and loyalty of a Greek hero.

Later, in the midst of her desperation, Talthybius arrives with the story of how Polyxena died so nobly that it caused even the Greeks to honor her. At this point comes this passage from Hecuba:

> O my Child,
> how shall I deal with this thronging crowd of blows,
> these terrors, each with its petition, clamoring
> for attention? If I try to cope with one,
> another shoulders in, and then a third
> comes on, distracting, each fresh wave
> breeding new successors as it breaks.
> But now,
> with this last blow I cannot cope at all,
> cannot forget your death, cannot stop
> crying –
> And yet a kind of comfort comes
> in knowing how well you died.
> But how strange it seems.
> Even worthless ground, given a gentle push
> from heaven, will harvest well, while fertile soil,
> starved of what it needs, bears badly.
> But human nature never seems to change;
> evil stays itself, evil to the end,
> and goodness good, its nature uncorrupted
> by any shock or blow, always the same,
> enduring excellence.
> Is it in our blood
> or something we acquire? But goodness can be taught,
> and any man who knows what goodness is
> knows evil too, because he judges
> from the good.
> But all this is the rambling nothing
> of despair.[6]

[6] Ibid., 521–3.

From this strained attempt to find some relief in the fact that Polyxena was able to face her death with nobility emerges a resolve in Hecuba to take control of her daughter's burial, to see to it that it is done fittingly. At this point, despite the betrayal of Odysseus, Hecuba has a moral order in terms of which she can honorably express her grief. What was good in her daughter stood out for all to see and could not be eclipsed by bad fortune, even to the end. Goodness stays good, its nature uncorrupted, she tells herself as consolation.

But Polyxena's character was not tested to the same degree as Hecuba's. At this point, Hecuba's emotions, themselves a mixture of despair and resolve, are beautiful modal expressions of her love and character. Yet things were to get even worse. She is to experience another betrayal, this time by Polymester. As she is preparing for her daughter's funeral, her servants find a body in the surf, which turns out to be that of her son, Polydorus. He had been murdered and his body thrown ignominiously into the sea by Polymester for the gold his father had sent along with him for safekeeping. Another layer of the moral order has been ruthlessly peeled away. It was one thing to be betrayed by Odysseus, but quite another to be betrayed by someone trusted as a friend. The most sensitive forms of trust are being undermined. Now Hecuba has only one child left, and she, Cassandra, is mad and a sexual servant among the Greeks. Yet Hecuba's hatred for Polymester still finds expression within the moral order. Now she wants justice.

When Agamemnon learns of what Polymester has done and the new tragedy that has fallen on Hecuba, he is deeply moved. But his expressions of pity are met with cold reality. "I died long ago," says Hecuba. "Nothing can touch me now."[7] These words do not yet mean that the good Hecuba is dead. Though she is past the point of despair regarding what her life was most centrally about, she still has a sense of justice that prevents the response of sheer revenge. She still has a footing in the moral order. What she wants now is for Agamemnon to enforce the law of the Greeks against those who mistreat their guests. But even this last attempt to deal with her losses in a way that expresses an honorable response is met with what Hecuba could only perceive as another betrayal. Agamemnon explains that though he would like nothing better than to do as she wishes, he is confined by

7 Ibid., 532.

Polymester's standing with the Greek forces. So with justice denied and no avenue of expression within the moral order, Hecuba turns to revenge with no thought of justice, asking Agamemnon for passive support in the form of protective exile after a meeting she has planned with Polymester.

Ignorant that he has been found out, Polymester is lured along with his children into a meeting with Hecuba, who pretends to inquire about her son's well-being and to offer the prospects of further wealth. Together with her handmaidens, she manages to separate the father from his children and springs an attack that leaves Polymester with his eyes gouged out and his children ruthlessly slaughtered. She has her revenge and sadistically delights in it. As Polymester grieves for his children and experiences the same devastation as Hecuba, she mocks him for his loss, showing no pity and no recognition of the children's innocence. Her hatred for Polymester is now pure malice, untempered by respect and concern for innocent parties. From a loving mother to a vengeful bitch, her metamorphosis is all but complete. Later, as predicted by the prophet Dionysus, she would climb to the mast of a ship, fall into the sea, and drown, after being transformed into a dog.

Unlike her daughter's, Hecuba's death reflects nothing resembling nobility. Given the circumstances, resort to uninstitutionalized justice might have been understood as justice nonetheless, but sadistic revenge involving the innocent is another thing altogether. So contrary to the principle that proved to be an empty platitude, goodness seems to have changed.

What are we to say about Hecuba? What does conceptual analysis provide regarding our normative concepts in the light of her transformation? Can we say in the end that she, despite appearances, was rotten from the start? Was she sheltered by good fortune, with only the downturn of events revealing that she was not so good after all?

Notice that we can say this with confidence about Medea, another of Euripides' characters.[8] Medea slaughtered her own children in a jealous rage to get revenge on her husband, Jason, for taking another

[8] See Euripides, *Medea,* translated by William Arrowsmith, in *The Complete Greek Tragedies,* edited by David Greene and Richmond Lattimore, vol. III, *Euripides* (Chicago: University of Chicago Press, 1992), 63–112.

woman as his bride. The subject of study in that tragedy was the character of immodest love and sexual passion. Love and passion not tempered by other concerns can lead a person to do awful things. Love modestly. Temper it with other love and other forms of regard. If not, then beware the outcome. Love unregulated is a source not of good but of evil. This is the lesson, and one we would all agree is worth learning. Nothing about love unregulated in the Medea story provides grounds for thinking that she was an example of the good undergoing a metamorphosis to something evil. The evil was there all along, awaiting only the relevant circumstances to manifest it. Moreover, there were plenty of advance signs of its presence. Later, Seneca was to write his own version of the play to push the Stoic line that love and passion do not come in modest versions. Given the right conditions, they invariably lead to excess and are therefore bad qualities to be extirpated from the life of a good person. In neither case is there anything about Medea's love that leads us to the conceptual result that the basic properties of goodness are such that they themselves can, under the right conditions, lead to what is bad or evil.

But notice that we do not have in the story of Hecuba what we have in the story of Medea. There is no advance sign of character flaws in Hecuba, and there is nothing to suggest that her love was unregulated by other concerns. Her love for Troy and the members of her family did not blind her to the worth of others. She accepted Helen the Greek as the wife of her son, Paris, and tempered her love for Troy with mercy for the foreigner Odysseus. Nothing suggests that she was vulnerable to fits of jealousy or unprovoked hatred. Indeed, the evidence confirms that her love for her family was regulated by respect and honor for a noble enemy. The explanation for her transformation seems traceable to the very qualities of love and respect.

Her grief and despair are modal expressions of her love for her husband and children and are not signs of immodest love or of qualities in her that we would want to remove from her character. Nor would we want to remove her respect for honor wherever it is found or the influence of respect in regulating the love she had for her loved ones. What, then, are we to make of her reaction to betrayal?

It was not extensive loss of loved ones that transformed Hecuba but the combination of such loss with persistent breach of trust that systematically undermined any moral order in which she could express what was honorable about her. Odysseus refused to treat her with the honor with which she had treated him; Polymester betrayed his commitment to Priam, his alleged friend; and Agamemnon declined to enforce Greek justice and the requirement that hosts honor their guests with protection. Though in death the Greeks honored Polyxena, in life they excluded Hecuba from any membership in the moral community of honor and respect. Denied access to an honorable death and honorable justice and bereft of her loved ones, she was left with revenge as the only modal expression of who she was. No one else in her family had faced these circumstances. Hecuba and her virtue inhabited a very unfriendly world, one over which she had only very limited control.

What happens to a person who starts as exceptionally loving and respectful when exposed to an environment filled with extensive fatal violence to loved ones and where betrayal replaces all the honorable means of response? If redness is the modal expression of litmus properties in an acidic solution, what are the modal expressions of love and respect in an environment brutal and devoid of basic moral support? There is an old expression that hell knows no fury like a woman scorned, but it may be more apt to say that hell knows no fury like a loving and respectful person put in a loveless world of complete betrayal. What are hatred and contempt expressions of in such an environment if not the death throes of love and respect? And in such an environment what would expressions of love and respect be if not hatred and contempt?

Does this mean that Hecuba in the end is good? No. We must not understand Hecuba to have been thinking that since institutional justice is not available, revenge as a form of extralegal justice is now what the moral order calls for. There comes a point at which her hatred and sense of revenge comes unhinged from the constraints of the moral order that were once central to who she was. I do not mean that hatred, anger, and contempt, and even some forms of revenge, cannot be modal expressions of love and respect, and even of morality. The soldiers who first liberated the concentration camps at the end of World War II were filled with rage against the agents of the Third Reich and took bloody steps to bring that regime to an end, but their hatred, rage, and contempt had not come unhinged in the way that Hecuba's had. Their actions and emotions were clear expressions of the moral order of which they were a part. However, Hecuba's treatment of the children and her taunting exhibit sadism not found among the soldiers. The good Hecuba died when all outlets to expressing what was good about her were systematically and persistently denied to her. It was only then that the metamorphosis occurred. Somewhere along the way, the burden of hatred that was fueled both by her love and by her sense of honor became too much to bear. It killed something inside her and gave birth to something dark and sinister. In taunting Polymester in the loss of his children, she was taunting the moral order that should have saved both his children and hers as well.

In this regard, it is an interesting exercise in both literary and moral imagination to consider how the remainder of the narrative might have been written had Euripides constructed the play in such a way that Odysseus granted any of Hecuba's requests or had Agamemnon enforced Greek justice. Of course, this would have been contrary to Euripides' central purpose: to investigate what happens to good people whose moral world is systematically undermined. More centrally, was the specific form of honor morality of his time worth the price it exacted because of what it did to women in particular? It is also an interesting exercise in historical imagination to consider what would have become of the soldiers of World War II had their moral order allowed no way of responding to the horrors they experienced.

That we might feel pity for the bitch of Cynossema, who was once Hecuba, says something. The pity that we feel for Polymester is not the same pity that we feel for her. We pity Polymester-the-grieving-father despite the fact that he is the same person he always was, Polymester-the-ruthless-opportunist. There was always some good with the bad. But what about our pity for Hecuba-the-bitch? Does it not recognize that what she has become, which is horrible, is an expression of what she once was but no longer is? We do not recoil at the soldiers' hatred and anger in their fight against the fascist murderers of the Third Reich, but we do recoil at Hecuba, while at the same time pitying her because we understand how such change is possible and what it expresses.

Clinical cases involving post-traumatic stress disorder (PTSD) shed some empirical light on these questions. What we know is that some people go off to war and come back changed for the worse. We also know that some people are victimized by other forms of violence and are subsequently changed in ways such that they are no longer the good people who by all appearances they once were.

There are countless stories of men who have gone off to war and come home changed. It was once thought that PTSD was unique to Vietnam War veterans,[9] but that thesis is no longer plausible. Studies have shown that there is every reason to believe that PTSD was evident in Civil War veterans and in all probability in veterans of all wars.[10] A common form of this delayed response to traumatic events is a violent distrust of others, a trait that we do not associate with good people, especially when those who are not trusted are entirely trustworthy. War veterans who went off to war apparently normal, decent people have come home to terrorize their wives and children or to victimize in criminal ways other members of society – some because they were haunted by fears they could not terminate, others because of a heightened need for excitement they could not live without. Are all these changes a result of the Medea effect, the effect of adverse conditions on prior character flaws, or is there another effect, the Hecuba effect, the effect of adverse conditions on good character?[11]

Consider the issue of trust. Not to be able to trust trustworthy people is a character flaw, and a very serious one at that. Not only does it undermine all meaningful relations with other people and thereby constitute a tragic loss to the person suffering it, it is also devastating to those who are distrusted, especially if they are loved ones. To be accused of betrayal is to be accused of one of the worst of wrongs. Dante reserved the deepest part of hell for those who betrayed

[9] See Jonathan Shay, *Achilles in Vietnam: Combat Trauma and the Undoing of Character* (New York: Scribners, 1995).

[10] See Eric Dean, *Shook Over Hell: Post-Traumatic Stress, Vietnam, and the Civil War* (Cambridge, Massachusetts: Harvard University Press, 1999).

[11] It is also an important fact that requires explanation that there have been countless numbers of men who have gone off to war as respectful, loving people who returned to be respectful, loving people. This should not be overlooked. But this does not show that goodness is pure. Even "undamaged" ex-soldiers have a very difficult time discussing their experiences. It might be that some people can return to a more normal life because they can psychologically compartmentalize their war experiences in a way that others cannot. It strains credulity, I think, to assume that those who cannot are either genetically abnormal or guilty of something that the others are not. There may be something about their experiences and their neurology that explains why they cannot stop experiencing the effects of the war. Only finely tuned narratives of their lives based on careful clinical investigation can settle these issues.

others.[12] What place he reserved for those who unjustly accused others of betrayal is unclear. But what is clear is that the consequences of distrust are tragic to all affected. Just imagine the double horror of a war veteran beating his child to death because he suspected him of betraying him to the enemy.[13] Given that this is a terrible character flaw, how might one acquire it?

To answer this question, it is important to keep in mind that the abandonment of theological concepts in understanding human value and the human condition requires at least two things, both having to do with the fact that we must see ourselves as natural organisms. The first is that we must accept as a naturalistic constraint on our account of human nature that our psychologies are a function of our neurological systems. Therefore, any inquiry about whether what is good about us can lead to our turning bad is constrained by whatever our neurological systems make possible. The second is that we must accept as a constraint on our account of the human condition that the extent of our vulnerability to moral metamorphosis is in part a function of the vicissitudes of nature in constructing the neurological underpinnings of our psychology. Just how friendly nature has been to human goodness is in large part an empirical question.

With these constraints in mind, consider Hecuba's case. We now know that one of the neurological underpinnings of both maternal and romantic affection in women is oxytocin and the neurological circuits activated by it. It is reasonable to believe that without oxytocin, a trusting attitude of women toward others would not be as it is. If, as Carol Gilligan has hypothesized, women and men start with different moral tasks, it may very well be due in part to their differences in regard to oxytocin levels.[14] If women begin their moral experience in connection with other people and inherit the task of gaining independence, and men begin their moral experience in independence and inherit

[12] See Dante, *The Inferno*, translated by John Ciardi (New York: New American Library, 1954), especially Cantos 32 and 33.

[13] Those who are tempted to think that we should admire Hecuba even in transformation cannot plausibly hold this view about some war veterans. That we excuse some of this behavior and find it repulsive shows that we do not admire the psychology from which it flows.

[14] See Carol Gilligan, *In a Different Voice: Psychological Theory and Women's Development* (Cambridge, Mass.: Harvard University Press, 1993).

the task of establishing connection, it may be due to the increased oxytocin circuitry in women.[15] This would make women and men vulnerable in different ways to betrayal. Trust in women might in the first instance be a sign of intimacy and in the second a sign of respect for independence. Whereas for men it might in the first instance be a sign of respect for independence and in the second a sign of intimacy. Betrayal by loved ones would be a shock to the more primitive psychology of women, and betrayal by those for whom they have respect for their independence, a shock to their developed psychology. Whereas betrayal by those for whom they have respect would be a shock to the more primitive psychology of men, and betrayal by those they love, a shock to their developed psychology. Which is the greater shock – one coming to a more primitive psychology or a more developed psychology – is hard to say. Primitive trust or trust established after considerable development are both very fundamental aspects of human psychology, and it is crucial to human development that both forms of trust be achieved and maintained.

The threat of betrayal, imagined or real, in certain environments puts enormous stress on any psychology in which the need and capacity for trust is instantiated. It is no accident, then, that fear of betrayal is a common form of fear that accompanies PTSD. Moreover, sustained stress can change the human brain and the psychology it underwrites in fundamental ways.

The stress response is a neuropsychological response that prepares the human organism to meet new challenges in its environment. When alerted, the brain begins its response in the hypothalamus with the release of a stress hormone, corticotropin-releasing hormone (CRH), which then activates the pituitary gland to secrete another stress hormone, adrenocorticotropic hormone (ACTH), which then signals the adrenal glands to secret another stress hormone, cortisol, which normally sends signals back to the hypothalamus to cease producing CRH and terminate the stress response. These chemical stages correspond to the three emotional stages of stress: the alarm stage, the resistance stage, and the exhaustion stage. When the stress response is protracted, neurons are exposed to a kind of hormonal toxicity that they are not

[15] See Candace B. Pert, *Molecules of Emotion: The Science Behind Mind-Body Medicine* (New York: Touchstone, 1997), 68.

designed to endure indefinitely. Actual destruction of parts of the brain can occur – the shrinkage of the hippocampus, which is crucial to explicit memory and learning, is one example. Take away your hippocampus entirely and you cannot learn anything new. The shrinkage of the hippocampus, however, is a symptom rather than the cause of some of the emotional effects of stress. Rather, the inability to terminate the emotions involved in the stress response is underwritten by the effects of stress on serotonin uptake.[16]

Serotonin is a neurotransmitter, which, when it is deficient in supply or is not taken up sufficiently by dendrites at their synaptic connections with axons, undermines a person's normal psychological functioning. Deficient serotonin uptake is implicated in both severe depression and asocial personality disorders involving a predilection to excessive violence. Often these disorders are the result of genetic predisposition, where there is an abnormality regarding the gene (a short form of the gene 5-HTT)[17] that encodes a serotonergic receptor.[18] But genetic predisposition is not always the culprit. Sustained stress can yield the same results, even among those who are normal in their genetic endowment. To oversimplify things: the neurological or neurochemical explanation for the difference between people like Medea and Hecuba that explains the differences in their narrative histories might be found in a different balance between their oxytocin and serotonin uptake capacities.[19] Imagine it is so. (There certainly is no conceptual reason

[16] See Joseph Ledoux, *The Emotional Brain* (New York: Touchstone, 1996); Jaak Panksepp, *Affective Neuroscience* (New York: Oxford University Press, 1998); Esther Sternberg, *The Balance Within* (New York: Freeman, 2000); *Principles of Neural Science*, fourth edition, edited by Eric R. Kandel, James H. Schwartz, and Thomas M. Jessell (New York: McGraw Hill, 2000); and Hans Seyle, *The Physiology and Pathology of Stress* (Montreal: ACTA, 1950) and *The Stress of Life* (New York: McGraw Hill, 1956).

[17] See Associated Press, "Gene Links Deep Depression and Traumatic Stress," *Daily Press* (Newport News, Virginia), July 18, 2003, A:4.

[18] See *Principles of Neural Science*, 50.

[19] One way in which this is an oversimplification is that there are other neurotransmitters involved. Another is that the balance actually involves not only a ratio between oxytocin and serotonin but also a certain level of serotonin as an individual variable. Both too little and too much serotonin are implicated in excessive violence. See *Principles of Neural Science*, 50.

Crocodiles go up to six months without eating in order to care for their young. Even in the midst of their hunger, normal crocodiles will carry their young in their mouths without eating them to provide them with security. Occasionally, some deviant crocodiles will eat their young at this point. What makes the difference? In all

to think that this could not be the case, and it is strongly suggested as an explanation by what we now know about neuropsychology.) The Medea effect, then, will be understood as the effect of adverse conditions on the basic properties of Medea's neuropsychology expressed as a certain genetic imbalance in her oxytocin and serotonin uptake capacities. Had she had the right kind of genetic balance to start with, she would not have been prone to distrust and subject to extreme jealousy in the way that she was.

But what about Hecuba? Assume that the basic properties of Hecuba's psychology were such that they could be expressed neuropsychologically as a certain ratio of oxytocin to serotonin uptake capacity, a capacity typical of a person not genetically disposed to emotional disorders. What is the modal expression of that ratio when put under stress, the stress of prolonged grief and distrust? It is entirely possible that without the oxytocin circuitry as a basic property of her neuropsychology she would not have experienced stress in the first place. It may also be that in humans such circuitry is essential to the ability to form trust in relationships. If so, then these very basic properties of Hecuba's psychology initiated the stress cycle that led to changes in her neurology that in turn resulted in her sadistic behavior. That is, it is entirely possible that the chemistry that makes trust possible in one environment is the very same chemistry that acts as a catalyst in another to initiate a metamorphosis to a psychology that is modally expressed as distrust, anger, rage, and sadism in that new environment.

A similar causal story may be true of some war veterans, even some who seem to have a heightened need for excitement. It may very well be that once a person has experienced a sustained level of awareness and alertness that is required in certain survival contexts, there is no way to go back to another way of life. The brain and its chemistry that were once in the kind of balance that underwrites normal and admirable creativity and drive (perhaps expressed neurologically as a certain testosterone to serotonin ratio) might under extremely stressful

probability, it is differences in their oxytocin and serotonin circuitry rather than differences in their appetites. Interestingly, only weeks after this period, when the young have become independent, most crocodiles will devour even their own. Love is only a seasonal thing in the crocodile breast. Medea's problem seems to have been that she had the serotonin but lacked the genetic encoding for well-functioning serotonin receptors.

conditions initiate a change to meet the stress that is irreversible. In these and other ways, good people might become bad because of what was originally good about them. To say without evidence that they were bad from the start is contrary to what is clearly possible, and in all probability true. It cannot, therefore, be a conceptual truth that nothing bad can issue from what is good about us.

Of course, some will say that this is just a regrettable fact about the limits of human nature itself but not a fact about goodness itself. Were humans perfect, the thought might go, such limitations and vulnerabilities would not exist. Moreover, the objection continues, there is no reason to think that the good cannot be pried off from the bad in a way that should discourage us from thinking that we are perfectible in the sense of having basic properties that cannot be corrupted by the environment. Goodness might be multiply realizable in the way that functionalism asserts that consciousness is. Mind, functionalists say, is to be understood in functional terms, rather than in terms of identity relations between mental states and physical states. Whether a physical state is a mental state is simply a matter of its function; thus our concept of the mental is not identical to any physical state. There is, then, no conceptual connection between having a mind and being in any particular physical state. Goodness might be thought of as similar, and hope of human purity might be sustained in the expectation that there can be alterations in our neurology that will facilitate the good yet prevent even the possibility of corruption.

I think the response in both cases is that there is no empirical reason at all for thinking that consciousness and goodness are multiply realizable in any very extensive way. If you want to study consciousness, it is better to study organisms than computers. The proof will ultimately be in the success of different research programs. The great thing about functionalism is that it points toward the empirical study of things that plausibly have mental properties as the basis for any real understanding of mental functions. Fans of computers have pursued one research program, and neuroscientists another. The best research program will no doubt employ both strategies, but the wise will place their bets more on the study of human organisms, and this seems the route currently being taken. If the best study of "mankind" is "man" in regard to the mind, the same is true about goodness. In some sense, goodness is, like mind, multiply realizable, but that it is multiply realizable in a way that would provide empirical reasons for thinking that the basic properties of human nature that underwrite what is good about persons can be purified is decidedly contrary to the evidence.

In this regard, it is important and interesting to think of what a purist hypothesis regarding our neuropsychology would be like. As Joseph Ledoux aptly puts it, there is no change in our psychology without a change in our neurology.[20] Dualists and materialists alike can accept this important truth. Those who do not are as intellectually foolish as the opponents of Galileo. Again, when theological concepts are abandoned, a central necessity of coming to an adequate understanding of the tragic nature of the human condition is coming to grips with the fact that we are biological organisms whose minds are functions of our brains, brains that are subject to the vicissitudes of evolution and chemical composition. Any plausible purist hypothesis has to accept this kind of naturalistic constraint, which no view that takes the human condition and tragedy seriously dares ignore.

In any event, what neurochemical purism would have to assert is one of two things. Either, first, goodness is the function of a pure goodness chemical and varies in the degree to which impurities have been eliminated, or, second, it is the function of a chemical balance, which once achieved is thereafter immune to change from within, regardless of variations in the environment. On the first view, admirable mother love would be a function of oxytocin on neural pathways unhampered by the need for other chemical support. But this is not what admirable mother love is in its neurological expression. It is the expression of a balance of chemicals that in different balances can have very undesirable expressions. What this shows is that we cannot think of human goodness as the elimination of impurities. This conceptual model just does not reflect the facts about the basic properties of human neuropsychology or about the human condition.

If, then, human goodness is to be conceptualized in a way that satisfies the naturalistic constraint on understanding the human condition, it must be conceptualized neuropsychologically as a balance. The question is whether that balance has the basic property of what we can call

[20] Ledoux has reminded me of this in personal correspondence about the very issues in this chapter.

pure equilibrium. Pure equilibrium would be a balance among variables that once achieved could be disrupted only by elements external to it. If all the variables in the universe were aligned in a certain balance and there were no other variables, the balance would be pure if there were nothing about the variables themselves that could introduce change that would disturb the balance. Purists of the second sort seem to think that goodness is a pure equilibrium in the sense that change of goodness is always due to the introduction of an impurity in the form of an external variable. But there is no reason to believe this, and significant reason not to believe it.

Some changes are changes in the variables internal to a balance, and other changes are not. Consider one that is not. A glass of water at room temperature constitutes a certain chemical balance in a certain environment. Add alcohol and that balanced is changed. This is a change in a balance due to the introduction of a variable external to the balance. Another change can be brought about by a change in the environment rather than a change in the variables internal to the balance. For example, increase the heat and hold other variables constant and the water will evaporate at a faster-than-normal rate. An example of a change in a neurological balance that is due to the introduction of an external variable might be the venom introduced by a snakebite or the influx of caffeine from too much coffee. Purists of the second sort have to believe that change in a neurological balance that underwrites goodness has to be a function of some external impurity introduced into the variables constituting the balance. Otherwise, goodness is vulnerable to the vicissitudes of fortune in virtue of its basic properties, and if it is vulnerable in this way to metamorphosis from good to bad, its value is impure.

A change in the environment, then, does not necessarily constitute a change in the variables internal to a balance. Rather, it may, and in fact does in many cases, trigger the variables in a balance themselves to initiate a change in the balance. The stress response is an excellent example of this kind of change. Without it, a loving parent would not be prone to alarm at a threat to her offspring. The very chemical balance that makes her care for her offspring in times of danger underwrites the processes involved in stress. Take this balance away, and you take away the care. Mother love, therefore, is not a pure equilibrium. We are left, then, with no reason to think of goodness as either the elimination of impurities or the achievement of a pure equilibrium. What is left is goodness as an impure balance.

Admirable mother love is a function not of some pure substance like oxytocin but of a balance between oxytocin and other variables such as the neurotransmitter serotonin. Moreover, it is not clear how it is even imaginable that goodness is pure without some conceptual illustration of how such purity is functionally achievable. If the evidence does not support goodness as either the elimination of impurities or a pure equilibrium, what else might it be but an impure balance? And it is not an objection available to purists to claim that there really is no clear way to distinguish between the environment and the variables involved in a balance. The second notion of purity demands that there is such a distinction.

What these observations that have led to the notion of an impure balance establish is twofold. The first is a strike against Kantian purity. Once we accept the naturalistic constraints on the study of human nature we have no way of conceiving of human goodness as a purity. To point toward God as a paradigm of pure goodness here is simply to confess one's ignorance; it is not to establish as possible something that is in no way observable, even indirectly. The same can be said for moral saints and Stoic sages of either the ancient or modern variety. The problem, then, is seeing what reason there is to believe in the purity of goodness other than the fact that it is a comforting thought. The second is a word of caution against overly optimistic recommendations to return to Aristotle and the Stoics for guidance, the project favored, as noted in the Aesthetic Prelude, by Martha Nussbaum. Once we see that human goodness must be conceived as an impure balance, we get a glimpse of just how precarious our goodness in its impurity might be, and we must be open to the possibility that the tragedians were closer to the truth on this matter than anything found in Aristotle or the Hellenistic thinkers.

This brings me briefly to Nussbaum's own treatment of Hecuba and of Aristotle's recognition of tragedy. Aristotle explicitly claimed that evil does not proceed from good character. He seemed to want to provide a philosophical alternative to competing schools of thought that maintained that living well is immune to luck. Plato before him and the Epicureans and the Stoics after him held such a view. But the good might be vulnerable in two ways, by attachments to external goods such as friends and loved ones or by a change in character from good to bad. Aristotle seems to have affirmed the former and denied the latter, at least in any deep way. This would limit the extent to which tragedy plays a role in Aristotle's ethical thought. It would make him a purist but not a supreme value purist. Nussbaum wants to interpret Aristotle in such a way that he affirms both the fragility of the good life and good character. That is the point of her discussion of the Hecuba case at the end of *The Fragility of Goodness.* Suppose we grant such a view, either as an interpretation of Aristotle (as I think we probably should not) or as a revision of his views for an ethics for our time, as I think we should.

The first thing to notice is that this makes tragedy more central to ethical thought than before, which is what I am recommending that a tragic ethics must do. This, however, is not enough. For one thing, it does not address the issue of how pervasive and perpetual the threat to good character is. I believe that it is pervasive and perpetual enough to chill a certain kind of optimism, the kind characteristic of Classical Greek ethics. A little thought on how pervasive and perpetual deep distrust is in the world should make the point. It seems to linger even in the absence of poverty. But second, as I will show in the next two chapters, there are other pervasive sources of tragic conflict. Along with the impurity of value, these sources move us more toward the Homeric mind, one that accepts the tragic fact that ethics is – and always will be – the perpetual task of accommodating the commitment to high values under pervasive threat.

Can we, then, afford the comforting thought of purity? What if the vulnerability of goodness runs as deep as all this suggests? What if what is good about us makes us vulnerable not only to grief, sorrow, depression, and the loss of the will to live in some contexts but in others to evil itself? Is it important that we know this, and what will we have gained by such knowledge?

I believe that it is crucial that we have true beliefs about the purity of value; we cannot afford the luxury of false beliefs in this regard. If value is pure, then we should do as much as we can to remove the impurities from our nature without removing the intrinsically good qualities. On the other hand, if goodness is impure, we should view the doctrine of purity as it is represented in both religious and secular garb as a pernicious fantasy and try to avoid the kinds of conditions that threaten to undermine the basic properties that we find most precious in ourselves and others. To take on the latter task is to recognize with Homer that human goodness occupies a world fraught with danger that requires constant vigilance. If we indulge in pernicious fantasies, whether Kantian, Stoic, or religious, regarding our goodness, we will do so only to make ourselves feel better when we could have prevented tragedies otherwise avoidable. Given what we currently know, the best bet is that value is impure and that we are better off believing that it is. Moreover, it is hard to see how belief in the purity of value – like belief in angels – is the product of inquiry.

To conclude these two chapters on supreme value pluralism, I refer back to some of the traditions that have influenced us. As I have indicated before, there are good and bad versions of the Enlightenment, Romantic, and Classical traditions. The Enlightenment tradition would have us live our lives in the light of the facts; the Romantic tradition would have us live our lives in a way that is not only properly thought but also passionately felt; and the Classical tradition would have us live our lives in a way that is as inclusive as possible of what we value and that can be chosen for itself as expressing most accurately what our lives are about. The moralism of supreme value pluralism accomplishes none of these goals. Rather, it represents a form of Romanticism of the worst sort. It so inflates the notion of human worth that it tragically eclipses our view of other values, and it naively promotes an ideal of purity that is anything but innocuous in its effects. It would have us think of our own worth in the way that the young Werther thought of his would-be lover: unmatched and untouchable. Such views, like some human relationships, cannot be sustained in the light of the facts about human valuing and about human psychology. They also distort our true feelings, much in the way that opiates do, addicting us to moralistic rhetoric rather than connecting us to reality in a way that can be sustained in both thought and feeling. And finally, they express our weaknesses rather than our strengths. Life without supreme value that is both constant and pure is not the nightmare the moralistic tradition would have us fear. It can be lived in the light of the facts, pursued with passion, and honestly expressed, or so I hope to show.

8

Best Life Pluralism and Reason's Regret

> What is never chosen as a means to something else we call more final than that which is chosen both as an end in itself and as a means to something else. What is always chosen as an end in itself and never as a means to something else is called final in an unqualified sense. For the present we define as "self-sufficient" that which taken by itself makes life something desirable and deficient in nothing.
>
> Aristotle, *Nicomachean Ethics* (1097a:30–35 and 1097b–15)

Even if there is no kind of value that is loftier than Werther's lover, always overriding and pure, it still might be true that there is some way of life that is better than any other at integrating the many things that give a good life its worth. The view that there is can be called best life pluralism. What follows is an investigation of the strengths of this view, including its advantages over the moralistic versions of supreme value pluralism, for an account of tragedy. At stake is the issue of whether a certain kind of project can succeed, namely, the project envisioned by Martha Nussbaum and many others of finding an ethic in the Classical Greek tradition that can serve as a model for modern persons in liberal democracies.[1] I will argue that it cannot succeed without moving tragic

[1] The group of thinkers engaged in this project can be divided into those who call themselves virtue ethicists and those who do not. Nussbaum has explicitly rejected virtue ethics as a distinct kind of moral theory but retains the pursuit of the Classical project. (See her article "Virtue Ethics: A Misleading Category?," *The Journal of Ethics* 3 [1999]: 163–201). Nor do I believe that Williams would have endorsed the virtue

concepts more to the center of ethical thought than its optimism can allow. Here the issue will be what is lost in even the best of lives.

With its heritage in the Classical Greek tradition, best life pluralism insists that the issue of how it is rational to act and feel must be put in the context of how acting and feeling fit into a way of life, which means that the aim of practical reason is the best life, or what the Greeks called *eudaimonia*. For them, the thought that actions and feelings could be rationally evaluated independent of a way of life in which those actions and feelings were related to some set of goods expressed by it was incomprehensible. About this, they were most certainly right. Alasdair McIntyre once said, in true classical spirit, that practical reason is narratival.[2] What he meant is that our actions and decisions are comprehensible to ourselves and others only as they can fit into a comprehensible story about our lives in which we are the characters and protagonists. This is no less true for us than for the Greeks; only the circumstances of our lives have changed. It is only within a narratival setting that practical conflicts among values emerge as comprehensible in the first place, and any resolution of such a conflict must take up the narrative there and resolve it in terms of a projected future or way of life that either furthers the narrative or ends it. It is in this sense that best life pluralism puts the emphasis on a way of life as the fundamental issue of practical reason. When combined with a pluralistic theory of value, best life pluralism is the view that there is some way of life that integrates a plurality of goods in the best possible balance and as a consequence gives us rational direction about how to act and feel in the context of living. Anything less is less than best, and less because it is a less integrated whole of a plurality of goods.

But what makes one life better than another and the best life better than all others?

According to the Classical tradition from which best life pluralism descends, the criteria for judging whether a life is the best life are the criteria of self-sufficiency and finality. As we have seen, the

ethics label, due in no small part to his philosophical aversion to the notion of moral theory. Among those who construe and endorse the Classical model as a virtue ethics are Alasdair MacIntyre, Christine Swanton, Philippa Foot, Rosalind Hursthouse, and Julia Annas.

[2] See Alasdair MacIntyre, "After Virtue," in his *After Virtue: A Study in Moral Theory*, Second edition (Notre Dame, Indiana: University of Notre Dame Press, 1997), 256–63.

self-sufficiency criterion has two dimensions: inclusiveness and expressiveness. Inclusiveness requires that the best life be inclusive of all the various kinds of goods that go into a good life. The idea is that the best life, if at all possible, should be lacking in nothing that is good in the sense that it honors and recognizes all that is good from a person's own point of view: nothing could be added to or subtracted from it in terms of what a person ultimately cares about to make it better. As a criterion of practical reason, a criterion of how to act and feel, inclusiveness is simply a function of the fact that we are the kind of animals that care about things and by caring want to include them in our lives if at all possible. Expressiveness requires that the best life include every good in a way that does not distort the kind of good it is. It is this second dimension of the self-sufficiency criterion that makes the Classical conception of practical reason an expressivist conception linked to the kind of transparency mentioned earlier: one's life is best lived and comprehensible to oneself and others when, as far as possible, it makes transparent what it is about. Of course, we must sometimes wear masks, but this is a banality hardly worth mentioning. The central point is that a *life* of disguise is a life of alienation, closer to being unbearable than best, and it is the life of disguise that Achilles rejected and Odysseus (as depicted by Euripides) accepted.

Both dimensions of the self-sufficiency criterion are illustrated in one of the arguments found among the Greeks against the view that the best life is the life dedicated solely to pleasure. The argument turns on a distinction between internal and external goods. Pleasure is an internal good because as an object of value it is a feature of the person who experiences it. Character is also an internal good when it is the object of self-respect. On the other hand, friends and loved ones are external goods because as objects of value they exist independent of the existence of the person who values them. A major argument among the ancients that the life dedicated solely to pleasure is not the best life was that it does not account for the value of friends as external goods. To omit friends from the good life is to leave out one of its most central elements, and to construe friends as a mere means to or source of pleasure is to distort the kind of good that friends are. For these reasons, hedonism is deficient in both dimensions of the self-sufficiency criterion: it leaves out the true value of friends in a loving person's life by misrepresenting what they mean to him. Here the insistence on transparency is the insistence that what is valued not be misrepresented, that the meaning of one's life and values not be distorted.

To be sure, there are those who are deeply self-deceived about what they care most about, but this does not show that transparency is not, even for them, a criterion of practical reason. What it shows is that it is a criterion that is harder for some people to meet than others. It is very important for such people that what in fact are misrepresentations are veridical expressions of what they value most. Both the mother who is truly loving and the one who is self-deceived about being truly loving take great steps to construct lives that express motherly care for their children. Sooner or later, the self-deceiver reveals to others and sometimes to herself that her life does not express what she thinks it does. And when such self-discovery occurs, reevaluation is invariably the response. This would not be so if transparency were not a criterion whereby we try to rationally assess how to act and feel about our lives. The search for meaning and the desire to express it run deep in the human heart, even when those meanings are fabricated by self-deception.

The finality criterion asserts that the best way of life is chosen for itself and not as a means to or as a part of something else. If a way of life is chosen because living it will get you into heaven or because it is the best means of promoting the greater social good, it is not the best life. It would in these cases be chosen for something thought to be more fundamentally good, and, according to eudaimonism, nothing is more fundamentally good than the best life.

The reason the best life is the most fundamental good is not that it is the best single good of many different goods but because it is the whole in which all goods have their proper places as parts. This is a very crucial point. As has been pointed out repeatedly by those deeply familiar with the ancient tradition, *eudaimonia* or living well is not to be interpreted as the ancient equivalent of the modern notion of happiness or some other notion of subjective well-being. Subjective well-being, on whatever construal, is merely one candidate for what might meet the criteria of self-sufficiency and finality. The best life, the one lived best, just is whatever way of life includes the complete set of things that are recognized as good, expresses the true value of those goods without distortion, and is chosen for itself and not for something else.

Subjective eudaimonists, such as the Epicureans, believed that some way of life that realizes a good identified with some subjective mental state meets these criteria; perfectionist eudaimonists, such as the Stoics, believed that the good in question is some state of human development; and objective eudaimonists, such as I believe Aristotle was, believed that the best life realizes a set of goods that include subjective mental states, states of human and nonhuman development, and external goods. On this last view, to live well is to live a life that includes all the things that are recognized as good, which includes things out there in the world other than one's own subjective states or states of one's own development. Moreover, the best way of life not only includes these things but expresses their value without distortion and is chosen just because it is the life that properly includes and expresses these goods and not for some other reason.

According to objectivist eudamonism, pleasure is bound to be distorted in its ultimate intrinsic importance when viewed apart from a life in which it is only one among a variety of goods. The same is true of any other good. Without an understanding of how each good in a multiple array of goods constitutes a part in a set of goods as a whole, there can be no understanding of the ultimate intrinsic worth of any particular good. Pleasure that excludes friendship is not pleasure properly valued, and friendship without intellectual pursuit is not friendship truly expressed. Only when a good is integrated with other goods as a set of goods that constitutes a whole can its ultimate value be specified, and goods can be seen as a whole only in the context of how they fit into a way of life that is chosen for itself and not for something else.

The value of life is as a whole and not as a sum. This is the most central point. Those who think of the value of family, friends, intellectual achievement, art, sport, or political engagement as various ways in which the real value of pleasure is realized must think of the value of life as a sum. They are like fools who would think that a beautiful symphony is just one beautiful note after another and that the one with the most notes is the best. On their view, the good life is just whatever life realizes the highest sum of pleasure (or subjective well-being) that has these goods as more or less reliable sources. The metaphor for value construed in this way is that of a ledger and its tallies or a wager and its odds. But what shows that life is not a sum is that this way of thinking of the value of these things distorts the kinds of goods they are. We get a clearer vision of the kinds of goods they are by understanding them as parts of a whole, where that whole is a life lived in a way that best accommodates all that is good in the way that it is good. The best life, then, is not the one that maximizes a sum of value but one that integrates as a whole the most inclusive set of goods in a way that does not distort their true value and that expresses some pattern of meaning and unity. The metaphors are artistic and organic: movements in a symphony, chapters in a novel, functions of an organ.

Since good reasons have already been given for rejecting monistic views that would reduce the standard for a good life to one variable such as subjective well-being or human development and for thinking that we do intrinsically value things external to us, neither subjective nor perfectionist eudaimonism can succeed. We are left, then, with objective eudaimonism as the most plausible version of best life pluralism.

Moreover, we must reject some assumptions that the ancients, including Aristotle, had for adopting a view of the best life in terms of which to live well was to flourish subjectively. The Classical Greeks had a view of human nature – Classical optimism, we might call it – that we cannot accept because it is predicated on a mistaken biology. The idea is best made clear by analogy. The nature of an acorn is such that when it is nourished in its proper environment it will grow to be an oak and flourish in the way typical of oaks in their natural environment. So too with all other natural kinds, including human beings. Human beings have a nature such that their natures are passed on to them by their parents as members of the species, and if they are allowed to develop in their natural environment with proper nurturing, they will flourish both physically and psychologically. What Aristotle seems to have thought is that though the good of human beings is essentially tied up with external goods as well as subjective goods, it is nonetheless true that if a human being develops properly in a favorable environment, he or she will flourish in the subjective sense. Why? Because Aristotle and the Classical Greeks had a very rosy and optimistic view of the harmony and unity of nature. They believed that a thing's nature is such that its full natural realization guarantees its flourishing. Nature is, in this sense, kind.

That this view has a great deal of appeal cannot be denied. It reflects a deep human longing, a belief that nature is motherly, that it gave birth to us, that it wants to nurture us, and that it will if only we will take our intended place in the natural scheme of things. The trick is to find our place in that scheme, and the thought is that nature is unkind and harsh only to those who live contrary to it. The question, of course, is whether any of this is true. Do we have reasons for believing that there is some natural process that endows us with a nature such that if we develop in a favorable environment we will flourish subjectively and be "happy" in this sense? One thing is for sure: we cannot have the reasons these ancients had for such a belief, for the simple reason that we cannot accept their biology and their view of the natural process that determines a thing's nature. They believed that species are fixed and eternal, that species are unchanging and propagated more or less intact through reproduction, and they also believed in the robust unity of our psychology that makes our psychological flourishing in our natural environment possible. Because of Darwin, we cannot believe the former and have very strong reasons for doubting the latter.

Our natures, whatever they are and especially the nature of our psychological traits, are not determined in the way that the ancients believed them to be. Our natures, including our psychological capacities, are the result of evolution and natural selection. Some of our psychological traits are selective, adaptive traits, traits that were essential to our having survived the battle against other biological competitors for adaptation in our natural environment. Other traits, both physical and psychological, also have an evolutionary history, but that history is not an adaptive one. The fact that we can whistle, for example, probably plays no role whatever in our reproductive success. What we now know is that some traits are adaptive traits and others are not, and we know that the "function" of adaptive traits is to ensure a competitive edge in the battle for reproduction.[3] This is a natural process central to both evolutionary biology and evolutionary psychology. The important point is that there is nothing about the natural selective process that guarantees the kind of robust unity of our psychology that is required to substantiate classical optimism and the motherly view of nature it presupposes. There is nothing about the process of natural selection that guarantees that the nature of human psychology will be

3 See Robert N. Brandon, *Adaptation and Environment* (Princeton, New Jersey: Princeton University Press, 1995).

such that if a member of the human (or any other) species develops in its natural environment, it will flourish psychologically in a way that we would associate with happiness or bliss. Indeed, the selective process might give a competitive edge in regard to reproduction to species that are psychologically conflicted. The desire for intimacy and the desire for sexual adventure are psychological traits that come easily to mind.[4] Nature is concerned for the unity of our psychology only to the degree that it is necessary to defeat competitors in the contest for reproduction, and good, flourishing reproducers may be better reproducers precisely because of psychological traits that make them less capable of flourishing subjectively.

What we lack that these ancients thought they had is any idea of a natural process that would guarantee a human psychology that is unified in a way that is robust enough to ensure happiness and subjective flourishing. Nothing we know about our place in nature and its processes ensures that if we pursue our deepest values, there will be no conflicts regarding the things we care most deeply about or that the conflicts will be so minimal that they do not threaten our subjective well-being and happiness. What we do know with confidence is that through the evolutionary process nature formed our nervous systems in a way that makes us carers-with-consciousness. In the impersonal rough-and-tumble of evolution, nature gave us brains that make us care about things in a variety of ways, and the very same brains make us conscious of our caring. Because of the brains that have been provided to us through the evolutionary process, we live under the burden of trying to understand and make sense of our lives in the light of the past and in anticipation of the future. That is what makes us practical reasoners. In all probability, the capacity for practical reason with its developed sensitivity to placing the present in the context of the past and the future is an adaptive capacity, a capacity that favors us over some natural competitors in the reproductive contest. Without being carers-with-consciousness (intelligent emoters and feelers, intelligent passionate creatures), without the kind of consciousness that makes us consider the present in the context of the past and the future when dealing with the things we are passionate about, and

[4] See Donald Symons, *The Evolution of Human Sexuality* (New York: Oxford University Press, 1979).

without the felt need to make sense of our lives, we would not be the kind of practical reasoners we are. And in all probability we would not have beaten out our natural competitors. In order to make us practical reasoners that would succeed in the reproductive contest, nature had to unify our psychology only so much. Beyond that, any integrative capacities we have or lack are left to other natural forces, and there is nothing to suggest that there is anything motherly about those forces. Indeed, what we know about those forces is that they are utterly and tragically indifferent to our happiness, as indifferent as the Homeric gods.

When nature made us practical reasoners it made us this: intelligent, passionate creatures who strive for a meaningful life in which all that we care about has a place in the way that we care about it. In this sense (but not in others), it made us seekers of the best life. The question is whether it made us care about things and fitted us to an environment in a way such that the best life for us guarantees our happiness if all our values are just realized. To understand the depth of this issue and to understand Darwin is to understand a great deal of the natural tragedy of the human condition. Nature designed us to care about a variety of things. It made us aware that our present is affected by the past and is projected into the future. It also made us desirous of understanding ourselves and others. By doing these things, it not only gave us a competitive edge over other species, it also left us with integrative tasks that often exceed our grasp. It left us struggling with the meaning of our lives in terms of what we care most about, which is not confined to reproduction. When it did this, it left us struggling with our values, trying to construct lives that could as far as possible include the things we care about in the way that we care about them and to make ourselves understood by ourselves and others.

The upshot is that we should reject Classical optimism and the notion that living in accordance with our nature will guarantee our happiness. There is no such guarantee. Nevertheless, we are still left with the task of living in accordance with our deepest values. To do so, we must make transparent the conflicts among our values and find a way to live with them rather than suppress them and suffer the consequences of such suppression. To insist on an ethics of virtue, as some people do, that finds its inspiration in the blissful assurance of ancient biology is a fantasy on all fours with the religious and moralistic fantasies of the past.[5] And it is, as we will see, no less pernicious. Whatever level of happiness we can expect must be a function of what we can expect in terms of the conflicting things we care about, which means, among other things, that our expectations of happiness should reflect both a knowledge of our place in nature and the tragic conflicts among our values. Whatever else being a secularist can mean for us now, it must mean taking Darwin seriously in these matters. The conflicts among our values are not simply the result of social arrangements that have somehow not been fitted to the perfect niche in nature that explains the absence of bliss. There is no such niche. Nature has "designed" us to care about conflicting things in a way such that the best life for us can never be one of bliss or anything approaching it.

But in rejecting Classical optimism, we should not fall prey to a kind of postmodern craze, call it postmodern pessimism, the view that our selves are so radically divided that aspirations to any kind of coherent, transparent life in which we live in accordance with our deepest values is just another fantasy. I suspect these views are generated less by a study of our place in nature than by discredited forms of social science and entrenched religious views that find abhorrent the very concept of nature itself. The idea that we care in such conflicting ways that no comprehensible life is accessible to us is the product not of scientific inquiry but of the loose imaginations of some literary critics. But be that as it may, rejecting the search for meaning and vitality in life is not an option for us. Listless and mindlessly incomprehensible lives are foreign to our nature. The history of human psychopathology proves it. So however conflicted we are, we are compelled by our nature to construct the most meaningful lives we can given what we care about. This is our fate.

Moreover, it is a tragic fate, one we must be diligent to understand.

The first step in such diligence is to gain a general idea of the kinds of goods we cherish and to ask what way of life, if there is one, most

[5] For views of this sort, see Philippa Foot, *Natural Goodness* (Oxford: Oxford University Press, 2001); Julia Annas, *The Morality of Happiness* (New York: Oxford University Press, 1993); Rosalind Hursthouse, *On Virtue Ethics* (Oxford: Oxford University Press, 2002); and G. E. M. Anscombe, "Modern Moral Philosophy," in his *Collected Philosophical Papers* (Minneapolis: University of Minnesota Press, 1981), 26–42. For a version of virtue ethics that does not take this form, see Christine Swanton, *Virtue Ethics: A Pluralistic View* (Oxford: Oxford University Press, 2003).

accommodates the largest array of these goods with minimal distortion. If best life pluralism is true, then for each and every individual, some way of life will stand out as the best way of life for that individual. It will stand out as the best way to live in the sense that it is more inclusive in accommodating what an individual cares about and expresses the importance of those values with less distortion than any other way of life for that person. Adjusted to correct the mistaken, optimistic claims the ancients made about human nature, best life pluralism does not assume that what meets the criteria of finality and self-sufficiency will result in a life of subjective flourishing. In this sense, it is open to tragic conflicts not found in ancient naturalism.

Nor does the revised notion of best life pluralism assume some species-wide good that the ancient version did. The revised notion of best life pluralism is open to the possibility of relativism, though it does not assume relativism in advance of some empirical inquiry regarding what people ultimately find it important that their lives express. And, as far as I can see, empirical inquiry about how deep values vary in human psychology is the only way to settle the issue of value relativism. It is just silly to think that such relativism is logically self-refuting, and it is something bordering on religious in the worst sense to think that relativism is false just because it might be disastrous. It might very well be disastrous, but the philosophical question is whether it is true.

It would certainly be some kind of defeat for best life pluralism if it could be shown that there is some widespread breakdown in the attempt to compare lives across persons. If relativism regarding good lives is epidemic – if Western and non-Western, masculine and feminine, Caucasian and non-Caucasian, old and young, deaf and hearing, and a host of other distinctions yield radically conflicting ways in which lives can be good from their own points of view but not from a shared point of view – then social disputes can hardly be resolved by appeal to shared ways of life. Something else would have to do that work, if anything could. But there is another, in some sense less ambitious, way of testing whether best life pluralism is true than by settling the issue of the scope and limits of relativism. Best life pluralism is false if it cannot account for a fairly prominent set of goods. That is, it fails if it cannot show that there is some way of life that is better than any other way of life at satisfying the criteria of self-sufficiency and finality regarding a fairly common set of goods that many people find upon reflection to be central to what their lives are about.

One way this might occur is if there are several equally good ways of life that accommodate these goods but no best life. Another is if incomparability obtains among the leading competitors for the best way of life. The latter possibility is directly relevant to the capacity of best life pluralism to account fully for our tragic sense. Best life pluralism is true only if ways of life are always comparable. Consequently, to evaluate it thoroughly, a return to the issue of incomparability will be necessary.

But before turning to that issue in the next chapter, consider the impressive resources available to best life pluralism, especially in comparison to supreme value pluralism, to account for tragic loss. Best life pluralism, as I am construing it here, recognizes that the inclusiveness dimension of the self-sufficiency criterion – that the best life is lacking in nothing good – cannot fully be met. It does so by being a form of pluralism. Recall that one form that tragedy can take is where choice of the greater good is such that what was rejected in the lesser good is not contained in the greater good. All forms of pluralism recognize this. Certainly, the Greek tragedians seemed fully aware of it. But with Plato, ethics started an intellectual journey that more and more sanitized our thinking regarding these unpleasantries. Even Aristotle seems to have idealized the best life in such a way that thoughts of a life lacking in no good thing were perfectly consistent with his sense of value. Best life pluralism, however, recognizes that whatever the best life is, some good things are lacking because the most central goods of life are plural and conflicting: having some goods at a certain degree of realization means lacking other goods at another degree of realization or not having them at all. Without this feature, best life pluralism would be at a serious loss to account for rational regret. That it has this feature makes it a powerful theory of value in the face of the problem of tragedy.

Consider how this is so.

To keep things simple, what way of life will integrate without loss two goods recognized by a person of a certain sort: a person – let's call him Gauguin – for whom his love for his children and his commitment to excellence as an artist are categorical values in the sense previously specified? To satisfy the self-sufficiency criterion, Gauguin's way of life will have to include two goods as categorical values, and his way of life must express these values without distortion. Unless we suppose that there is a way of life that allows Gauguin to be the best parent he could be and the best artist he could be, we must suppose that the best way of life for him is such that it allows him to be a good, maybe even excellent, parent and artist, but not both the best parent and the best artist he could be.

Realizing this, we might imagine our Gauguin attempting to integrate his life around his family and his art by completely subordinating one of these goods to the other. For example, he might be completely dedicated as a parent and then be what he can as an artist. The thought is that he would make no compromises when it comes to his children for the sake of his art. Given the demands of parenting, it is simply implausible that art could be very central to his life if this is how he solved the integration problem, the problem of integrating two categorical goods into his way of life.[6] A similar point applies to the inadequacy of just the opposite set of priorities. The best life for such a person is going to be one that involves significant loss, no matter what the best life is for him. If he totally subordinates his art to his family, the resulting mediocrity and lack of excellence at his art is a significant loss. If he totally subordinates his family to his art, the ways in which his children suffer from his lack of attention will be a tragic loss. Neither way of life will be self-sufficient in the inclusive sense.

However, it does not follow from this that there is no best life for Gauguin. He might be able to live with a compromise that allows both categorical goods to have a role in his life to some important degree. Assume that he can make such a compromise and that this turns out to be the best life available to him. What loss will such a life entail? The compromise gives him both some level of goodness as a parent and some level of excellence as an artist with which he can live. Given that both values are categorical values for him (that they are central to his psychology in terms of what he finds important and central to what his life is about), any compromise is going to involve loss in terms of a categorical good, and his way of life will express this if it satisfies the expressiveness criterion, which by assumption it will,

6 See my *Agent Centered Morality* for a more extensive discussion of what I call "the integration problem."

if best life pluralism is true. Therefore, the best way of life for him will express tragic loss. In its compromise, it will express that there is something good of categorical importance contained in an alternative way of life that is not expressed in the best life for him. He could have been a better parent on some alternative way of life or a better artist on another alternative way of life. Parenting and creative work are plural and conflicting values, and the way of life that satisfies the self-sufficiency criterion in both its inclusive and expressive dimensions will express the depth of how they conflict. The best life, then, for a person like our Gauguin is not a life without loss, even tragic loss. Some very significant good is necessarily missing to some significant degree.

Of course, the best life for some other Gauguin, perhaps the real one, would leave no room for compromise, in which case the tragic loss would be all the greater. The same applies to anyone who is committed to excellence, whether at art, or at philosophy, athletics, politics, science, or whatever, and who is a deeply loving parent. On the one hand, if complete subordination of one value to the other is the best way of life available, then tragedy is the result of the inability to satisfy in a significant way the inclusiveness criterion. On the other hand, if compromise is the best way of life available, the expressiveness criterion will reflect a sense of loss of what is included in other ways of life that is not included in the best way of life in regard to both values. Life, if lived in the light of the facts as the Enlightenment tradition would have us live it, will be lived with regret for what is lost in the lesser good, despite the fact that the good of that life outweighs the bad of that life (if in fact that is the case). But consolation will be found in the thought that what is in the greater good is indeed better. In that way, life can be lived with passion, as the Romantic tradition would have it (again on the assumption that the best life is on balance good). The comparative judgment at the heart of best life pluralism, therefore, accommodates the three central requirements in the Enlightenment, Romantic, and Classical traditions for even a tragic life that is on balance good – a life truly thought, passionately felt, and honestly expressed.

The point is compounded when we note that for most of us the plurality of goods at stake is far more complex than for our Gauguin, which means that our integration problems are far more complex and render us far more vulnerable to tragic loss, even in the best way of life we can adopt. Most people do not have the passion for art or excellence that Gauguin had, but most people want to be very good at something. The thought that one is utterly mediocre at everything is, for most people, a terrifying thought. Excellence to some degree at something is therefore a good that is to be included in the best life for almost anyone. This is the important grain of truth in perfectionism, a truth we cannot afford to ignore. Moreover, various personal commitments that express a variety of forms of love are part of what almost anyone finds important in life. Being a loving friend, spouse, parent, sibling, and neighbor are matters of utmost importance to almost all of us. In addition, most of us care very deeply about persons in terms of respecting them as agents of their own lives. We also care about persons in the sense that we have sympathy for them in terms of their vulnerability to the vicissitudes of fate that lie outside their control. A similar sympathy for the weal and woe of the so-called lower animals is also something that most of us find important. When aesthetic considerations and considerations of play and mere pleasure are added to the list, most of us find what Barbara Herman has aptly called our "deliberative field," the domain of things we find important and of high value in life, is filled with a plurality of goods that conflict in ways that make compromise necessary for even a minimally worthwhile life, let alone the best life.[7]

Now assume that when we bring the criteria of self-sufficiency and finality to this deliberative field in order to integrate these plural and conflicting values, we find that there is some best life that does not treat any good as a supreme value in the way that supreme value pluralism would but that nonetheless satisfies the criteria of self-sufficiency and finality in a way that makes that way of life the one most worth living. The first thing to note is that there must be some compromise on the part of all the values involved. They conflict in ways that make it impossible to realize all of them maximally. The best way of life will express that each value accommodated by that way of life is a compromise and that there are alternative ways of life that are less good but that express values not included in the greater good of the best life. We could have been better off regarding any one of these very

7 See Barbara Herman, *The Practice of Moral Judgment* (Cambridge, Massachusetts: Harvard University Press, 1993), 152, 166, 168, 172, 179–83, 191–4, 196–202.

important goods on some other way of life, but not on the whole. Best life pluralism has the very desirable feature of making us realize this in a way that expresses both regret and passion for life. In the light of the facts of human valuing, this attitude seems a very compelling view of how life is properly felt in the light of the facts.

It is mere pernicious fantasy to persist in the belief that our lives, however well lived, do not include significant loss. Moreover, it is important that we proportion our emotions of regret at the loss and of joy at the gain to the value of what is lost and what is gained. The realism in Romantic realism requires this, not that we map our emotions to some external metaphysical realm of value but that we sustain our values in the light of the facts. To pretend that what is in the lesser good is not really a loss of value is to invite the worst forms of denial, and it can lead to the inability to accept the losses in a way that allows us to live our lives with passion.

Isaiah Berlin maintained in his memorable essay "The Pursuit of the Ideal" that the concept of utopia is incoherent.[8] What he meant was that the nature of value itself is such that the realization of some important values involves the inability to realize other important values. Something good is going to be missing in even the best possible political arrangement. The same can be said for a good life. Some people lead miserable lives because they want life to provide what nothing can provide – a life where nothing good is missing. When they notice that something good is missing, they automatically conclude that they are not living the best life and become dissatisfied with it. Such people have not learned to proportion their emotions to the loss of value involved. They fail to see the consolation in the greater good. Others have a sense of cheerfulness that is oblivious to the loss incurred. The dangers of such denial are many, but two are worthy of special note.

People who have to believe that the best life leaves no room for sorrow have a hard time facing the facts about the sources of sorrow. The first danger of this is that it puts their own well-being in jeopardy. When the facts finally do come flooding in, these people are often crushed by the consequences. Cynicism and despair take the place

[8] See Isaiah Berlin, "The Pursuit of the Ideal," in his *The Proper Study of Mankind*, edited by Henry Hardy and Roger Hausheer (New York: Farrar, Straus and Giroux, 1998), 1–16.

of their naivety, diminishing the good life they could have if only they could accept some fundamental facts about the human condition. The second danger is that if they are able to sustain their naivety, it is often the result of their blindness to the sources of sorrow, thus jeopardizing the well-being of others. Pernicious fantasy and philosophical opiates in this regard are therefore doubly dangerous.

It might be objected here, however, that the Gauguin case is not convincing, that the conclusions drawn from it are mere hyperbole. Why should we think that the kind of compromise a loving parent and dedicated artist might have to make would be one where the loss involved would reach tragic proportions? Why think this about any conflict between parental love and the commitment to excellence of any sort?

The first response to such an objection takes the form of addressing it head on. No doubt there are some people for whom the best life as a loving parent and a person committed to excellence is such that there is loss, but the loss does not reach tragic proportions. Some degree of not being the best parent is not a tragic loss to parent or child, and some degree of not being the best artist (or whatever) is not a tragic failing either. Even so, it is all too easy to overlook the fact that it is hard to be even a good parent, let alone an excellent one. The same can be said for being an artist or anything else that requires excellence. The margin for failure when trying to integrate both into one's life is not as great as the objection makes it seem. Children require hours and hours of attention to their basic needs, especially in their earliest years, and excellence at art or music or science or philosophy or athletics requires hours and hours of work in relative isolation from the concerns of parenthood. Being good, let alone excellent, at both parenthood and art is a very difficult task.

The best evidence that such a task often involves tragic loss is the history of women and men as primary and secondary care givers. The artistic, scientific, philosophical, political, and literary talent left undeveloped by both the joys and burdens of motherhood is staggering to consider. The same can be said for the losses in family intimacy from the joys and burdens of the work that fathers have engaged in to provide secondary care. Excellence gained has all too often meant intimacy lost, and, of course, the reverse is also true. Moreover, our ongoing contemporary struggle to redefine parental roles across gender difference shows that good compromises are anything but easy to find, even when all parties are making sincere and sustained efforts. Significant loss looms, it seems, no matter what the compromise. The worry many individuals have in this regard is that what is lost in the compromise tends to invite the thought that it would be better just to choose which of the goods to include in one's life. And surely that should show that the tension between these goods is a tragic tension between a basic level of excellence and intimacy, even among people of relative privilege.

But if this kind of conflict is not convincing that ordinary life involves tragic loss of lesser goods even when best lived, other kinds of conflicts should be. What is needed to support best life pluralism in its account of tragic loss is the following:

Suppose you could accurately envision the best, the second-best, and the third-best ways of life for you to live, given what you care most deeply about upon reflection and given your circumstances. Now assume, quite plausibly, that there is a pair of things (probably more) that you care about categorically and that conflict to some important degree. The best way of life will be the one that includes and expresses that pair of values, including the tension between them, in combination better than any other way of life. Now suppose that the second-best way of life would include and express one of those values considered on its own better than either the best way of life or the third-best way of life, and that the third-best way of life would include and express the other value considered on its own better than the best way of life or the second-best way of life. For example, the best way of life is where you are both a good parent and a somewhat accomplished person, say, a good musician, teacher, surgeon, or simply a reasonably well-educated person; the second-best, an excellent parent and an unaccomplished person; and the third-best, a highly accomplished person and a poor parent. (Think of your own examples, if others make more sense to you.)

Notice that where both values are categorical, no matter which way of life is the best life it will include a value deficit in the following sense: there will be another way of life in which what is lost in the lesser good as a way of life is not contained in the greater good as a way of life. In the example, the second-best way of life as a lesser good will include value not contained in either the best way of life or the third-best way of life, namely, being an excellent parent. So too for the third-best way of life: as the lesser good, it contains good not contained in either the best way of life as the greater good or the second-best way of life, namely, being a highly accomplished person. The greater good (by assumption for the sake of the example) that is contained in the best way of life that is not contained in the second- or third-best way of life is the good of being both a somewhat accomplished person and a good parent. There is one surplus of value in the second-best way of life and another surplus of value in the third-best way of life that are not contained in the best way of life as the greater good. The loss of this surplus that comes with adopting the best way of life can be called the value deficit of the best life. Any form of pluralism is going to yield the notion of there being a value deficit of this sort due to conflicting values even in the best life.

The question of central focus here is whether the value deficit of the best life reaches tragic proportions. Remember that we are trying to construe best life pluralism in a way that accommodates the facts about tragic loss. If there is a best life that includes and expresses all of what we care about most, yet its value deficit does not reach the tragic level, then ancient optimism is preserved. The fantasy of bliss (or at least near-bliss) will be ours for the having if we only live well, just as the ancient optimists and the religious tradition would have it. But if best life pluralism as it is being construed here is true, any best life relative to some paired set of goods is one for which the value deficit of that way of life involves tragic loss. The degree of tragedy of this sort that is a part of ordinary life is gauged by the extent of the tragic value deficit in the best lives of contemporary persons. If the degree of tragedy is pervasive and perpetual, as I will show that it is, then the lessons of the classical ethics will be important but limited: we should retain their general conception of practical reason regarding the criteria of finality and self-sufficiency, but we should reject their optimism. We should recognize that the task of ethics is pervasively and perpetually sensitive to the tragic losses involved in our choices.

Consider just two paired set of goods: (i) liberty and security and (ii) equality and cultural achievement. A consideration of these two pairs at this point should drive home the central point that any best life for contemporary people will contain a tragic value deficit.

Everyone who has any concern for sustaining a life cares about some degree of liberty and some degree of security. That the former is highly prized in the West does not undermine the claim that Westerners also value security. So the question is this: in the best life, what system of liberties and securities constitutes the best balance of these important goods? It will not do to object that these are not two different kinds of goods on the grounds that what is at stake is really different kinds of liberties – freedom from constraint and freedom from risk – rather than liberty on the one hand and some other good on the other. Even if we construe the conflict as being between different kinds of liberties, there is still a plurality of goods that conflict in ways that mean that both cannot be fully realized. The greatest system of freedom from constraint cannot be realized in the safest possible world. This is just a fundamental truth about these goods and the world in which we live.

People differ on these values. Some people who are horrified at risk want a relatively risk-free way of life that includes fewer liberties to pursue more dangerous options. Others who find a very secure life the worst form of drudgery want a way of life filled with risk and more abundant opportunity. How do we show respect for people and their differences on these two values when we create a system of liberties within a way of life? Again, it does not matter whether this conflict is between respect for people's choices, on the one hand, and sympathy for them in terms of their vulnerability to risk, on the other, or whether the conflict is between our respect for them in terms of two different kinds of liberty. Either way, there is a conflict. People differ on these things, and whatever way of life we adopt is going to involve putting some people at risk that they face with great anxiety and constraining the freedom of others in ways that they find deeply oppressive. Assuming that the best way of life for those who care about others in regard to these goods is a compromise, then there are at least two alternative ways of life that include goods that are not included in the best way of life: more liberty in one way of life and less risk of harm in the other. The question at this point is whether the loss of the lesser good reaches tragic proportions, and it is hard to entertain the notion that it does not.

If supreme value pluralism is false, then the best life will not be one in which one of these goods is completely subordinated to the other. Consider what would not be included and expressed in a way of life in which freedom from constraint is absolute in relationship to security from harm. The terror of and for those who are even modestly risk-averse would appear in that way of life as a clear expression that something good was missing that was not worth the price of the system of liberties. Now consider what would not be included in the safest possible world even for those who need only a modest amount of adventure in their lives. The boredom of that way of life would express its deficiencies for those who were not extremely risk-averse, and toleration of that boredom for the sake of the security of the extremely risk-averse would be an affront to our sense of respect for those not so intent on security. These observations should show once again that supreme value pluralism in this regard is simply incompatible with our sense of the relative importance of these goods. No way of life that totally subordinates either of these considerations to the other will satisfy the inclusiveness and expressiveness requirement of self-sufficiency. The best life relative to these goods is therefore a way of life that involves a compromise to achieve a balance of these goods.

But, again, any way of life relative to any set of goods is going to involve a value deficit, and the question is whether that deficit reaches tragic proportions. In this case, it is hard to see how any compromise, no matter what it turns out to be, avoids someone losing in a tragic way. It is one thing to see a total ban on public smoking as an acceptable dimension of the best form of public life. No one benefits categorically from smoking in public, and the liberty lost is anything but tragic. No doubt there are other liberties that when denied for the sake of risk averted have similar consequences. But consider the war on terrorism that began as a response to the attacks on New York City and Washington, D.C., on September 11, 2001. What system of civil liberties is included in a way of life that will adequately cope with terrorism of this sort? Is it remotely plausible that, whatever set that system is, there are no tragic risks that are not averted in that system that would be averted in a more restricted system? And is it remotely plausible that there are important liberties restricted in that system that would be unrestricted in some other system? Only the most naive could think that the value deficit in this regard is not a tragic one. Reflections on life in Northern Ireland in the recent past and in the current Middle East should make the point clear.

Of course, the best life does not have to cope with terrorism. Ordinary life under terrorist threat is not ordinary life. Nevertheless, ordinary life of whatever variety does have to cope with great danger of tragic loss as a result of liberty exercised. At what age do we impose a ban on alcohol consumption to protect the general public? Libertarians and totalitarians will have their absolute answers to this question, but we will reject them. We will compromise, and we would not compromise unless we took both values to be of the highest order. Do we take the lives lost to drunken drivers who are over twenty-one years of age (the age of maturity in most U.S. states) any less seriously than those that are lost to underage drunken drivers? Is the liberty gained by those who have reached the age of twenty-one important enough for the tragic loss of life involved, but the liberty lost by those who are only twenty suddenly less important? To be sure, the statistics might show that we will save more lives by setting the age at one point rather than another, but the point is that what is lost in the way of liberty will be very similar for those close to the cutoff point. How can it be a tragic loss of liberty that outweighs the loss of life in the case of those who have reached majority age and not a tragic loss of liberty for those who have not quite yet reached that age?

Consider also the liberty of association and the risks of association. At what age do we say that someone is a self-determining adult in deciding who her lovers will be? The risks are enormous, and the right is precious. Suppose that, for purposes of social policy and our way of life in regard to these two values, there is some age at which we should restrict the liberty of association that will best balance our concern for both the liberty and the risks of association. Assume that the age is eighteen and that we adjust our system of liberties to reflect this. The harms incurred after eighteen can be just as devastating as those incurred at seventeen and the liberty denied to seventeen-year-olds is very similar to the liberty denied to eighteen-year-olds. Why, then, should we think that in the one case the liberty denied is tragic but in the other it is not? Why think that the harms incurred at eighteen are not tragic but those at seventeen are?

A similar analysis applies to a broad range of liberties and risks: the liberty to decide the level of one's education and the risks of ignorance, the liberty to decide which career one will pursue and the risks of failure, the liberty to decide whether to have children and the risks of their misfortune, and the liberty to decide one's political associations and the risks of corruption are a few of the many ways in which liberty and security can be paired in ways that mean that what is lost in the best ways of incorporating these goods into a coherent way of life involves a value deficit with tragic dimensions. Any system of liberties is going to reflect a range of options that are cherished because of the goods they make available. The greater the goods, the more cherished the liberty. But, then, the more cherished the goods made accessible through liberty, the more the risk. There is no way of life regulated by the best system of liberties that can confine the loss to less than tragic proportions, and there never will be. High value is perpetually and pervasively at risk, a central feature that a tragic ethics must keep before us and of which Achilles was acutely aware.

Totalitarianism is no solution to this problem, although it is a mistake not to understand the good that a well-designed totalitarianism would provide. It would save a lot of lives that are lost and prevent a lot of human misery that is the result of the frivolous use of civil liberties, and, make no mistake about it, the best life does allow for some frivolous use of civil liberties. The instinct to totally eradicate such frivolity is one of the seeds of totalitarianism. "First, cause no harm" is its motto. But if totalitarianism is a mistake, it is so because it refuses to accept the fact that some level of liberty that puts people at risk of great harm from frivolous uses of that liberty is a categorical good of the best life.

Something is similarly true with regard to a completely libertarian view of the value of liberty. This way of life preserves some good that neither totalitarianism nor the best life can preserve. Under the libertarian way of life, some lives that are lived exceptionally well that will not be preserved under either totalitarianism or the compromise that balances the goods of liberty and security will be preserved. That the loss of these exceptional lives is not tragic is just hard to believe. Our desire that our system of liberties could in many regards be greater is evidence that what could be preserved in an alternative way of life is of enormous value. That our regret of this fact runs so deep shows that we consider the loss a tragic one. There is just no way around it: the best life, if there is one, in which liberty and security are balanced is one for which there is an alternative way of life in which there is a level of either liberty or security that is not contained in the best life, and the loss of that liberty or security is a tragic loss, a loss of the lesser good not contained in the greater good.

Now consider the other paired set of values: equality and the appreciation and achievement of excellence.

All of us are in some sense egalitarians. We all believe that persons are important because they are persons and that treating persons differently because of their personhood requires some relevant difference in their value as persons. Some believe that there is no relevant difference in the value of persons, and this is reflected in their very strong sense of substantive equality. Others believe that there are relevant differences in the intrinsic value of persons, and they have a different sense of substantive equality. But there are few people who believe that it is of no intrinsic importance that a person is a person. One of the legacies of Christianity is that it leaves us with the task of working out a plausible conception of human equality. It is a value that on some interpretation, we will never forsake.

On the other hand, one of the major legacies of our Greek heritage is a tradition that treasures the achievement and appreciation of excellence. Cultural splendor, let us say, exists where art, science, and philosophy produce great music, architecture, and poetry, great advances in physics, biology, and technology, and great essays on the meaning of life, the nature of consciousness, and political theory. Cultural splendor exists where Homer, Plato, Aristotle, Thucydides, Shakespeare, Mozart, Beethoven, Galileo, da Vinci, Curie, Descartes, Newton, Darwin, Gibbon, Kant, Nietzsche, and Austin are among the few whose names and achievements are immortalized, where countless others go unnoticed and are forever forgotten. It also exists where Albert Einstein, Henry Ford, George Gershwin, Louis Armstrong, Charlie Parker, Ella Fitzgerald, e. e. cummings, Tennessee Williams, W. B. Yeats, Maria Callas, Mohamed Ali, and Michael Jordan stand above others in their achievements, and where others remain lost in obscurity. A way of life that does not include some significant level of cultural splendor, the achievement and appreciation of greatness in art, science, philosophy, and other enterprises, is one that we can look upon only with despair.

But it cannot be denied that on any plausible interpretation equality and cultural splendor are conflicting values. Of course, they do not always conflict. One sometimes supports the other. Some inegalitarian arrangements are pernicious to excellence. When natural talent is suppressed because of a class system that is brittle and has mainly to do with inheritance rather than merit, the arts and sciences and other areas of endeavor will suffer a dearth of available talent. The best will not rise to the surface. Opportunity denied will be excellence lost. But sometimes excellence is lost because equality is gained, and equality is gained because excellence is lost. The question is whether such a loss of either equality or excellence is a tragic one.

Nietzsche was well aware of the historical fact that cultural splendor, the pride of any past civilization, was built on the back of human misery. Moreover, the splendor was unequally appreciated and the misery unequally borne. When we admire, as we do, the great architectural achievements of the Greeks, the Egyptians, and the Mayans, we need to see how those achievements reflected ways of life that made those achievements possible. They were anything but egalitarian. For one thing, they involved slavery as an essential part of life. Without slavery, there could not have been, under the historical circumstances, those achievements. Cultural splendor would have been lost. How anyone can deny that the loss of such splendor would not have been tragic is completely perplexing. Whether its loss would have been justified on grounds of equality is one thing, but whether it would have been the loss of something of enormous value is another. When the Taliban of Afghanistan destroyed centuries-old Buddhist statues, the world recoiled at the loss. Moreover, the loss was not mitigated by the awareness that the work that went into constructing those works of art was in all probability forced labor that cost many, many lives and much human misery. So if we were able to go back in history and eliminate from past civilizations the inequalities that we now view with horror, and if we decided that doing so would be best, we would have changed the course of history in a way that resulted in a tragic loss of cultural splendor for the greater good of equality.

Does this mean that equality is for us a supreme value?

None of us is likely to take seriously the "Nietzschean" view that excellence is the supreme value to which all other values must be subordinated. So there is no reason to refute that option. But the view that equality is a supreme value relative to other values is a widespread view deeply imbedded in our Christian past. If we are all of the same moral worth, how can excellence be a competing value? Are we not left with the option of pursuing cultural excellence only in a way that is consistent with the equal worth of persons? Would anything be lost in contemporary historical circumstances if we insisted on a strictly egalitarian enforcement of the equal worth of persons as a constraint on how far we can pursue and appreciate excellence?

Before any answers to these questions can be informed answers, the costs must be considered. We certainly do not now need slavery in order to achieve cultural splendor, but can we have a meaningfully shared cultural life where our way of life expresses only cultural mediocrity or cultural pablum?

To ensure cultural excellence, standards have to be high, so high that failure to gain excellence is more the norm than the exception. This is a sobering fact, a fact that many people just cannot accept. But it is a fact. Not only is it true that not everyone can be a Beethoven or an Einstein, it is also true that not everyone can be a rock star or a professional athlete. The culture in which everyone is a professional athlete or a rock star is a culture in which Michael Jordan is not allowed to excel and the latest version of Madonna is distinguishable from the girl next door only by her sexual bravado. A thoroughly egalitarian pop culture is like pop science; it is no culture at all. And a culture in which everyone is guaranteed fifteen minutes of fame is a culture doomed to dullness, mediocrity, and obscurity. The probability of failure, not to mention its possibility, is pervasive in any culture that achieves and appreciates excellence. There is simply no changing this fact, even after technology has eliminated the need for slave labor and, in some cases, the demand for talent. When equality completely trumps excellence, mere entertainment rushes to fill the cultural void.

With this in mind, how are we to integrate equality and cultural excellence into a coherent way of life that expresses the distinct value of each as the kinds of goods they are? We might establish some practice of equality, of what it is to treat persons as equals independent of a concern for cultural excellence, and accept whatever level of excellence comes out of it. How we would specify that system of equality is itself problematic, but suppose it could be done. We would not accept it unless some threshold level of cultural excellence were the result. If the result were cultural drivel or mere entertainment, we would eventually reevaluate our system of equality as the boredom and embarrassment of mediocrity exacted its toll on our sensibilities. What this shows is that cultural excellence is a distinct value, a source of importance in our lives that is separate from equality. If this is so, then we cannot solve the integration problem just by having the importance of cultural excellence be a function of some notion of equality.

Assuming for the sake of argument that there is some minimal level that would be acceptable, what are the implications for how to accommodate equality? One plausible way of treating the issue of equality in relation to cultural excellence is by setting some threshold level of excellence as a minimal goal of social policy and then institute a system of equality in regard to opportunities to achieve and appreciate cultural excellence at that level.[9] The idea is that the means to cultural achievement and appreciation that reaches the threshold level must be equally available to all who are capable of reaching that level. This is probably the most optimistic kind of project we can imagine in regard to reconciling these two values. And it is probably too optimistic, but imagine that it could be successful. What kind of solution would it be? What kind of losses would it entail, and what kinds of goods would it provide?

The first thing to note is that this is not strictly an egalitarian solution. It does not treat equality as a supreme value. Supreme value pluralism would make no compromises in equality in order to reach a threshold level of cultural excellence as a distinct good. That it is a distinct good is reflected in one way by the fact that it is a constraint on an acceptable notion of equality that for most of us there is some threshold level of cultural excellence in even a minimally good way of life. Another way in which the distinctness of equality and cultural excellence is demonstrated is by the fact that some people are philistines who do not care about incorporating cultural excellence into their way of life at all, and we are as unwilling to let them hold cultural excellence hostage as we are to let egoists hold hostage the common good.[10] Accepting some threshold level of cultural excellence as an

9 I am not thinking here that there should be a government agency for cultural excellence, but that the basic institutions of society should be designed in a way that at least allows for cultural excellence. Tax breaks for the support of the arts or science might be one way to promote such excellence without the government trying to produce what it considers to be cultural excellence.

10 Unequal outcomes of excellence cannot therefore be fully justified on the grounds that the inequalities benefit the culturally uninterested, though some inequalities might be justified on the grounds that the greater share of cultural excellence enjoyed by some provides a good of excellence for the disadvantaged that they would not otherwise enjoy.

independent good in the best shared way of life shows a willingness to compromise on the good of equality, if such a compromise is necessary. That it is necessary even in modern societies with advanced economies should be clear upon reflection.

Though there are many, consider only one dimension of this need. Consider the issue of standards for academic performance in our public universities. This is an issue of growing concern in the United States. Grade inflation – the subject of much recent discussion at Harvard and elsewhere – is only the tip of an iceburg that hides declining standards of academic performance. Several variables contribute to this, not the least of which is the fact that the teaching performance of university faculty is now almost entirely the result of numerical scores on student teaching evaluations. Being a good teacher is a function of achieving somewhere between a 4.0 and a 5.0 on a five-point scale on such evaluations. The standards for good teaching, then, are whatever students demand as a reward for such evaluations. The least-educated people are setting the standards that the educated people must meet, when it should be the other way around. This is the cost of doing business when higher education is construed as an ever-expanding industry.

But why think of education as an ever-expanding industry? One reason might be greed. There is money in the practice, and those benefitting, including faculty members and administrators, do not want to give up the source. So when the Democratic administration under Bill Clinton and the Republican administration under George W. Bush employ rhetoric that sets as a desirable goal in the United States that everyone have an undergraduate degree, it is not difficult to see how those in higher education might be tempted to go along. But greed aside, there is another, more noble value at work: the desire that the goods of excellence be equally available to all. When greed can be covered by rhetoric attached to a noble value, it is all the more difficult to control because it is more difficult to detect, even in oneself.

The nobility of equality not withstanding, it is one of the most pernicious fantasies of our time that it would be good for everyone to have a university education. Suppose we reduced the goal to 50 percent of the adult population. What would the consequences be? Certainly there would be an increased demand for Ph.D.'s, which are now in great surplus. There would have to be more professors to teach the greater number of students. This, of course, would mean that the average talent level of those with a Ph.D. would be lowered. In this regard, higher education is no different from baseball: the higher the percentage of citizens who can make a living as major league baseball players, the lower the quality of baseball played. Contraction becomes an option when fans get bored with the quality of baseball and refuse to pay the price of admission. Of course, this raises the question no one seems to be willing to ask: what percentage of the population is capable of playing baseball at a level that sustains the excellence of the game? A similar question applies to higher education: what percentage of the population is capable of spending thirty to thirty-five years in diligent and intense intellectual study at a very high level? One piece of evidence that it is considerably less than what even the current academic market demands is the intellectual burnout among current university faculty members. The ugly truth is that we now accommodate outright incompetence, not to mention mediocrity, among graduate students and tenured faculty members in order to keep the wheels of the higher education industry going.

Why?

The most generous answer is a misguided egalitarian ideal, one that is so focused on equality that it has lost sight of the kind of excellence higher education should provide. To get excellence properly back into the way of life that adequately includes and expresses both equality and cultural excellence, we have to ask how high academic standards should be. So what should they be?

In order for cultural achievement and appreciation to be available to anyone in any advanced Western society of any size and any level of diversity, whether they are members of the economically best-off class or members of the economically worst-off class, the standards for earning a university degree must be such that some significant number of people who cherish cultural excellence will fail. We are now reluctant to let many fail, even if they do not care about cultural excellence at all. The games of basketball and hockey would become parodies of themselves if the standards for play at the professional level did not disappoint many in their desire to play with Michael Jordan and Wayne Gretzky. For similar reasons, science, art, history, philosophy, music, and many other areas of cultural achievement would become only vestiges of culture in a world of Lake Woebegon where all the children are above average. Walking onto the court with Michael Jordan or taking to the ice with Wayne Gretzky, or many lesser athletes, means taking failure into your own hands. The same is true when confronting the problems of science, the challenges of art, and the pains of philosophical inquiry. The way of life that includes excellence at these things and the opportunity to appreciate such excellence includes more failure than success. This is just the tragic truth of the matter: excellence is born in a crucible.

Any practice that does not recognize this truth only adds to the tragedy. If we lower the standards, we deny the goods they make possible. For the talented but economically worst-off, lowering the standards comes as a double loss. Having gained the opportunity to study, they arrive at our universities only to be confronted with an educational system that often leaves them in the lurch. Little will platitudes about equality serve them in their quest for the kind of education they need to live lives they can find ultimately worth pursuing. By catering to their current appetites for popular culture, we leave them developed only for lives in which "fun" soon fades to jaded desperation.

Is the loss in excellence tragic? Yes, the equality gained is quality lost, and the loss is just too much to justify the gain. But whatever the solution is, there will be tragic loss in its wake. To raise standards to a level adequate to cultural excellence will introduce a kind of competition for a cherished good that not even the majority of talented people can attain. Many will be crushed by the demands of excellence. Kindness has a place in the halls of excellence, but it is a limited one. And though meanness is not essential, cultural excellence is a brutally demanding enterprise that is incompatible with the warmth of a nursery. The net result is that if the threshold of achievement is lowered to where it is readily available to all, then there is a tragic loss of excellence, and if it is set too high, there is a tragic loss in the access to excellence and its appreciation.

Most every intelligent person would upon reflection accept this claim. But what is more tragic is that no matter where the threshold is set, there will be both tragic loss of excellence and tragic loss of access to its achievement and appreciation. The refusal to recognize that there is a tragic value deficit in any possible way of life relative to the goods of equality and cultural excellence is itself a great tragedy. It is the tragedy of pernicious fantasy in which the lesser good is substituted for the greater good because we just refuse to accept that even the best life involves tragic loss owing to the plural and conflicting nature of our values. The realization of some best life relative to the goods of equality and cultural excellence makes impossible the realization of some alternative way of life in which there is more equality and less cultural excellence and some other way of life in which there is more cultural excellence and less equality. To think that the loss of what is included in the lesser goods of these second- and third-best ways of life that is not included in the best life is not tragic is to trivialize the values at stake. At the same time, not to recognize that what is included in the best life is better than what is included in the alternative ways of life is to lose the ability to proportion our sense of loss to our sense of gain. It is this inability that prevents us from asking the hard questions about how it is best to live in regard to equality and excellence. As a result, we cannot get the problem enough into focus to begin seeking meaningful solutions. This itself is a great loss of tragic proportions, one that is fed by the pernicious fantasy that in the best life there are no occasions for sorrow of the sort discussed here, when, in fact, they are pervasive and perpetual.

The same point is multiplied by the number of things we value deeply. Any best life that integrates the goods of liberty and security, equality and excellence, sympathy for human suffering and sympathy for animal suffering, love and respect, pleasure and devotion, and many other values that we care about deeply faces an integrative task that will incur tragic losses in terms of each and every one of these things that we cherish. The result is that the more conflict there is among important values, the greater the tragic nature of any best life there might be in regard to them. What must be remembered, however, is that if best life pluralism is true, then even in the clear recognition of tragedy there is the consolation that the best life contains a surplus of good over bad. We should, therefore, recognize our grounds for sorrow and regret, but our regret should be rational regret: it should be tempered by the joy taken in the greater good. That should give us some passion for life. It allows us not to see our losses as waste.

What, then, should we say about best life pluralism as conceived here, and what are its implications for current philosophers who recommend a return to our Greek heritage for contemporary guidance? First, we should note that the power of best life pluralism takes its energy from a central concept of Classical Greek ethics: the ethical task is living a life that best accommodates all that we hold dear in the way that we hold things dear. The Classical Greeks were right about this. But, second, we must note that best life pluralism progresses by moving backward toward Homer in recognizing the pervasive and perpetually tragic nature of the human condition in ways that Classical Greek optimism could not abide. Consequently, any call to return to the Greeks for moral guidance in a world with our values will have to move more toward a tragic ethics than is currently being advocated. The question remains, however, if we can retain some passion for life if best life pluralism is false, as I believe it is.

9

Tragic Pluralism and Reason's Grief

> Non-Religious Ethics is at a very early stage. . . . Since we cannot know how Ethics will develop, it is not irrational to have high hopes.
>
> Derek Parfit, *Reasons and Persons*

> I can only say that those who rest on such comfortable beds of dogma are victims of self-induced myopia, blinkers that may make for contentment, but not for understanding what it is to be human.
>
> Isaiah Berlin, "The Pursuit of the Ideal"

We have come as far as we can in making sense of tragedy without invoking incomparability, and it is important to see the direction in which the previous observations have driven us, what they have driven us from, and what they are driving us to. The superficiality of nihilism, the bleakness of pessimism, the simplicity of monism, the arrogance of supreme value moralism have all been found wanting. With the exception of some forms of pessimism, they all invoke or descend from a religious paradigm that makes all tragedy intelligible as the interruption of bliss. This is the paradigm we are being driven from, and the one we are being driven to remains to be seen.

On the sunniest religious view, the best of all possible worlds is one in which there is no occasion for sorrow and no place for tragedy: the Garden of Eden before the Fall and Heaven in the hereafter. The world that exists between the innocent beginning of human history and the blissful eternity that awaits is tragic because of the circumstances of life, not because of the nature of what we value itself. Monism best fits this picture, envisioning the possibility of a world full of the one good thing and completely devoid of the bad. It might appear to be a paradigm shift away from this view to reject the religious assumptions about the innocent beginning and the blissful hereafter. A change in metaphysics, as it were. But not so. As long as we continue to think that tragedy is intelligible as a lack of the kind of bliss that the religious tradition envisions, we are still caught in the grips of a paradigm we need to escape. To have high hopes of approximating that vision (however short we might fall) is to have learned nothing at all from the history of tragedy. Indeed, it is to insist that nonreligious ethics stay mired in an early, even primitive stage of development, no matter what the secular trappings. The lesson here is the diversity and complexity of value.

The interruption of bliss, then, is no way to make tragedy intelligible, or for that matter even unintelligible. Remember that nihilism is the view that nothing is worthy of commitment in such a way that loss could ever merit a tragic response. The heights of bliss reach only the peaks of amusement for the nihilist, and the fall is less than a thud. Tragedy is unintelligible because the loss of the life of optimal bliss is nothing to get worked up over. Trapped within the sunny paradigm, the nihilist is thereby robbed of his own iconoclastic ambitions, and thus even that amusement is lost.

Then there is the arrogance of supreme value moralism, which elevates the sunny paradigm to a postulate of practical reason. The highest good, according to Kant, is not virtue but the combination of virtue and the bliss of happiness. The best world, the world in terms of which the deficiencies of all other worlds is to be measured, is the world in which virtue, which does not come in degrees, is matched by a fitting level of bliss. Both rational choice and tragedy are intelligible only against the background of thoughts about unsought but unblemished reward. When secular versions of the Kantian tradition abandon the bliss paradigm (or what John Kekes has memorably called "the transcendental temptation"),[1] they have shifted to a new paradigm of reconciliation. On this view, when bliss is not possible, we can still be reconciled to the tragic loss of the lesser good because of its

[1] See John Kekes, *The Art of Life* (Ithaca, New York: Cornell University Press, 2002), 88.

subordination to a supreme value expressed in the greater good. But, as we have seen, it is very hard to make intelligible the view that there is some value that is pure and overriding in a way that makes either bliss or reconciliation of this sort intelligible. All this, of course, raises questions about secular attempts to revise Kant or any other transcendental illusion. Even as a regulative ideal rather than as a metaphysical thesis, the view is puzzling. Ironically, its sunny genealogy and its inflationary ambitions cast a shadow across its future. The lesson here is the deflation of value.

Other deflationary currents come from reflections on pessimism, on the one hand, and best life pluralism, on the other. Once we get any realistic appreciation for the complexity and diversity of value, the difficulties of achieving a net balance, from any point of view, of the good over the bad are so daunting that it makes the sunny legacy look pathetically naive and irresponsible. That we might achieve a good life for ourselves and others, viewed from the perspective of pessimism, should provide grounds for celebration, not disappointment. But the sunny legacy makes such an achievement look at best like a consolation prize hardly worth pursuing, rendering the lesson here the deflation of expectations.

Understood as including a tragic value deficit in even the best of lives, the great advance of best life pluralism is that it yields to the deflationary pressure regarding value and expectation. It does so as a direct result of accepting the implications of the complexity and diversity of value. If the best life we can expect is on balance a good life in regard to the things we care most deeply about, we should see ourselves as having grounds for joy and passion, even in the clear acceptance of tragic loss. Tragedy viewed either as the interruption of bliss or as reconciliation by subordinating lesser goods to a supreme value robs us of the joy of having achieved a good life. It does so, on the one hand, by not taking the problem of pessimism seriously and, on the other, by making us think that there is something much better than an overall good life called bliss, the vague desire for which undermines the appreciation of just how good a good life is. And where instead of evoking the bliss paradigm it evokes reconciliation by subordination, it does so only by grossly distorting our values.

Sometimes it is instructive to get a little perspective at a distance. Step back and take stock is the thought. Consider the issue more naturalistically. That there is life of any sort on Earth is in itself against all cosmic odds, but that through the blind forces of nature and the imperfect cooperation of fellow human beings we get any kind of chance at a good life is nothing short of staggering. To expect anything like a set of values and circumstances that hold out the prospects of bliss seems like the insatiable demands of a spoiled child. At this point, then, the sunny inflationary paradigms of bliss or reconciliation by subordination should have dimmed considerably, allowing another kind of light to direct our lives. The death of these old pernicious fantasies is not only not horrible but positively liberating. We should not expect to find bliss or to escape tragedy, just any kind of decent shot at a good life – and that is good indeed. Viewing the human condition as providing the opportunity for a good life against all cosmic odds is much different from viewing it as a fall from the Garden of Eden. This is a central feature of the deflationary shift that is elevating.

What best life pluralism represents, therefore, is a shift to a kind of reconciliation paradigm distinct from that associated with supreme value pluralism. Less sunny but still positive, it recommends that we make the loss of the lesser good not contained in the greater good intelligible as the cost of reconciling the conflicts among our values for the sake of living the best life possible. The movement of the paradigm shift is from the sunny inflationary paradigm that makes tragedy intelligible as the loss of bliss to an increasingly deflationary paradigm: first to a paradigm of reconciliation by subordination, then to a paradigm of reconciliation by integration. What remains to be seen is whether even the integration paradigm is too sunny, as I believe it is.

Best life pluralism is a very powerful theory, the most potent version of pluralism of those that assume that practical options are always comparable. It recognizes that even if there is a best life, it contains a value deficit of tragic proportions. It implies, however, that all other tragedy takes the form of the lesser good or evil prevailing over the greater good. Were this true, the only form of grief to which we would be vulnerable other than that evoked by the loss of the greater good would be eliminable by rational choice. Were we rational, we would never have to grieve over choices in which we placed the lesser good or evil over the greater good, and we could always have the consolation of reason that, given the circumstances, we did what we believed to be the best.

Tragic pluralism denies this in a disturbing way. It does so by denying that the consolation of reason for tragic loss is always available to us, even when we act as rationally as possible. It strips us of the fantasies that prevent us from seeing what is involved in our values that is difficult but necessary for us to face. Some forms of tragic choice yield tragic losses because the options are incomparable – choice between them is unintelligible – in which case the rational emotional response, the response that best satisfies the expressiveness criterion, is a kind of grief, not mere regret. Grief (of the sort in question) is the response to unintelligible loss. In these cases, we have to choose, but there are no rational grounds for choosing, and what is lost in one good relative to what is gained in the other is incomparable. Without the consolation of reason, grief replaces regret as the appropriate response to unintelligible loss. The challenge for tragic pluralism is to avoid pessimism, and to meet this challenge it must show that a life properly thought and expressed can be passionately lived in the face of unintelligible loss. Its burden is to reconcile reason's grief with the avoidance of despair. This, I think, is the greatest challenge posed by the problem of tragedy to the twenty-first century.

The first task facing tragic pluralism is the negative task of showing that best life pluralism is false, that, after all, the belief that there is a best life is just another illusion. The second task is to show that reason's grief is not despair; it is consistent with a life of passion, true belief, and honest expression. In what follows, I will take up both these tasks, first by showing abstractly that there is a test for incomparability, and second by showing how incomparability arises regarding some of the most tragic conflicts confronting humanity in the twenty-first century. In Chapter 10, I will take up the issue of the avoidance of despair.

Regarding the abstract task: recall that the *tracking thesis* asserts that our ability to make rational choices between practical options requires that we are able to compare the value of those options. The *trichotomy thesis* asserts that when we compare options, we are limited to three value relations that might exist between them: A is either better than, worse than, or equal to B, which is to say that A is either more worthy of choice than B, less worthy of choice than B, or equally worthy of choice as B. Finally, the *ubiquity thesis* asserts that rational choice is always in principle possible. What should be clear at this point is that best life pluralism asserts that all three theses are true. By contrast, tragic pluralism asserts that though the tracking thesis is true, the ubiquity thesis is false because sometimes practical options are such that neither option is either better than, worse than, or equal to the other just because they are sometimes incomparable.

In Chapter 2, the explanation for why practical options might be incomparable was presented in terms of value vagueness. Value vagueness is not some spooky metaphysical malady but a function of the fact that we and our values godlessly and blindly evolved out of the soup of the universe. Again, a godless and nonmetaphysical, naturalistic paradigm is the way to make sense of the phenomena. Value vagueness is a psychological limitation of our higher-order valuing capacities, our inability to determine choice even when all epistemic and psychological conditions are favorable. Despite knowing all the relevant facts and despite being psychologically unencumbered relative to the issues involved in the choice situation, we know *that* the options are relevant to choice, we know *why* they are relevant to choice, but we do not know *how* relevant they are to choice. Incomparability and value vagueness, then, are due to inherent limitations of our integrative capacities, our psychological capacities to integrate the plural and conflicting modes of regard we have for ourselves and the things we cherish in our environment. Such limitations are just something we should expect when we reflect from the perspective of the naturalistic paradigm as opposed to the religious one. Viewed from this perspective, to make it a condition of reconciliation with the world, social or natural, that the world always be seen as both reasonable and rational borders on the absurd. If we are going to be at all reconciled with the world, we simply must accept the fact that it is a part of the human condition that the world sometimes makes demands on us that nature did not prepare us to meet. Grief is the expression of our limitations in this regard. A very different kind of expression is despair. Despair, I will argue in the next chapter, is an expression of the comparative judgment that the bad hopelessly prevails over the good. Rational regret, grief, and despair, then, are very different emotional and valuational assessments of the human condition best made sense of on a nonreligious paradigm that involves incomparability.

Consider the issue of regret and grief. On the one hand, if best life pluralism is true, then rational regret is sometimes in order because what is contained in the lesser good is not contained in the greater good. Nevertheless, we have the consolation of reason that the greater good is indeed greater than what is lost, and in this sense the loss is intelligible to us. It is intelligible as loss but not as waste, since it is sacrificed for the greater good. Moreover, we need never grieve: if we are rational in our choices, our losses are always intelligible in a way that prevents grief, which is not to say that regret for the loss will not be deeply painful. On the other hand, if tragic pluralism is true, then grief, a sense of loss without the consolation of reason, will be in order because value vagueness and incomparability make it false that there is some best life regarding the things we care most deeply about. Some losses will not be intelligible in the terms that best life pluralism requires. The lesson here is that this is something we should expect. The question at this point is, how do we test to see if incomparability does undermine the ubiquity of practical reason to direct our lives in a way that makes grief rather than regret the appropriate response to some losses and thus makes best life pluralism false and tragic pluralism true?

Whatever the test is, if tragic pluralism is true, we should expect two things from it. First, when employed, it should involve a breakdown in the ability to compare values that are different in kind. And second, it should reflect a different way of thinking about our values and, in that sense, represent a new paradigm.

Regarding the first point: many have argued as though difference in kind itself makes comparison between values impossible.[2] Put simplistically, the thought is that you cannot compare apples and oranges. But Ruth Chang has shown that this is not true by appeal to what she calls notable-nominal comparisons.[3] Notable-nominal comparisons involve comparisons of different kinds of values. This makes them especially important to any form of pluralism, because pluralism rightly maintains that we are often in the position of having to make decisions involving conflicts among plural values. Notable-nominal comparisons establish that comparisons between things that at first seem incomparable are sometimes possible. The fundamental thought is that you can

[2] A good example is found in Elizabeth Anderson, *Value in Ethics and Economics* (Cambridge, Massachusetts: Harvard University Press, 1993), 1–59.

[3] See Ruth Chang, "Introduction," in *Incommensurability, Incomparability, and Practical Reason*, edited by Ruth Chang (Cambridge, Massachusetts: Harvard University Press, 1997).

in fact sometimes compare apples and oranges: a really good apple is better than a very mediocre orange.

Consider the difficulty involved in comparing two artists who work in different art forms. Who was the most creative artistically, Mozart or Michelangelo? One might conclude from the difficulty of making such an assessment that composers and painters are incomparable in regard to the covering value of artistic creativity. But surely this is false, at least at some level. Consider the comparison between Michelangelo and Average Joe Painter. Michelangelo is a notable painter, and Average Joe a nominal one. When compared in regard to creativity as an artist, Michelangelo is clearly better than Average Joe. But what about Mozart and Average Joe in regard to artistic creativity? If we assume that painting is Average Joe's only artistic endeavor, surely we still want to say that Mozart is better in terms of artistic creativity than Average Joe, despite the fact that they work in different art forms. So what looked impossible at first turns out not to be. It may still be true that we cannot fine-tune a comparison between Mozart and Michelangelo in terms of artistic creativity, but it will not be for the general reason that incomparability prevents comparisons across art forms. A notable-nominal comparison has disabused us of that notion.

Moreover, this understanding of notable-nominal comparisons provides an abstract formulation of what I will call *the tuning test* for determiing whether incomparability obtains between conflicting values. What I want to emphasize most is that when applied to conflicts among some of our most cherished values, the tuning test constitutes a paradigm shift away from a prominent understanding of Western culture and its values. The shift has two central elements: a shift away from thinking that the plurality of Western culture and its values is to be explained by a supreme value like equality (or liberty or humanity), and a shift away from thinking that our most central values can always provide rational guidance even when we are fully informed. Continuing a tradition begun by John Locke, both John Rawls and Ronald Dworkin have insisted that Western culture and its liberal democracies are to be understood as experiments in equality as the fundamental, inviolable cultural value.[4] Isaiah Berlin, however, maintained that

4 For John Rawls, see *A Theory of Justice* (Cambridge, Massachusetts: Harvard University Press, 1971), and for Ronald Dworkin, see *Sovereign Virtue: The Theory and Practice of Equality* (Cambridge, Massachusetts: Harvard University Press, 2002).

liberty and equality were distinct, conflicting values and that it is the way in which the central values of Western culture conflict that make Western culture both what it is and something worth preserving.[5] A major goal of my theory of tragedy is to support a shift to Berlin's paradigm away from the paradigm of Rawls and Dworkin. It is a shift away from the religious paradigm and its secular progeny, a shift to expecting equality, liberty, fraternity, excellence, and everything else we hold dear to come at a heavy cost to each. But more positively, it is a shift toward a way of life that we can think of as good and worth pursuing with some passion, despite the fact that it is riddled with tragedy and despite the fact that its being best, in any of its forms, is unintelligible.

With this in mind, we can test for both comparability and incomparability between conflicting values by taking the following steps:

1. Start with a notable case of A and a nominal case of B, where A is clearly superior to B (a really good apple and a very mediocre orange).
2. Find a device for imagining tradeoffs whereby improvements in B result in diminishments in A (improving the orange-tastiness of the orange diminishes the apple-tastiness of the apple because of tradeoffs in maintaining the orchards).
3. See what kinds of value relations are revealed by the trade-offs and whether there are zones of vagueness and incomparability.

If A and B (any paired set of values) are different kinds of values, and if we find that we can fine-tune a notable-nominal comparison between them by marginal units of improvement in the nominal value and by marginal units of diminishment in the notable value and that we can always make a comparative choice between them, then they are always comparable, and the foundation of best life pluralism is secure. But if in fine-tuning the values under favorable epistemic and psychological conditions (where improvements in the nominal value come at the cost of the notable value) we are unable at some points to choose between the values so tuned, then incomparability obtains due to value vagueness. The range in the tuning process in which such vagueness appears is a zone of vagueness and incomparability relative

5 See Isaiah Berlin, "Two Concepts of Liberty," in his *Four Essays on Liberty* (London: Oxford University Press, 1969), 118–72.

to those values. In such a zone, the consolation of a comparative reason for a choice between the values is lost, and the foundation for best life pluralism is undermined, with tragic pluralism waiting in the wings.

What is crucial to the tuning test is that it recognizes that incomparability is always a breakdown in the ability to compare. This means that under favorable circumstances, comparability, clarity, and choice are the rule; incomparability, value vagueness, and stultified choice, the exception. If this is true, then some contemporary claims against reason are grossly exaggerated, but the central point remains that if comparative reason breaks down over important values in ways that undermine our ability to integrate our modes of concern and choose between different ways of life, then best life pluralism is just another destructive delusion.

Without a clear case of incomparability, all this talk about the need for a new paradigm will seem contrived and dubious. But there is a clear case, and it is one alluded to earlier, the one represented most graphically by the question, how many decent people is your most cherished loved one worth? I know of no more powerful way of establishing the vivid force of incomparability than this. The question puts two of our most precious values in conflict and forces us to choose. On the one hand, we have value (A), love for our loved ones, and, on the other, (B), respect for other decent people. What does the tuning test reveal about the value relationship between these two important values?

Consider the following imaginary device for tuning the values. Imagine yourself in the horrible position of trying to rescue your most precious loved one from among a large number of other decent people whose lives are also at stake. It is September 11, 2001, and your daughter works in the World Trade Center. Just moments after the attack, you are trying desperately to get into one of the buildings to rescue her and to help as many other people as you can before the towers collapse. Because of her location in the building, it will take you longer to rescue her than it would for you to rescue any number of other people. Indeed, the longer you spend on rescuing her, the more other decent people will lose their lives for lack of your rescuing them, with the number increasing exponentially as time passes. Similarly, the more time you spend rescuing others, the more you put your daughter at risk of not being rescued at all. Whether there were in fact cases like this during this event, I do not know. But I am virtually certain that as I write there are people going through this very process along the southern coast of Asia in the wake of the recent tsunamis that struck there.

In the imagined circumstances, rescuing your daughter is a notable case of (A), the value of your loved one, because saving her will be a complete success in terms of that value in the context. As to (B), the value of other decent people's lives and the respect you have for them, a nominal case would be saving one other person. Now suppose you knew that you could improve (B) by diminishing (A): the more time you spend on others, the lower the chances of saving your daughter. Would such knowledge allow you to make comparisons between the values?

Surely in some cases it would. If you knew that taking the time to save one other equally decent person first would have a 100 percent chance of costing your daughter her life, you would clearly save your daughter first. However, suppose the risk of your daughter dying by your rescuing one other person first was only a .001 probability and that the success of the other rescue was certain. Surely vivid awareness of such probabilities would reverse the priorities. But now notice how complex the variables can get. Suppose we increase the probabilities of success of rescuing ever-higher numbers of other decent people first at the cost of ever-increasing probabilities that your daughter will die? What version of moral mathematics gives us the formula, even with the vivid awareness of all the facts and probabilities, for comparisons that will allow us to answer the question: how many decent people is your most cherished loved one worth?

The conclusions we should draw from reflection on this case are powerful and clear. If monism, supreme value pluralism, best life pluralism, or any view that claims that values are always comparable were true, there would be a definite answer to this question. But there is not. Nothing could be clearer than this, and nothing said in the remainder of this book is intended to make the argument any stronger. I know of nothing that could.

What else, then, should we conclude? First, that different values are at stake and in conflict. So monism, the view that value is one and not many, is false. Second, that your loved one is more intrinsically valuable to you (as loved ones are to any loving and respectful person) than one other decent person and less valuable than thousands and thousands of other such people. Just think of how your priorities would be effected by the vivid awareness that there is one chance in a billion that you could save your daughter but a certainty that you could rescue thousands of other people who would otherwise certainly perish. Neither love for your loved ones nor respect for other decent people always overrides the other, regardless of the context. So supreme value pluralism is false. Third, that there is a vast zone in the trade-offs between the two values in which you would simply be stultified by the choice. As time passes and the cost to others for saving your daughter increases, the more anxiety increases about the comparative judgment. At some point, despite your vivid awareness of all the relevant facts, including the probabilities of success, you would simply be unable to choose between the options and be stultified by the choice, which shows that within that zone the options are incomparable. So best life pluralism is false. No matter what choice is made, there is a tragic loss, but within a range of possibilities that loss cannot be compared to what is gained. The lesser good and the greater good cannot be distinguished, rendering the loss unintelligible and the consolation of reason's regret inaccessible. We are left, then, with reason's grief and to further contemplate the implications of this kind of tragedy for an ethical outlook.

Anyone looking for a stronger argument for incomparability than this will have to find it elsewhere. I cannot see that it is anything less than definitive on the issue. Even so, these conclusions would not be far-reaching if incomparability were confined to rare cases of the sort imagined in the World Trade Center or tsunami examples. But what I will show is that incomparability is anything but rare in regard to a number of important values and choices we increasingly face. With this in mind, it is time now to consider some of the tragic choices before us in the twenty-first century and whether best life pluralism or tragic pluralism best recognizes the losses we incur in these conflicts and most ably equips us to act and feel appropriately in regard to them. In all these cases, there is a parallel to the question, how many decent people is your most cherished loved one worth?, which should solidify the argument that a paradigm shift in our understanding of tragedy is one of the most urgent needs in contemporary life.

Consider first how this is so regarding conflicts between values we have already discussed in the context of best life pluralism: liberty versus security and equality versus cultural excellence. If best life pluralism were sufficient to account for all losses in regard to these values, incomparability would not be needed for making sense of how to act and feel in regard to them. However, the more incomparability is needed, the stronger the case is for a paradigm shift in thinking about our values.

LIBERTY VERSUS SECURITY

Two ways of thinking of the relationship between liberty and security bring with them a bright-liner's mentality and descend from the supreme value tradition rooted in our religious past. One is that the only thing that can limit liberty is liberty itself, and the other is that we should first do no harm. On either of these views, it is blasphemous to suggest that the values might be traded off against each other and that the tuning test is an appropriate way of dealing with them. But, given the lessons from Galileo and numerous other thinkers, we should have learned by now that blasphemous thoughts are often the only road to progress. In order to see where they lead, I start with conclusions drawn in the previous chapter regarding liberty and security and the very powerful account that best life pluralism gives of the difficulties of integrating them: (i) liberty and security are distinct values; (ii) neither is strictly superior to the other; and (iii) any best life in regard to them would itself involve a value deficit of tragic proportions. All these conclusions have been argued for already, and there is no need to repeat those arguments here. The current interest is in what some device for the tuning test might reveal about the relations between these values and whether, despite its enormous appeal, we should reject best life pluralism and its consolations for tragic loss.

Consider first some of the dimensions of liberty and security. One of the things we value is the absence of interference. We want a way of life that leaves us plenty of room to take our own chances, to determine our own course, and to be left alone by others in this regard. We also value self-realization and the resources to effect such realization. It is, after all, one thing to be free of interference in pursuing self-realization and quite another to have the resources and opportunities to effect it. Finally, we also value not being harmed in fundamental ways through physical injury, death, or psychological terror. These are three distinct values. Where we have not experienced any interference from others or any loss of resources and opportunities for self-realization, we can still suffer physical injury, death, or psychological terror. Of course, there are relationships among these concerns, but they are nonetheless three distinct values. The first involves the value of negative liberty; the second, the value of positive liberty; and the third, the value of security against physical injury, death, and psychological terror.[6]

Now consider what the value relation is between negative freedom and security from harm as these values are revealed in what we care about after careful reflection. Any system of civil liberties involves a negative liberties factor and a harm factor. To provide security from harm, we sometimes have to restrict civil liberties by interfering with dangerous activities, activities that cause physical injury, death, or psychological terror. We adjust both the liberty factor and the harm factor to accommodate a balance between them.

The worldwide war on terrorism involves a conflict between security from the harms of physical injury, death, and psychological terror, on the one hand, and the civil liberties of all those affected by the war, friend and foe alike, on the other. It is simplistic, of course, to say that this is all the war involves, and I do not mean to imply that it is. But this conflict is one of the war's salient features with which we are currently grappling. How are we to think of how to resolve it?

One way is to think of civil liberties as absolute rights that are inviolable under any circumstances. That is one bright-liner point of view, and one that few if any intelligent people will accept. Another, equally unacceptable view is that civil liberties pale so much in comparison to the value of security that their infringement can be comfortably accommodated. What this shows is that for every bright-liner peering across one side of the moral border, there is another peering back on the other side. Media images of Joseph McCarthy and Larry Flint come to mind. Most of us are going to reject both these views without the need for a lot of reflection, which confirms the point that neither of these values is strictly superior to the other.

To get our bearings on what the relation is between these values, we need to construct a notable-nominal comparison between security and negative liberty and find a device for the tuning test in which

[6] See ibid.

improvements in the nominal value come at a cost of diminishments in the notable value. A notable case, A, of negative liberty might be one in which a very large number of people enjoy a very low level of interference, and a nominal case, B, of security might be one in which a large number of people are put at some significant level of risk. The more harms at which we are willing to put ourselves and others at risk for a wider range of liberties for a larger number of people, the more we value liberty over security. A notable-nominal comparison in this regard would be one in which extensive liberty from interference is weighed off against security from minor risks of harm. That comparison is easy to make. Extensive negative liberty is superior to security from minor harms. But what if we tune the values incrementally? We increase the value of security by increasing the harms that come with liberty until we finally realize that our liberties are such that they are one causal factor in intolerable terrorist harm. We will then find that the tuning has reversed our priorities. For many in the Western world, especially in the United States, this point came on September 11, 2001. What happened was a shock to our conceptual resources, a paradigm shift away from thinking that liberty is a supreme value to the realization that liberty, too, must be weighed off against other values, and it will be some time before the full effects of that paradigm shift are clearly realized. Thinking in terms of the tuning test is a paradigm shift of no small political significance.

The question we face now is how to conduct a war in which both the value of liberty and the value of security must be constantly weighed. What is the zone in which that war can be rationally fought, given our values? If the tuning of these values is to accommodate anything like the kind of pluralistic societies upon which Western culture is based, they will reveal that the value of liberty is vastly but not strictly superior to that of security. To how much harm are we willing to put ourselves at risk for the sake of accommodating non-Western values, and how much risk of harm are we willing to put those who do not have Western values for the sake of preserving the liberty central to our pluralistic societies? In this sense, our desire to accommodate plurality explains in part why we have gone so far in making ourselves and others so vulnerable. But there are limits, as recent events have shown. Moreover, as the world becomes smaller and smaller and the needs for Western and non-Western accommodation become greater and greater, the more and more difficult it will be to make the comparative judgment of when liberty is vastly superior to security. Why? Because the cost of tolerating non-Western values increases in the currency of harm (physical injury, death, and psychological terror) as these are the means of power that a competitive culture has to defend or aggrandize itself. This, I believe, is one of the most tragic problems facing all of humanity in the twenty-first century.

But if I am right, it is best to think of the value zone in which the current war on terrorism is being fought as one with vague borders between zones of rational necessity, unrelieved by equally acceptable options. And the truth is that while we can tune these values in a way that rules out many options, we have no idea at all, none at all, of how to tune the liberty factor and the harm factor in a way that yields anything like a best life in regard to civil liberties and security from harm. There is no such life. It is a mistake, then, to hope for such guidance and a pernicious fantasy to insist on it. The most we can hope for is to avoid the clear case in which the bad prevails over the good. To insist on more because of utopian instincts, or religious optimism, or classical naivete about human nature and the best life, is to invite more tragedy by refusing to accept the fact that some tragedy is ineliminable.

When we are as a matter of fact able to judge that liberty is inferior to security, we should not be paralyzed by the loss of such an important value. We must regret it, even grieve it in the sense of an intense emotional response to a significant loss, but we should be consoled by the fact that in these circumstances security is the greater good. When we forgo our own liberty to protect non-Western countries against harm, we should be clear on the cases. Forgoing liberty to some degree to remedy the Palestinian issue, on whatever turns out to be a reasonable solution to that problem, is one thing. To protect our liberties against those who hate secularism, harbor terrorists, and impose the kind of repressive theocracy implemented by the Talliban regime is quite another. That is a compromise we cannot make. Liberty, theirs and ours, is that superior to the risk of harm.The very course of Western culture is at stake, and it is foolish to think otherwise. Nevertheless, our negative liberty to pursue frivolous elements of Western lifestyles that come at a direct, significant cost of physical injury, death, and psychological terror to members of non-Western cultures is vastly inferior to the value of their security. How much of this sort of evil exists, then, is an important part of the war against terrorism. It is certainly not the kind of liberty on which to base Western culture. Nor do I believe that Western culture is based on this notion of negative liberty, though there are certainly effects of this sort. Moreover, the practical task of sorting out those elements from the more positive elements is itself a daunting task. What we have to stand on guard against, then, are conceptions of negative liberty that do not adequately express a value on which to base Western pluralistic culture. We must do the best we can not to let the bad prevail over the good. The problem is that a great deal of this war, and of future conflicts between the secular Western world, and the religious non-Western world is going to be fought near and around zones in which we value vaguely regarding different fronts of the war. This is a tragedy of a different sort. We cannot console ourselves with reasons here, nor with pernicious hopes of utopian solutions.

But there are two things we can do. We can avoid the tragedy of compounding tragedy. We can try to understand each other as honestly toiling with our incapacitiy to cope with these difficulties. We can resist the bright-liner's self-assuredness and sanctimonious intolerance. This goes for bright-liners on both sides of the political divide. When we do and when we bring ourselves to act without reasons, we can at least understand that we are trapped in one of the tragedies of the human condition. The best we can expect, then, in the coming decades regarding Western and non-Western cultures is a very high level of tension over tragic losses from each point of view. This is just the tragic truth of the matter.

Indeed, we should expect a great deal of tension within Western culture itself over these issues, which is exactly what we are seeing. One way to understand the clash between Western Europe, on the one hand, and the United States and Great Britain, on the other, regarding the latest war in Iraq is a bright-liner's understanding. Robert Kagan has described one way of interpreting the dispute.[7] For historical reasons that are easy to understand, Europeans, according to Kagan, have adopted the Kantian framework of perpetual peace based on international law. From that perspective, we hear the rhetoric claiming that

[7] See Robert Kagan, *Of Paradise and Power: America and Europe in the New World Order* (New York: Knopf, 2003).

it is just unfathomable how anyone could reject such an idea in favor of brute force. For other historical reasons that are equally easy to understand, British-American rhetoric has appealed to a hard-headed Hobbesian model for toughly resisting intransigent regimes that are clearly inhumane on any set of values. The rhetoric from both camps reflects a bright-liner's mentality about what the most central values of Western culture are. The longing on both sides is for a set of values that marks the moral borders of life in crisp, bright colors for all but the most depraved to see.

By contrast, however, I suspect that the tension we see between the United States and Europe over the war is symptomatic of a different problem, one that can be traced to the vagueness of our values and to incomparability. Just as you would be torn if asked to decide how many decent people your most cherished loved one is worth, the social psychology of a culture can be torn over the vagueness that permeates its values and that arises in hard cases. When we are torn as a culture, we run for the shelter of conceptual schemes that shield us from the facts about our own values that are hard to face. All the jokes about the French being cowards (despite the fact that more French soldiers died during World War II than American soldiers have in all American wars) and all the French and German rhetoric about America and fascism are not comparisons that actually have any rational basis in Western values. They do not issue from some clear vision of a best life relative to our values. Rather, they are more likely the disguised effects of reason's grief on Western culture itself. It is important that we understand this and adjust our rhetoric accordingly. Unfortunately, it has become fashionable to think that skill at such rhetoric is a sign of belonging to the intellectual class, when nothing could be further from the truth. The shriller the rhetoric, the dumber the speaker, regardless of the language, English or French.

The second thing we can do is work as hard as we can to eliminate all the sources that contribute to these kinds of conflicts. This is a very complex problem involving comparisons of different cultures. For now, it is important to realize that to take on this task we must first recognize the particular kind of horror these conflicts cause. There is the loss of liberty and the loss of security, but there is also the horror of sometimes having no way to compare the options in order to cope with the problem. This, I fear, is one of the most serious tragedies facing the twenty-first century. Rational hope of utopia regarding liberty and security is dead, leaving part of the problem of tragedy for the twenty-first century to be that of finding grounds for hope other than in the pernicious, utopian fantasies of lingering traditions. The truth is that there is neither an American nor a European vision of a best life in regard to Western values, and our rhetoric should reflect a paradigm shift in our thinking about these things. We simply must scale down what we can reasonably expect. In so doing, we may avoid more tragedies than we otherwise would.

The same, I believe, applies to other ways in which liberty and security conflict. Think of the value of a market economy and the value of a social security net. Gone are the days in which faith in a completely unfettered economy is plausible. Also gone are the days in which faith in extensively planned economies can be maintained with any degree of credulity. To linger over these hopes is to indulge in fantasy at a time when history demands that we move on. It is to refuse to recognize that both laissez-faire and Marxism are failed social experiments, despite what the confident and faithful remnants of these traditions say. We are left, then, with trying to balance the benefits of a market economy with the need for some kind of security net, and there never will be a clear political formula, however complex, for the desired balance, whether it be some form of American capitalism or of European social democracy.

Consider how this is revealed in a notable-nominal comparison patterned after an example made famous by the late Robert Nozick. In the example, Wilt Chamberlain, the great American basketball player, is able to amass a huge fortune through numerous, small voluntary exchanges that cost no particular individual anything that he or she is unwilling to pay to watch Chamberlain play basketball.[8] The lesson is supposed to be that a libertarian economic system ensures that there are no harms that are not voluntarily accepted. But, of course, as Nozick was aware, there are harms that are the indirect result of such exchanges. Wealth and power will accumulate not only in ways that undermine any semblance of democratic representation, but also in ways that endanger the health and basic welfare of those at the bottom of the social scale. The problem is how to design an economic system

[8] See Robert Nozick, *Anarchy, State, and Utopia* (New York: Basic Books, 1974), 161–3.

that avoids the pitfalls both of economies fully planned by the government and of economies that allow wealth and power to accumulate in ways that undermine an acceptable level of security for those who are less fortunate in economic competition. Obsession with security leads to one kind of disaster, and obsession with negative liberty and noninterference to another.

So how are we, even when we have gained all the facts, to tune a market system with controls that will result in an acceptable security net for those who are harmed by the system? This is one of the unavoidable tragic issues of the twenty-first century. It will be worse if we approach the problem thinking that there is some vision of a best life in this regard. There is not. We can certainly know that sometimes the harms involved in economic freedom are just too much to bear and that some of these harms can be eliminated. We can also know that sometimes the harms involved are just the cost of liberty that we value more. In either case, we are guided by our tragic sense, which is far more reliable than visions of utopia. In these clear cases, we accept the tragic loss either of liberty enjoyed or of harm averted for the sake of a clearly greater good. But that greater good is not the best life, nor is it informed by some vision of a best life. Rather, it is informed by a sense that some losses are too much to bear. The problem, however, is that historically, at least on a global scale, we have no idea where we stand on the scale of comparison. We do not know how to calculate the facts, let alone the values.[9] But assume that we could calculate the facts and that we could implement a desirable economic system without flaw or corruption. What is our sense of where the trade-off between these two values reaches a point at which the cost of liberty is just too much? How many lives is some level of liberty worth? We have no idea how to answer this question in any remotely precise way. Why? Because we care about both liberty and security, but our values and the ways in which we care about things did not evolve in a context that equipped us for such decisions. The most we can do is to try to avoid tragedy that we can clearly avoid, and we cannot always judge even what this

[9] Gregory Kavka makes a claim like this regarding the Gulf War of the early 1990s in his article "Was the Gulf War a Just War?," *Journal of Social Philosophy* 22, no. 1 (Spring 1991): 20–9.

is. In this regard, best life pluralism has us think in ways that do not fit the problems facing us.

The problem we now face is how we avoid despair regarding conflicts between liberty and security when plagued by value vagueness. Later, I will try to say how. Here it is important to point out how we cannot avoid it. We cannot afford the simpleminded view that when something exists that is bad, there is some way of arranging things that would be better because the bad would be eliminated. Even best life pluralism accepts the fact of tragic value deficit, even in the best life. But we cannot afford to pretend any longer that we actually have any remote idea of what a best way of life would be like in regard to liberty and security in the actual world in which trade-offs are necessary between them. Sometimes – rather often, in fact – we cannot tell which is the superior value. This means that the first step in avoiding despair is divesting ourselves of utopian fantasies in which it is clear that all that is bad is necessitated by the greater good. It also means divesting ourselves of the rhetoric that encourages that delusion. Even our rhetoric needs to be revised to accommodate the tragedy of vagueness, and this is nowhere more crucial than in the rhetoric regarding liberty and security. When our rhetoric does express this vagueness, it will also express the extent to which we in the West hold liberty superior to security and the reasons for it. That rhetoric will serve both as a warning and as a comfort to those who now oppose Western practices. It will serve as a warning to militant theocracies, foreign or domestic, that see secular democracy itself as a target to be eliminated, and it will serve as a source of dialogue for victims of a kind of liberty that a defensible liberty would not condone. The current state of the rhetoric on all sides of the political divide is largely and tragically that of the old bright-liner's self-assuredness, especially (and sadly) in so-called intellectual circles.

At this point, these observations on conflicts between liberty and security are intended to show that my claims for the necessity of a paradigm shift are predicated not on a fictitious rendering of the World Trade Center example, but on the very real conflicts we are actually facing. Moreover, the case for the shift is further extended by a reconsideration of conflicts between equality and cultural excellence.

EQUALITY VERSUS CULTURAL EXCELLENCE

William Faulkner once made the blasphemous comparison that Keat's poem "Ode on a Greecian Urn" is worth, in his words, "any number of old ladies."[10] That the point could just as well have been made in terms of middle-aged male golfers does not detract from the blasphemy. Nor is his point confined to Keats. I take it that he would have thought the same about the exemplars of cultural excellence from Homer to Shakespeare, from Plato to Kant, from Bach to Gershwin, and from Bacon to Einstein. The heart of his claim is that cultural excellence on the whole is worth some price in the currency of human equality. And therein lies the blasphemy. It offends both our religious and secular egalitarian traditions. Whether it is the view that we are all equally God's children or that we are all equal members of the Kingdom of Ends, even the suggestion that equality is not an uncompromising and inviolable value is such anathema to our predominant conceptual scheme that submitting equality to a comparison test with any other value, let alone cultural excellence, is very nearly unthinkable. Only people with fascist tendencies of some sort could even entertain the possibility that equality is not strictly superior to all other values. There can be no doubt, then, that any serious consideration of the tuning test is already a paradigm shift in our thinking about equality in its relationship to cultural excellence.

But before testing Faulkner's blasphemy or anyone else's claim about these two kinds of values, we should recognize that they do not always conflict. Opponents of one are often opponents of the other. The Nazis are a good example. Working from a completely nonegalitarian paradigm, they scoffed at the notion of human equality, and their rhetoric strongly suggested that cultural excellence was strictly and not just vastly superior to human equality. Yet what the Nazis did to the art treasures of Europe is enough by itself to record them as perhaps the worst philistines in history.[11] Liberating Europe from the Nazis was a victory not only for human equality but also for cultural excellence.

[10] See Joseph Blotner, *Faulkner: A Biography* (New York: Vintage, 1991), 619.

[11] Lynn H. Nicholas, *The Rape of Europa: The Fate of Europe's Treasures in the Third Reich and the Second World War* (New York: Vintage, 1995).

The history of communist Russia, however, is not so one-dimensional in the lesson it teaches. Consider the Marxist principle of distribution, "From each according to ability and to each according to need." This is an egalitarian principle if ever there was one. Does it come at a cost to cultural excellence? Historically it has, when cultural excellence and its expression have not been counted among the basic human values or when such values have been delayed until the coming of socialist utopia. Like it or not, state-enforced equality of one sort or another has been a constant opponent of art as a form of cultural excellence since the time of Plato, and it has flourished throughout the twentieth century and into the twenty-first.

I am not thinking of artists who, as political activists, opposed repressive regimes. The value of political expression is a different value than the value of cultural excellence that I have in mind. Art as protest is one thing, but the more cultural value of art lies elsewhere. Part of that value is the expression, creation, and cultivation of beauty, the subject of Keat's poem, and it is beauty and its place in life that has been a major target of totalitarian oppression. Totalitarians despise Romantics because they think of them as bourgeois, as too personal, as taken with a petty, nonpolitcal conception of the beautiful and the sublime. Of course, they fail to note that the Romantic poetry of the late eighteenth and early nineteenth centuries was itself (among other more central things) an expression of political opposition to the dehumanizing influences of the industrial revolution. Still, the values the Romantics sought to restore and to make more central in life were aesthetic and personal, not political. And it is this vision that many totalitarians of the twentieth century saw as one of the greatest threats to socialist equality. But in the end, Zhivago was more like the Russian peasant than the Bolsheviks, despite his aristocratic heritage. What he wanted most was to live the personal life and write his poetry about it.[12] He, like the Russian peasant, recognized that even a modest life dedicated to the personal and the beautiful is vastly superior to an impersonal, drab egalitarianism, no matter what else it offers. The same might be said about other cultures.

Cultural bleakness, then, can be the offspring of Nazi arrogance, but it can also be the progeny of egalitarian ideals politically enforced.

[12] Boris Leonidovich Pasternak, *Doctor Zhivago* (New York: Pantheon, 1997).

Perhaps the solution is a system of liberties that lets the best of cultural expression rise to the top. I have no doubt that this is true and that some form of liberal democracy with a significant egalitarian component will win the battle for our allegiance in this regard. Still, the question remains how to judge any system of liberties in terms of the balance achieved between the value of equality and the value of cultural excellence.

Consider a notable-nominal comparison and how it might be tuned. A tuning device might be a set of standards for academic performance requisite for undergraduate university degrees in the humanities. No doubt there are other devices we might employ, but this is one that is instructive. Humanities degrees are crucial because they involve disciplines that are central to cultural excellence. This is not to denigrate technical or professional degrees. They, too, have a crucial role in our lives, even regarding cultural excellence. But focusing on disciplines like history, philosophy, literature, art, psychology, and the sciences explicitly recognizes those areas in which the true, the good, and the beautiful are pursued for their own sake rather than for their extrinsic benefits, whether those benefits are understood as profit or social welfare. The thought is this: the level of understanding, appreciation, and achievement of the average humanities graduate should be a good predictor in modern, advanced societies of what to expect in the way of cultural excellence. The higher that average level, the greater the cultural excellence that should be expected. I say "should" because at least one of the central functions of higher education should be the promotion and preservation of cultural excellence. Higher education should not just be about job training, sports entertainment, and the career advancement of professional academics.

How we set the standards will determine the balance between equality and cultural excellence and will function as a tuning device for relating these two important values. Moreover, no matter how we set the standards, there is going to be tragic loss. This was revealed in the discussion of best life pluralism. Yet the issue remains: where do we draw the line and by what criteria can it be drawn precisely or with anything approaching precision?

As any conscientious academic knows, this is one of the most agonizing issues facing higher education today. One way to settle it is by drawing some baseline in terms of one of the values beyond which we are just unwilling to make any further compromises for the sake of the other value. Only so much inequality is tolerable, and only so much cultural mediocrity can be stomached. But where is the line, and how clear are the borders it draws?

Suppose we start with the view that equality is vastly superior to cultural excellence. This view is the direct opposite of the one expressed by Faulkner and seems to be the prevailing view in American universities. Can we test this hypothesis as an expression of our considered opinion of the relationship between these two values? As heretical as it sounds, I think we can do so with a notable-nominal comparison.

Imagine a notable case, A, of equality as one in which half the population of the United States has a university degree of some sort and has gainful employment as a result, and that this college-educated group is demographically diverse with proportionate representation of minorities, and add to this that overall unemployment and poverty rates are at historic lows. As a nominal case, B, of cultural excellence, imagine a society in which the average humanities graduate could not carry on a reasonably intelligent conversation of any substantial duration regarding any two of the following topics – Shakespeare's contribution to literature and the English language, the distinction between Keynesian and supply-side economics, the major religions of the world, the Enlightenment, the significance of the American Civil War in the history of warfare, the role of the Bill of Rights in defining American constitutional democracy, Darwin's theory of natural selection, Plato's *Republic*, any Greek drama, Germany's contribution to classical music, the Bible or the Koran, existentialism, any period in the history of painting, the role of African Americans in the development of jazz, behaviorism and psychoanalysis, the differences between Malcolm X and Martin Luther King, different forms of feminism, three major developments in astronomy, the major population shifts in world history, how to determine the validity and soundness of an argument, or three different ways to construct a paragraph – but could tell you the latest standings in the National Basketball Association, balance a checkbook, retain a self-supporting job in a highly litigious climate, operate a TV remote without assistance, and conscientiously form a political opinion based entirely on CNN commentary. What should be clear is that the nominal case of cultural excellence is not much, and that we would never sacrifice A for B. We would never lower the high, equitable standard of living in A for B's cultural mediocrity. It would seem, then, that improvements in B would have to be great for us to violate equality.

But what if A comes at the cost of B or something less? What if the average university graduate has little grasp of science, music, philosophy, and the history of our own culture and other cultures? What if in order to get A we have to tolerate standards that result in the cultural mediocrity of B or worse?

Both Soviet communism and liberal market democracies have been experiments in egalitarianism. The latter is ongoing; the former, for a variety of reasons, is now defunct. The Soviet egalitarian experiment had unforseen costs in terms of the human spirit and the value of cultural excellence, and for this we rightly criticize it. Might current trends in liberal market economies that promise another egalitarian vision also have unforseen costs in the same regard? Which is better, culturally speaking: a society in which cultural bleakness is the result of suppressed expression or one in which it is the result of enforced neutrality regarding anything anyone wants to call culture?[13] In monitoring our development, should we consider how we might tune the options in such a way that the costs in terms of cultural excellence are at some point just too high to pay for greater overall equality?

The problem is that even as things stand now we are facing difficulties. The equality percentage measured in terms of the percentage of degree recipients is less than fifty percent, and the average university graduate in the humanities from all public universities cannot carry on a reasonably intelligent conversation of any duration on any two of the topics mentioned, even including the less demanding topics. Though I have no hard proof of this, today's average humanities graduate probably has less historical awareness than the average high school graduate of forty to fifty years ago. The problem will be exacerbated as we increase the demands on either of the values. If we set academic standards in a way that ensures the notable case of equality, we will not get anything like a nominally acceptable case of cultural excellence.

[13] In conversation, Max de Gaynesford has put a similar point in political terms. Which is better: a society in which you cannot say what you believe or a society in which you can anything you please but no one listens? To think that there are not unforseen dangers to any political way of life, including any form of Western liberal democracy, is the worst form of naivety.

This is a causal claim, one I would be happy to have refuted. But the current state of higher education strongly suggests that it is true. Does this mean that the nominal case of cultural excellence sets too high a mark? If so, then what would a nominal case be that defined an acceptable baseline? Consider how to tune the values to arrive at a coherent balance: any plausible baseline of cultural excellence is going to put significant strains on the demands of equality. This, I believe, is one of the most significant conflicts facing us in the twenty-first century.

Our current thinking seems to be that equality and excellence are always friendly values. They are not, and this is something that will become more and more apparent as more and more inequalities of certain sorts are eliminated. Here I am not talking about inequalities that express discrimination based on race or gender or something of that sort. I am talking about general inequalities whose elimination moves toward equality of income and equality of education across the populations of pluralist, liberal democracies. The fact is that pluralist equality of outcome comes at the cost of cultural excellence, even cultural competence.

Despite these observations, trends in the United States are moving in a dangerously different direction. Two trends are especially worrisome. The first is in how the performance of pubic higher education is evaluated by the general citizenry and their political representatives. Performance is evaluated very heavily in terms of graduation rates. The factory model – the more graduates produced at the least cost, the better – is clearly implied. Nothing, however, could be more shortsighted. The ideal implicit in this view is both market-oriented and egalitarian in the crassest sense: the goal is realized when everyone has a degree at the least monetary expense. The lesson is that unbridled marketing of education can be as leveling in its cultural effects as communist egalitarianism. The result, of course, is cultural disaster.

Politicians cannot have it both ways. They cannot insist both that we produce more college graduates and that we raise standards. To add insult to injury, they want us to do this with less and less support. The task for politicians as representatives of the public good is to tune the values so that the trade-offs result in a comparative judgment with a rational foundation. We are now flirting with the tragedy of the bad or lesser good prevailing over the greater good. But we should realize that there is no bright-line criterion that will infallibly tell us the clear point at which the trade-offs are rational. Public political discourse on this topic would be better served by an understanding of how vagueness can enter these issues. Perhaps it is the fear of that vagueness that preserves the pernicious fantasies exacerbating these problems.

The second worrisome trend is within higher education itself, and it involves the concept of diversity. It is one thing to value diversity for the contribution it makes to education and cultural excellence; it is another to value all cultural perspectives equally. What is the nature of a pluralistic culture in which respect for diversity means that no cultural perspective can be expressed if it is found to be offensive to another cultural perspective? The result, of course, is homogeneous cultural pablum in which no culture is honestly expressed. So it is not just politicians and those outside higher education who cannot have it both ways. The easy rhetoric of diversity often spoken by educators themselves belies a lack of awareness of the conflict between the values at stake. If we set the standards in a way that equalizes all cultural competitors, the higher forms of cultural expression simply will not rise to the top. The result will be that universities will turn out career professionals who are intellectual frauds, full of vinegar and little salt.

How much diversity we can tolerate is a good tuning device for testing the comparative relations that obtain between equality and cultural excellence. When it comes at the cost of cultural excellence, the more cultural neutrality we require for the sake of diversity, the more we value equality over cultural excellence. Assuming that some system of liberties regarding cultural expression is the solution to the problem of how to achieve an acceptable balance between equality and cultural excellence, tolerance for diversity will also reveal how much liberty is to be valued in this regard as well. In fact, tolerance for diversity is a good tuning device for a number of values.

History is on a collision course regarding these two values, and as shocking as it may be to contemporary sentiments, it is anything but clear that the value of equality is vastly, let alone strictly, superior to the value of cultural excellence. What I mean by this is that it is anything but clear that after careful reflection we would tune the options in a way that showed that we vastly prefer the elimination of inequalities to the advancement of cultural excellence. The more we compromise on the standards in the humanities, the more the direction of the culture is put into the hands of the culturally ignorant. This is what we are currently doing. And we are doing it in the name of empowerment and equality. Instead of mouthing platitudes about equality, what we should be doing is asking the hard question about the proper balance between equality and excellence. We can no more afford platitudinous morality than the delusions from which it emanates.

Where should the line be drawn? No doubt there are those who have bright-line answers to this question. And like bright-liners of all sorts, they seek to moralize the environment in which these issues are at stake so that open discussion of other ways of thinking about these problems cannot be openly discussed and meaningfully considered. To question the absolute value of equality is just out of the question to many people, especially to many academics. To do so is to raise suspicions about one's moral standing. It is to raise suspicions that you do not care about equality at all. It is to raise the specter of old forms of elitism. But is it not possible that historically we need a new form of elitism rather than a blind form of egalitarianism?[14] Those who recognize the real nature of the conflict between equality and cultural excellence will realize that the borders between good and evil here are vague and that historically we are facing these borders in ways that we never have before. The history of equality has brought us a long way in reducing the tragic consequences of old aristocracies. But the West is now facing a new form of tragedy, the tragedy of egalitarianism run amok trampling the value of cultural excellence. Have we gone so far in the equal distribution of higher education that we have designed standards that put us on the verge of a cultural wasteland?

We should realize that there is no nontragic solution to this problem. If we overvalue excellence in relation to equality or equality in relation to excellence, there is the tragedy of the lesser good or evil triumphing over the greater good. And if we value each as we should where comparisons are clear, there is the tragedy of excellence lost where equality is achieved or inequality endured where excellence is gained; in either case, there is the loss of the lesser good not contained in the greater good. Finally, even where we know *that* the options are important to our choice and *why* they are important to our choice, there is the tragedy of not knowing *how* important particular tunings

[14] It can be argued that this is what the American Revolution was about. See Gordon S. Wood, *The Radicalism of the American Revolution* (New York: Knopf, 1992).

of equality and excellence are to our choice at the most reflective level of practical reason. This is tragedy expressed as reason's grief, but it is not the tragedy of despair. The tragedy of despair is where the bad triumphs over the good without hope of reversal. We are not yet at that point in regard to this kind of conflict, even if we are at a point at which our decisions more and more face the zones of vagueness.

On this topic, I leave you with this thought: go to the beautiful city of Prague in the Czech Republic and observe a tragedy averted. The one I have in mind is architectural. During their occupation, the communists (for once) had the good sense to keep their particular brand of egalitarian housing on the outer rims of the city, where the drabness of those quarters and the lives that are often lived within them find relief in a vista that opens onto the old city-centre, whose architecture and beauty are the very antithesis of Soviet aspirations. Then go to an unnamed American university where college students flock to a cinema complex to watch the latest Hollywood fare in what was once a thriving opera house. Paint me then your picture of the way of life that best integrates the goods of cultural excellence and equality. You will find it hard to focus.

The same difficulty of focus spreads to any picture of a best life regarding other values we have. Peter Singer and others are right to bring our attention to the suffering of lower animals and the tragedy of it. But as we struggle with the conflict between preventing the suffering of lower animals and promoting human well-being, we will find that these are distinct values that sometimes conflict and that we cannot always tune them in ways that allow for comparative choice. We will discover the same when we focus on conflicts between fairness and various forms of loyalty, and on conflicts between various forms of personal relationships: family, friends, and neighbors. I do not pretend to have settled the particulars of any of these issues, but only to have made the case for a new paradigm for thinking about them, one founded on a new paradigm for understanding tragedy, for how to think and act and feel in regard to loss where high value is pervasively and perpetually at risk. What the paradigm shift achieves that no other paradigm does is the right kind of sensitivity to value. This means accepting grief of a certain sort as a natural response to the human condition and the conflicts among our values, including conflicts not dealt with here. Ironically, it means accepting that our deepest values themselves, like the Homeric gods, are often hostile to human excellence and well-being.

But if tragic pluralism is to represent an ethic as a way of living, an ongoing way of thinking, acting, and feeling, it must include grief without surrendering to despair. How this is possible is the final issue I will address.

10

Postscript on the Future

The Idea of Progress and the Avoidance of Despair

> Cultural criticism finds itself faced with the final stage of the dialectic of culture and barbarism. To write poetry after Auschwitz is barbaric. And this corrodes even the knowledge of why it has become impossible to write poetry today. Absolute reification, which presupposed intellectual progress as one of its elements, is now preparing to absorb the mind entirely.
>
> Theodor Adorno, "Cultural Criticism and Society"

> If the idea of progress does die in the West, so will a great deal else that we have long cherished in this civilization.
>
> Robert Nisbet, *History of the Idea of Progress*

> It is not sufficient to simply cite the Holocaust and expect discourse on the question of progress or rationality in human history to end, much as the horror of this event should make us pause and contemplate.
>
> Francis Fukuyama, *The End of History and the Last Man*

Despair is a special form of response to significant loss, distinct from both reason's regret and reason's grief. Reason's regret is the rational/emotional response to tragic loss where what is lost in the lesser good is not contained in the greater good. Reason's grief is the response to unintelligible loss, where what might be gained is incomparable to what might be lost. And reason's despair is the response to tragic loss when it is rational to think that the bad hopelessly outweighs the good. When no hope is left for the light of goodness to penetrate the darkness of cruelty, of suffering, of loneliness, of mediocrity, of ugliness, and injustice, despair comes not as a relief but as a bitter rejection of life. It is one thing, then, to face death and embrace it with some satisfaction as the natural end to a good life that has run its course (even in the clear recognition of goods it did not contain). It is quite another to be dragged from life with regrets about what it lacks in regard to the things that matter most. Both are rational/emotional attitudes that function under successful comparison, with the former affirming life and the latter rejecting it. To understand grief as a response to loss, we must understand it as affirming life without successful comparison. Otherwise, tragic pluralism cannot be a life-affirming ethic.

One recourse might be taken in the idea of progress. The thought is something like this: as long as there is no convincing case that the bad hopelessly outweighs the good, we can affirm life in the hope of progress, in the hope that the future can bring more good than evil. We can live through unintelligible loss by focusing on whatever good we can find that is not clearly outweighed by the bad. And this is something we can do at both the personal and the global level. What needs explaining when our values are vague is the will to live without pernicious fantasies.

On the personal level, the line between grief and despair often hangs by a gossamer thread. How much loss we are already living with influences the effect of new loss and the will to try again. Forgetting old sources of regret, returning to cherished goods, or finding new ones becomes increasingly difficult as tragedy mounts. Still, there is the fact that we get one and only one life, which gives us considerable pause at giving up on some source of joy that might lie hidden in the mist of a vague horizon. Even the slightest hope arms us against despair in coping with grief, as long as there is some good in our lives that penetrates the dark awareness of what we cannot now retrieve. Unless, then, the weight of loss so fully burdens our capacity to see some good in life, our grief does not usually mount to despair. We are defenseless, however, if we lack the irrational capacity to latch onto whatever is good in our lives when faced with incomparable loss where the worth of life is in the balance.

The fact is that there are people who live by exercising this capacity every day. They are latching on to whatever prospects they can find to avoid giving up on their one and only lives. Lost loved ones, failed aspirations, thwarted causes, beauty and excellence defiled – all are burdens of grief borne only by an irrational attachment to some glimmer of goodness that allows a degree of hope that the future will be better.

What happens in these cases is that a glimmer of current goodness becomes an object of intense focus that pushes the comparative task into the background. As long as comparison is held before consciousness with a full view of what is at stake, life and its prospects are utterly unintelligible. A mother in a developing country persists in her fight against the despair of poverty by focusing on the love of her children. Or a patient suffering from cancer finds some relief from his pain by focusing on the beauty of a rainbow or a musical symphony. In these and other examples, I have in mind cases in which if the issue of comparison were to come before consciousness, vagueness of the person's values would not allow a resolution of the question of whether life is still worth pursuing. Here the will to live is aided neither by comparison nor by blind hope in the future but by the presence of some good that deflects the focus on comparison. That there is some good, that it is not all bad, seems to carry the hour, even if it cannot shoulder the day. For the latter, some degree of hope in progress is required. At the border of grief and despair, then, the psychological dialectic of the will to live gains its pulse at the personal level by a slight glimpse of goodness and a glimmer of hope.

But what of the global level? Is the idea of progress dead and with it our defense against despair?

For some, perhaps even many intellectuals the idea of progress is now like the idea of Santa Claus, something we could believe only in our infancy. After Auschwitz and the other horrors of the twentieth century, the criticism is that the idea of progress is a notion only Americans can entertain. Our naive optimism is often attributed to the mistaken belief that no devastating war has been fought on our own soil. This and our relative wealth have sheltered us from the harsh realities of which others are so starkly aware. Or so the story goes. The lesson is supposed to be that only people who have known the darkest tragedies from a considerable distance are capable of believing in progress. Any serious person simply does not entertain the idea anymore.

Of course, there is a good bit of fact as well as fiction in this view of American optimism. There is a distinctive American religiosity that seems undaunted by the problem of evil and naively views the lack of faith as mere obstinance. It seems never to have occurred to this kind of religious mind that many people simply cannot believe in God and ultimate redemption any more. The thought that things might not turn out well is not only one that is foreign to this religious mentality, but also one that reflects in those to whom it does occur a kind of spiritual and moral inferiority.

There is, however, another side to the American experience. The American Civil war was among the bloodiest wars in history and one that is indelibly engraved in the Southern mind. What we did in defense of slavery and in the name of freedom is not unlike what Europeans did in the name of culture to the Jews. We have our shame, and we have made our sacrifices. The fields at Gettysburg and the shores of Normandy are laced with both. Even so, it must be recognized that there is an appreciation in Europe of the significance of Auschwitz and other twentieth-century horrors that is not as fully realized in American thought. It shows in the issues our moral philosophers spend most of their time focusing on. The previously mentioned negligence of the problem of pessimism in favor of worn debates between utilitarians and neo-Kantians is only one case in point. Another is the careers of academic philosophers still dedicated to some version of theodicy predicated on developments in possible-world semantics.[1] For these thinkers, the problem of evil is either solved a priori or awaits evidence that is not yet in, despite the awful facts of the twentieth century. Viewed from this perspective, it is hard to dismiss charges of American shallowness as the mere product of self-indulgent European gloominess.

But shallowness can attend pessimism as well as optimism, and in defense of the analytic tradition, a distinction should be noted. There is a difference between recognizing Primo Levy's response to Auschwitz and Adorno's. For Levy, Auschwitz brought down the curtain on any hope in theodicy and on any doubt that the evidence is in on divine Providence: belief in an all-powerful, all-knowing, wholly good God after Auschwitz was impossible. Adorno, however, went further than Levy: his target was not Leibniz and his progeny but Hegel and his.

[1] For a good discussion of contemporary views and the history of the problem, see Susan Neiman, *Evil: An Alternative History of Philosophy* (Princeton, New Jersey: Princeton University Press, 2002).

The barbarism of poetry to which he referred is any defense of the idea of progress that justifies the more central horrors of the twentieth century as a necessary stage in the dialectic of historical progress. On their respective points, Levy and Adorno are right. It is too late in history to believe these things.

Where, then, is the shallowness of some forms of European pessimism? It is this: Nothing that is true in Adorno's rejection of Hegelian "poetry" after Auschwitz dooms the idea of progress. Kojeve may have believed in the dialectical necessity of such horrors, but Fukuyama certainly does not.[2] It is even doubtful that Hegel himself would have thought that in order for history to have a direction, it must be governed by a dialectic so cunning that nothing is left to chance. What is undeniably clear is that the most intelligent contemporary defenders of the idea of progress cannot be saddled with the charge of such naivete. The issue is not whether utopia is possible. It isn't. Nor is the issue whether all things serve the good. They do not. Rather, the issue is whether there is enough good in the world as it now stands to penetrate the darkness of our doubts about whether we can recover from our losses, including Auschwitz, and make progress to a world that is on the whole more good than evil. To jettison the idea of progress because a certain form of Hegelian optimism is easily dismissed cannot be defended as an inferential necessity. Nor is it dictated by the evidence. Unlike the theological problem or the secular prospects for utopia, the evidence is not in that the good cannot outweigh the bad. This is why Fukuyama is right to insist that the discussion of the idea of progress cannot be terminated with a simple gesture toward the Holocaust and other modern horrors, a gesture wholly adequate to dismiss other naive forms of optimism, whether secular or religious.

How, therefore, should we think of the idea of progress?

Whether the idea was born in the early Enlightenment, as J. D. Bury claimed,[3] or was present from the start in the Greek precedents to Western culture, as Robert Nisbet contended,[4] one thing is clear:

[2] See Alexander Kojeve, "Introduction," translated by James H. Nichols, Jr., in *Introduction to the Reading of Hegel*, edited by Alan Bloom (Ithaca, New York: Cornell University Press, 1980).

[3] See J. B. Bury, *The Idea of Progress* (New York: Dover, 1932).

[4] See Robert Nisbet, *History of the Idea of Progress* (New Brunswick, New Jersey: Transaction, 1994).

the focus brought to the issue in sixteenth- and seventeenth-century Europe has been a central feature of debate in modernity in a way that it never was before. In fact, it is no exaggeration to say that modernity can be defined in part by the issue of progress. Not to understand this is not to understand much of what has gone on in the West from the Protestant reformation down to this very day. Even stronger: it is not to understand perhaps the most central philosophical issue of our time. Can we live without the idea of progress, and if we cannot, how must that idea be understood? If we can, what is to replace it? Much of what now divides America and Europe, on the one hand, and the Western and non-Western worlds, on the other, turns on this very issue.[5] The remainder of what I have to say here is an attempt not so much to fully answer these questions as to try and get them intelligently framed. In doing so, I hope to add to the claim with which I started: that the problem of tragedy is the most important philosophical problem currently before us.

It might be thought that surely we can live without the idea of progress because historically even very advanced cultures have. The Greeks, it has been asserted, did not believe in progress but had what we might call a view of history as decadence, a fall from a golden age. Similarly, one way of understanding Christianity takes the same form: the effects of the Fall from the Garden of Eden will be remedied not through gradual progress but by an apocalyptic intervention.

The problem with golden-age-to-decadence views of history is that debates over the decline of the cultures strongly influenced by them reincarnate the debate over the need for the idea of progress. Did these cultures decline because they lacked an adequate way of thinking about the future? If so, then we are back to thinking about how to project our lives and our culture in time. Moreover, it is just ludicrous at this point in history to think that there was once a golden age of human flourishing that we should try to get back to. Whether it is communitarian longings for the age of the Greek polis, or romantic dreams of Rousseau's state of nature, or the golden age of Islam as envisioned by Sayyid Qutb, Osama bin Laden, and their followers, conceptions of a golden past are as riddled with incoherence as those

5 For Robert Kagan's interpretation of this conflict, see his book *Of Paradise and Power: America and Europe in the New World Order* (New York: Knopf, 2003).

of a golden future.[6] As Berlin claimed, utopia is incoherent, whether envisioned as yet to come or seen through a rearview mirror. There has never been a paradise, and there never will be. Whatever decadence is, it is not a fall from perfection, and the direction of history is not to be understood as a rotting corpse. To view the future with this kind of pessimism is to be as naive about the past as Adorno thought Hegel to have been about the future.

Moreover, even if history is cyclical rather than linear, any culture will need a sense of progress and regress in terms of which to assess its direction. This is as true for contemporary non-Western cultures that do not have a linear view of history as it is for cultures of the Western world.

For us, then, what can the idea of progress be?

First, it must start with an acceptance of the idea of progress in knowledge, especially scientific knowledge. We can now only smile with intellectual amusement at the very serious debate during the early Enlightenment about whether modern people could ever be as knowledgeable as the ancients.[7] Before progress in scientific knowledge could proceed, the historical reverence for the ancient intellect had to loosen its grip on European expectations. Now it is beyond question that scientific knowledge is currently at a stage unparalleled in history and growing exponentially. Moreover, even non-Western cultures have accepted the need to modernize their economies in order to survive in the age of globalization, and they recognize that progress in science is essential to progress in economic competition. Of course, it is anything but clear that any notion of progress applies to what we call the arts in the way that it does to science, just as it is anything but clear that progress in scientific knowledge will lead ineluctably, as Enlightenment optimists believed, to progress in value and the human condition. What is clear, however, is that any notion of progress that survives will have to survive in the light of a great deal of scientific knowledge that will be impossible to ignore.

For one thing, knowledge of what we are like (in this sense, knowledge of human nature) will in the future come not so much from

[6] For a discussion of Sayyid Qutb, see Paul Berman, *Terror and Liberalism* (New York: Norton, 2003).

[7] See Bury's discussion of this topic in *The Idea of Progress*, 40, 48, 53, 78, 90, 101, 119.

philosophy and metaphysics, or from theology and revelation, as from an emerging scientific psychology. As neuropsychology increasingly gains the ability to explain psychological functions, our cultural conceptions of what we are will have to sustain themselves in the light of such knowledge. To be sure, there will be work for philosophers to do in conceptualizing what we are (work much different than the interminable labor over the ontological status of qualia), but it will have to be done in the clear awareness that we are a function of our nervous systems. We do not transcend nature but are a part of it. Old transcendent concepts will die because of the progress in such knowledge.

Similarly, transcendent concepts of both natural and social history will die as a result of progress in scientific knowledge. There are now heated debates regarding the "carrying capacity" of the Earth: what population can be sustained at what level of well-being. As things currently stand, the science is extremely unsettled on this issue. That will change. We will know within the not-too-distant future the answers to questions of this sort, and we will have to live in the light of such knowledge. Whatever hopes we can formulate will have to conform to what we cannot help but believe as a result of the progress of science. Just as the telescope killed Ptolemy's astronomy, the progress of science will kill many false hopes and views we have of ourselves, our history, and what we can expect. We will no longer be able to believe that the resources of nature are inexhaustible. And we will have to formulate our concept of hope accordingly: is our view of the future with the good prevailing over the bad consistent with the facts of what we will know about natural scarcity? If it is not, we will not be able to sustain our hope in such a future. What we will know will kill it.

The central point is this: as we study nature scientifically, including ourselves and our psychology, our knowledge of ourselves and what to expect will increase. Because of the distribution of such knowledge in modern societies, it will become a stable expectation of our social psychology that certain kinds of questions that were formerly the domain of priests and philosophers are to be resolved only with the blessings of science. It is not that we will think that scientific understanding is the only kind of understanding. Far from it. Rather, it is that whatever "truths" there are must be compatible with scientific truth, and there are scientific truths about what we are like that we will not be able to ignore. We are already deeper into such a psychology than many will admit: even die-hard social constructionists in our finest English departments take their antidepressants.

A second, more important point is this: increased understanding of our own psychology as a result of scientific progress will lead to an increased understanding of our values and the conflicts among them. As a result, we will have to adjust our idea of progress in the human condition in the light of that knowledge, including our understanding of political progress. What cannot be overemphasized as a general point is that historical conflict will distinguish very clearly between real expectations and political, religious, and moral platitudes. More specifically, the weaning from platitudinous moral and political rhetoric will require us to give up any Enlightenment expectations that scientific knowledge of our psychology and the values embedded there provides any foundation for utopian expectations. Nowhere will this adjustment be more evident than in what we can expect regarding the development of Western liberal democracies and international relations.

My concluding comments are meant to show that our concept of tragedy is indispensable to the task of formulating a concept of the direction of history for the foreseeable future that promises some relief from despair without recourse to philosophical opiates. What is needed is a vision not of utopia but of a world in which the good outweighs the bad.

One view of political history is that it is essentially over. Largely precipitated by the end of the Cold War, which was symbolized by the destruction of the Berlin Wall in 1989, an almost euphoric optimism arose in the West with the perception that liberal democracy had finally triumphed over its only real rival, Soviet communism. Berlin was the gateway to the East through which political history would flow on the tide of liberal democracy, never again to ebb. Best expressed by Francis Fukuyama in his book *The End of History and the Last Man*, the view asserts, roughly, that there have been three basic dialectical forces directing history to this point, all of which terminate in global political liberalism characterized in part by market economies.[8] Growth in scientific knowledge, the success of expanding market economies,

[8] Francis Fukuyama, *The End of History and the Last Man* (New York: The Free Press, 1992).

and the human quest for recognition are those forces. The inability to cope with them has made obsolete or moribund all other political forms: monarchy, dictatorship, communism, theocracy, forms of social democracy with significantly planned economies, even democracies that practice protectionist economic policies. Progress in scientific knowledge has produced a largely technological economy that requires a global market for its constant expansion. However, it is the human quest for recognition that has channeled the economic currents of history toward liberal democracy.

On one tradition of liberalism descending from the British Enlightenment (from Hobbes, Locke, and Adam Smith), the movement toward democracy and equality emanates from market economies that were designed to meet the demands of desire. On this view, frustrated desire has slowly but surely deposited undemocratic and nonmarket economies on the trash heap of history. The need for bread and the love of luxury have fueled a movement that has undermined forms of government and economic arrangements that entrench gross inequalities in social, economic, cultural, and political status. The "last man" of history on this view is the contented member of a constantly expanding bourgeois class.

In contrast to this view of liberalism stands another that Fukuyama would have us see as descending from Hegel. The real struggle in history has not been so much between those who have their desire for the bourgeois life satisfied and those who do not. To think this is to miss the real dialectical force at work in history. The more central struggle is between the powerful and the powerless in their struggle for recognition: the struggle between the master and the slave. The struggle for freedom has been most centrally not about freedom from the frustrated desire for bread and luxury but about the freedom that comes when the struggle between the master and the slave is terminated in an acceptable mutual recognition, which can happen only when they can see each other as equals. The otiose forms of political and economic arrangements can trace their most central failures to their incapacity to accommodate the quest for recognition. The idea is that any political form instantiates a pattern of recognition and that those that instantiate forms that cannot adequately accommodate the quest for recognition will fail. Only those that instantiate an acceptable conception of equality will succeed.

Some will fail because they further the inegalitarian struggle between "masters" and "slaves." Others will fail because the conceptions of equality they make available do not reflect what we truly value about ourselves. Both the economy and the "democracy" of the American South failed because neither could satisfy the quest for recognition by African Americans. Soviet communism failed because it reduced its notion of equality to that of need and sought to crush any quest for recognition that did not suit the demands of dialectical materialism. In the end, its economy could not meet even the basic material needs of its citizens, nor could its political form contain the quest for recognition. The real dialectical forces of history, then, lead to liberal democracies that do not fight the progress of science, that recognize the global nature of a technological economy, and that express a form of equality that can terminate the quest for recognition in a way that no other political form can. Fukuyama's claim is that only liberal democracies can do this, and for many the shining example of such a democracy is America. For them, America is leading the way to the final political stage of history by wedding a conception of global economics to the quest for mutual recognition.

But just as the Terror burst the bubble of optimism that accompanied the French Revolution, the genocides that occurred in the Balkans with the breakup of the Soviet Union introduced countercurrents in views on the direction of history. Samuel Huntington's *The Clash of Civilizations and the Remaking of World Order* sees in the events following the Cold War not the ascendency of the West but rather its decline, which stands his view in stark contrast to Fukuyama's liberal optimism.[9] The Berlin Wall was not a dam restricting the flow of liberal political ideology toward its final destination. To the contrary, what it contained were the forces of cultural identity. Before the destruction of the Wall, political alignments were drawn on the basis of ideology and superpower relations. Since then, they are being drawn on the basis of culture and civilization, which means that the flow of history from the direction of the West is ebbing and soon to be reversed.

9 Samuel P. Huntington, *The Clash of Civilizations and the Remaking of the World Order* (New York: Touchstone, 1996).

As Huntington aptly puts it, "The 1990s have seen the eruption of a global identity crisis."[10] Now that it is no longer necessary to take sides in the struggle between two superpowers, each country now asks who are we? rather than whose side are we on? And the answer to this question can come only in terms of the most fundamental sources of identity, which, for Huntington, are culture rather than ideology or political power. Power can stem the tide of cultural identity only for so long. When Soviet power collapsed, it was not liberal ideology that swept the Balkans but a wave of cultural resentment. Moreover, the point generalizes globally. The economic and military power of the West has suppressed non-Western cultural identity for what will turn out to be only a fairly brief moment in human history. As other civilizations modernize by mastering Western science, market economies, and the technology that both produce, the cultural influence of the West will subside. Modernization does not mean Westernization. Western dominance of economic and military power relations will subside, and the more normal sources of cultural identity – language, blood ties, and religion – will return to play their more normal historical roles. The modernization of Asia and Islam (and possibly Indian Hinduism) will create economic, military, and political forces far more formidable in opposing the progress of liberal democracy than the old Soviet communism.

We have, then, two opposing views of the direction of history. Fukuyama's view is linear, and Huntington's is cyclical. But both employ a conception of progress. For Fukuyama, progress is defined in terms of the global success of the West over the political forms of the non-Western world, the success of liberal democracy over its political rivals. When complete, the political journey of history will have eliminated not only the divine right of kings, but also communist totalitarianism, all forms of theocracy, Confucian and Hindu-style hierarchies, and all nonliberal forms of democracy. What will remain is a universal culture whose variety will be limited only by what can be expressed in liberal democratic form.

For Huntington, on the other hand, the West can survive only by accepting a view of progress that is compatible with a cyclical view of history and by seeing where the West is in its cycle. This means

[10] Huntington, *Clash of Civilizations*, 125.

accepting two different views of progress: one in international relations with non-Western civilizations and one within Western culture itself.

As to the issue of relations with non-Western civilizations: the West must abandon its quest for universal dominance and accept modus vivendi strategies for resolving conflicts. This means abstracting from differences and resolving disputes with the non-Western world on the basis of commonalities. To ensure this, the West should accept a certain level of nuclear proliferation and wider representation of non-Western cultures in the United Nations. A core state from each of the world's civilizations should have access to nuclear arms, further proliferation should not be tolerated, and each civilization should have adequate representation in the UN. This would contain the dialectical forces of history in a way that best preserves the chances for peace. The central point is that there is a difference between the uniqueness of Western culture and its universal status. If the West insists on the latter, it will lose the former: the modernization but not the Westernization of the non-Western world will deal the West a humiliating defeat.

As to the issue of internal progress within Western civilization: the West, like every other distinct culture, must reaffirm its own unique cultural identity instead of trying to accommodate all cultures within its own cultural sphere. For the West, everything depends on whether America can reassert its commitment to and find its identity in what Huntington calls the American Creed: liberty, democracy, individualism, equality before the law, constitutionalism, and private property.[11] The multiculturalism movement in America is only a sign of its identity crisis rather than a solution to a real problem. It is one thing to abstract from differences in order to settle disputes and preserve the peace with foreign countries. It is quite another to base a civilization and its internal relations on such a practice. A culture whose core is simply what survives modus vivendi is no culture at all. To think so is to refuse to accept the fact that different cultural forms represent conflicting sets of values and ways of life, a refusal that is based on some insidious fantasy that when all is said and done there are no deep cultural differences. But there are. Different cultures cannot occupy the

[11] For a contrasting view of America, see John Gray, *False Dawn* (New York: The New Press, 1998).

same cultural space. That is what makes them different cultures. They advocate conflicting ways of life.

The issue of progress for the West, then, is whether America can accept a diffusion of power that results in modus vivendi relations with non-Western civilizations and have the strength of will to refuse to be all things to all cultures at home.

I will not try here to settle the dispute between these and other competing views of progress. Rather, I want most to suggest how the issue of progress is best understood from the perspective of the problem of tragedy. If what I have said previously is anywhere near correct, then the central problem every civilization faces is carving out a way of life that is on balance good. It is not about producing utopia or even the best possible way of life. There is no such life.

What does this say about progress from any Western point of view?

The first thing to notice is that it does not rule out a linear view of political history in one sense. It may very well be that, for Fukuyama's reasons or those of others (Amartya Sen's, for example), all authoritarian political forms are bound to collapse under the weight of their moral costs and that only liberal forms of democracy can survive the test of time. It may turn out to be true (though I hazard no guess here about whether it is) that there is an historical progression *away* from political forms that are not liberally democratic. That is one kind of linear historical direction. However, it is not necessarily a direction of linear progress toward a state of political equilibrium.

The reason it is not is that not all forms of liberal democracy are compatible, and no form of liberal democracy (or any other political form) is completely stable. The conflicting nature of our values and the looming problem of incomparability ensure both. So even if it turns out that all roads lead to liberal democracy, not all roads lead to the same balance of liberal democratic values. In fact, if what I have said previously is true, liberal democracy is a project still imperfectly understood. It has yet to be given a completely secular interpretation in the light of the problems it faces, and, in all probability, it has yet to have found its best forms. Still trying to construe equality as a supreme political value strictly superior to all others, it fails to appreciate how the value of equality can conflict with other democratic values within a liberal tradition. It is this part of its Christian heritage that it cannot quite shed. But it must.

A basic mistake made in this regard by Fukuyama concerns the struggle for recognition. According to the Hegelian tradition, what the slave wants is appropriate recognition, and the historical struggle over this issue will cease only when all parties recognize each other as equals.

Despite the allure of these claims about recognition, there are very good reasons for viewing them with suspicion. The master-slave metaphor for understanding the forces of history is deeply misleading. What the slave wants (initially at least) is a decent life, to live a good life in accordance with his deepest values. It is the refusal of the master to grant him even this that keeps the struggle going, and there is much to understand from this point about the tragedy of valuing equality too much.

As a way of understanding the dialectical forces of history, the master-slave metaphor leads us to think of all inequality relations as master-slave relations. Accordingly, any culture deeply guided by the metaphor in its sense of history will see any evidence of advantage either as oppression or as prima facie evidence of oppression, the very antithesis of progress. But why should we think this?

If I am living a good life in terms of my deepest values and you are living a better life according to your deepest values, why should I think that I am your slave? Moreover, why should I think this even if my living a comparatively inferior life is a direct consequence of your living a comparatively superior one? Suppose you have more control over your life than I do over mine, maybe even considerably more control. But what if despite that advantage you are unable to force me into choices that result in my not having a good life. How am I your slave? It seems the worst sort of rhetoric to say that I am. In order to make me your slave, you must not only have some control over my life, you must have it to a degree that either prevents me from choosing my way of life at all or forces me to choose one that is not on my values a good life. The central point is this: I can prevent anyone from oppressing me if I can embrace my life as good in the light of my deepest values. This is the grain of truth in Stoicism. Within certain parameters of choice, it is up to us whether we are being oppressed by our circumstances, including the behavior of others. Try as you may, if you cannot make me take a certain attitude toward the value of my life, you cannot oppress me. Where Stoicism goes wrong is in asserting that a good person can never be prevented by others from living a life in accordance with his or her deepest values. Still, within wide parameters of inequalities, master-slave relations are impossible where the disadvantaged are able to see their lives as on balance good in terms of their deepest values and choose them for that reason.

But suppose I do not embrace my life despite the fact that it would be good if only I would embrace it and choose it in that sense. Instead, I refuse to embrace it because the control you have over your life prevents me from being able to choose a different life. Then it seems to me that I have made myself your slave. Why? Because I have made equality so important as to eclipse other things I value. This is the tragedy of the bad prevailing over the good. Concern for equality is bad when it prevents you from appreciating the good. To value equality as the supreme guiding force of history is to set in motion a dialectic that will never find its rest even in the presence of much that is good in life. In that way, the passion for equality can sometimes take the same form as greed, an insatiable appetite for that which cannot fulfill, a life of bondage. What must be learned and remembered is that within a range of freedom, others cannot make you their slave if you do not let them. This is why freedom is sometimes more important than equality. However, some inequalities prevent this range of freedom. This is why some inequality relations are master-slave relations and others are not. It is also why some inequalities are insidious in just this sense and others are not. Yet when the dialectic is controlled by the flow toward equality as an inviolable value rather than toward lives that are on balance good and away from insidious inequalities, alienation and envy are bound to spoil the good that is there for the embracing. Those criticisms of Western culture that focus on its greed for material goods can be seen as penetrating to a deeper point when applied to the concept of equality.

How should this influence our understanding of progress?

Neither individually nor culturally can we expect the value of equality to carry the weight of history that is being put on it by some currents in Western culture. It is one thing to insist on eliminating insidious inequalities that result in oppression worthy of the name of slavery (or anything close to it), but quite another to view one's life as a life of slavery so long as political institutions allow some other people to have advantages. This does not mean that we should not oppose insidious inequalities and even some that are not. We should. But when doing so, it is important to know the relative importance of equality vis-à-vis other values. We cannot even raise this issue if we view equality as the supreme goal of political history. And to insist, as John Rawls did, that any inequalities must be justified in terms of some larger set of equalities for all is to insist that all goods be cashed in terms of one kind of currency, or at least held hostage to it. For some, it is money; for others, equality. Both can lead to a culture ruled by a kind of greed.

An illuminating test case is the status of women.

Consider first two kinds of issues that come up in Western culture, especially in the United States: the gender wage gap and the problem of the glass ceiling. It seems plausible that if the average wage gap between men and women were to pass a certain threshold, we could be sure that some women would be unable to enjoy the range of freedom necessary to have lives that are on balance good from their own points of view because of systematic problems in our basic institutions. If this is true, then the wage gap at a certain threshold is reliable evidence that there are practices that are insidious because they constitute oppression. It is important, then, to know what the effects are on the life prospects of men and women relative to different thresholds regarding the wage gap. A one percent difference in the wage gap is inegalitarian, but it is just implausible that it constitutes evidence that women are the slaves of men. (Of course, the same thing might be true if the gap went in the other direction, unless more financial responsibility accrued to one gender rather than to the other.) The more general point is that in order to judge how important it is to eliminate an inequality or to judge its moral status, it is important to know its effects on other values. A woman confined to earning 71 percent of what is in reality a subsistence wage for a single man while she raises children their father has abandoned is being oppressed. She is enslaved to a way of life that is one of constant struggle in terms of what it is most centrally about.

Now consider the problem of the glass ceiling. This is a problem at very high levels of management in American business. The very top earners in high management positions are largely men. Women have advanced to a certain level in management with very good salaries, but have not been able to crack the glass ceiling and get into the upper echelons of earners. Does this mean that women are the slaves of men in our society or that these women are the slaves of these men? I cannot see that either is the case. That does not mean that the practice is unobjectionable. But not every objectionable inequality is a matter of oppression. If some cannot see their lives as good at the kinds of salaries that are just below the glass ceiling, I doubt very seriously that they are going to be viewed as good at salaries above the ceiling. To think of yourself as a slave at those salaries is to have enslaved yourself. It is to covet one kind of equality (no one being above you) more than other things that are more valuable. The real worry about those salaries, both those above and those just below the glass ceiling, is their effects on the life prospects of those who do not earn anything like either salary. Do the practices that make these salaries possible unnecessarily enslave other people, both men and women, in the sense that they restrict the range of freedom in which some people can construct a life that is on balance good? If they do not, then whatever issue of fairness or equality is at stake in the advantageous salaries some mangers earn, it is one that is far less important than the unfairness and oppression of slavery.[12]

What these observations are intended to show, despite how they might be employed by the rhetoricians of bourgeois conceptions of slavery, is that there is a kind of obsession with equality among some currents of Western culture that is anything but a dialectical force leading to political and cultural equilibrium. Just the opposite. It is a recipe for unending dissatisfaction that leads some people to view themselves as victims of oppression when on any scale of well-being they are among the most privileged people on Earth. If this is the notion of equality we are communicating to non-Western cultures, it is no wonder that they find it repulsive and a sign of Western decadence. A conception of equality that cultivates constant comparison as the driving force of social awareness will choke the life out of any culture it infects. It will not set it free, nor will it liberate the rest of the world if used to justify foreign policy in the name of spreading democracy.

[12] The issue of the glass ceiling is usually framed in terms of salaries, and it is within this framework that I have discussed the issue. However, it might be framed differently, in terms of leadership roles denied and talents undeveloped. So framed, there is real tragedy as well as injustice. Nonetheless, I do not think that either the tragedy or the injustice is explained very well in terms of master-slave relations. Nor, for that matter, is the tragedy explained very well in terms of inequality.

Rather, it will enslave other cultures and constitute a certain brand of Christian imperialism.

There is, however, another view of the effects of inequalities on women that makes it very difficult to see the American obsession with multiculturalism as any kind of progress at all, and the point is compounded regarding Huntington's modus vivendi view of progress in international relations with non-Western cultures.

Consider first the multiculturalists who caution against cultural imperialism and encourage cultural inclusiveness. The problem here is that there is a tension between these goals, especially in regard to the status of women. Consider two cultures, the Chinese and the Islamic. What notion of inclusiveness takes women's lives seriously and includes the attitudes toward women that are central to these two cultures? If anyone is guilty of cultural imperialism, it is the naive multiculturalist who assumes that the attitudes toward women in these cultures are not really central to their cultural values. It is to insist that we are all really Western at heart. Or worse: that it is the West that has it fundamentally wrong, that the Master's golf tournament is a clear sign that patriarchal oppression still reigns in the West, whereas the conditions in China that give it the highest suicide rate among women in the world are simply benign expressions of a different, little-understood view of femininity.

And what about homosexuals, and Jews, and atheists? What is it to value the meaningful lives of homosexuals, Jews, and atheists and to encourage inclusiveness of cultural currents that disvalue the meaningful lives of homosexuals, Jews, and atheists? What is at stake in these questions, whether they apply to women, homosexuals, Jews, atheists, or others are two values that are central to Western culture's being what it is: secularism and individualism. Without the secular value of the separation of church and state that is central to Western culture, there could not be the kind of tolerance that allows for the acceptance of people of different faiths and of people with no religious faith at all that we enjoy in the West. The fact is that it is a requirement of Western cultural inclusiveness that no religion that does not accept the separation of church and state be tolerated within its cultural space. To be sure, there are people in the West, some of whom are religious fundamentalists (whose Christianity has not yet been Westernized) and others who are advocates of some vague version of multiculturalism, who would reverse this. But people who really understand values that are foundational to the West reject these countercurrents, as we should, no matter how shrill the claims about Western decadence. It is the Western value of secularism that has allowed us to solve our problem of the religious wars. Are the multiculturalists suggesting that we abandon this value, and if so, what is being recommended about the inclusiveness of individuals regardless of their gender, sexual orientation, or religious affiliation? Some forms of Islam may internalize secularism in the way that Western Christianity once did, but if they do, then there will be, in this regard at least, a distinction between Western and non-Western Islam, just as there is a distinction between Western and non-Western Christianity. The current struggle in Iran over women's rights is a struggle over the degree to which Islam should be Westernized in this regard. Multiculturalists need to make up their minds about what their cultural values are. They cannot simply mouth incoherent platitudes regarding inclusiveness. Which conception of inclusiveness? is the question. If not a Western secular conception, then what?

Similarly with regard to individualism. That Western individualism has some very ugly faces, few would deny. But what is the nonindividualist alternative? Western attitudes of inclusiveness could not be what they are in regard to benefits for people regardless of gender, sexual orientation, religious affiliation, and the like were it not for the value we place on individualism, a certain notion of the primacy of the individual over the group. Some individuals do not belong to groups that have enough power to protect themselves. Are the multiculturalists suggesting that we abandon a notion of inclusiveness that protects these people, and if so, what is to become of women, homosexuals, atheists, and other people found undesirable according to many non-Western cultures? To be sure, we should be very pluralistic, but this does not mean that we should be multicultural. Cultures differ on their criteria for inclusiveness that determine the kind of pluralism reflected in the culture, and the West has its own unique criteria. Huntington, then, is right: we should be one culture, namely, the West, with our own criteria of inclusiveness. To get clear on this much is progress. We should design our basic institutions in a way that undermines insidious inequalities and disvalues the strains in other cultures that underwrite them. And we should insist that multiculturalists make clear what their conception of inclusiveness is that would deny Western values of secularism and individualism. My guess is that any revisions we make in these values as a result of what we can learn from other cultures will be variations on familiar Western themes. As things now stand, especially on American university campuses, multiculturalism all too often is the name for an academic industry, a cult of conformity that suppresses rational debate about the relative merits of different cultural values and different conceptions of inclusiveness. That we can learn from other cultures, few would deny. If that is what multiculturalism is, then that is one thing, a very good thing. But if multiculturalism means rejecting the time-tested values of secular pluralism, that is quite another.

But what about moving toward modus vivendi relations with non-Western cultures? Should we dig in our heels, even at the risk of endangering international peace, and insist that they move toward liberal democracies where the problem of the glass ceiling and the issue of all-male golf clubs are high on the social agenda? If the toleration of glass ceilings and all-male golf clubs in foreign countries were the price of world peace, all but a few feminists of a rather bourgeois variety would agree, I believe, that the benefits would far outweigh the costs. But that, of course, is not the way things are. It is one thing to insist on the realization of equality and quite another to insist on the eradication of certain kinds of inequality, namely, those that do constitute oppression of the master-slave variety.

Consider, again, the plight of women in some of the civilizations enumerated by Huntington and his claim that it is possible for the non-Western world to modernize without Westernizing. There are purely economic reasons for doubting that either the Islamic world or Confucian China can modernize without accepting some of the more central Western values in regard to women. Why? Because, if for no other reason, the status of women is absolutely crucial to solving the problems of overpopulation that plague most non-Western cultures. Nor is it clear that in order to modernize the non-Western world can internalize the value of scientific inquiry and not ask the kinds of questions that such inquiry would answer in a way that would challenge non-Western beliefs about the differences between men and women (not to mention the differences and similarities between heterosexuals and homosexuals). But let us suppose that I am wrong and that

Huntington is right, that both China and Islam (non-Western Islam) can modernize without changing any central values, including values in regard to women and how reliable knowledge of what we are like is gained. How is the West supposed to tolerate this, given Western values? Suppose the price of peace that results from modus vivendi is not the inequality of glass ceilings and a few all-male golf clubs but various forms of what can only be seen as oppression by a civilization that has built its very foundation on eliminating insidious forms of inequality.

According to Huntington, modus vivendi emerges as power diffuses, and the West should see this as progress. Why? Because of the prospects for peace. But then the ugly head of comparison arises once again: what is the comparative value of securing international peace at the price of entrenching inequalities and their effects once disproportionate power is out of the West's hands? This question cannot be answered with simpleminded warnings against cultural imperialism. The issue is not how we are to spread the gospel of a certain form of liberal democracy until we convert all the "heathen," but what are the limits of our tolerance for what we cannot help but see as intolerable. In fact, the question just is what is intolerable, given our values? Every culture has to answer this question, and the West is no exception. Moreover, how the West answers this question will determine the fate of billions.

If the West had the power to prevent a civilization from practicing slavery of the sort that existed in the American antebellum South or worse, would it be cultural imperialism to use that power to eliminate that kind of insidious inequality if the use of force were the only means of doing so, even if doing so came at some risk to the equalities and the way of life enjoyed in the West? Or would surrendering our power advantage to secure international peace in order to preserve our own way of life at home constitute a betrayal of those enslaved as a result of the kind of status quo modus vivendi might allow? If supporting the shah of Iran was wrong because of the realist foreign policy that was used to justify it, why is modus vivendi suddenly attractive if the consequences lead to insidious inequalities and effects in various parts of the world as bad or worse as those under the shah? If modus vivendi were to leave the concentration camps of North Korea intact, would it be worth the price in the peace it would make possible? These are hard questions the defenders of modus vivendi and multiculturalism seem unwilling to ask. But ask them we must.

Just as we must ask other hard questions about conflicts among our values. War is a terrible thing, but sometimes peace is worse. It depends on the price. As Samantha Power has recently made all too clear, the question, how much peace is the cost of genocide worth? is one that the West and the rest of the world simply must answer.[13] If the West ever gets to the point that it can accept some kinds of insidious inequality in the name of peace, it will have sold its soul. It will have lost the will, as totalitarians of various sorts have constantly predicted of the West, to find anything intolerable enough to fight over. Our idea of progress does not have to be about making our own form of liberal democracy universal, but it both can and must retain a notion that some forms of inhumanity, such as genocide, are simply intolerable. To move away from them is progress. Avoiding an overly ambitious universalism is only one of the dangers facing contemporary liberalism; another is a pernicious isolationism that is fundamentally inconsistent with its entire tradition. There is no escaping this. The distinction between progress as moving away from insidious inequalities and progress as viewing equality as the only form of recognition short of slavery should help us see the point.

The problem, of course, is that it is not always clear whether an inequality is insidious to the point that eliminating it is worth the risk of endangering international peace and unleashing the dogs of war. It is unclear not only because we do not know the outcome in advance, but also because we cannot always have any clear idea of whether the likely outcome is on balance good or bad. Which brings us back to the issue of despair. In cases where comparison is not possible, we cannot be guided by our notion of progress, even when we have given up all our political hallucinations about utopia and the end of history and accepted a much more modest view of progress. So what we are we to do?

We can try to see what good there has been and currently is in our most fundamental Western values and hope that in defending these things, while at the same time eliminating insidious values within our own culture, we can reach a point where a clear view of progress in the

[13] See Samantha Power, *A Problem from Hell* (New York: Basic Books, 2002).

circumstances that we face might emerge. But as it is for the woman in the developing country who maintains the will to live without clear grounds for hope by focusing on the good that is the love of her children, it is the primary focus on the good that is crucial under conditions of moral vagueness. Currently, Western reflective consciousness, as opposed to the forces of unreflective optimism, is so blinded by a focus on our flaws that it risks paralysis in the face of hard comparisons. If public rhetoric among our intellectuals is any gauge of our cultural psychology on these matters, many of our intellectual elites seem to think that the good can be promoted by simply focusing on Western flaws. Politically, if we could only replace the party of pious religiosity with the party of obsessive guilt, enlightenment could begin to flow in ways that the Berlin Wall never began to contain! Of course, nothing could be further from the truth. Or more dangerous. Cheap guilt, like religious piety, is no substitute for keeping one's eye on the good even when it is unclear whether the good outweighs the bad. We cannot, however, have even this defense against despair if we lack the knowledge of what our values are and how they can conflict, a point that applies both to those who studiously focus on the bad and to those who refuse to see it. And this is perhaps the greatest tragedy we now face, the ignorance of our own values.

The cure for our ignorance is understanding and accepting tragic pluralism in regard to the things that we care most deeply about. This begins with accepting the fact that ultimately things are not going to turn out well for humanity and then appreciating how rare and precious is the opportunity for a life in which the good has some legitimate chance of outweighing the bad.

We would do well in this regard to put our values and our history in a broader context. In *The Life and Death of Planet Earth*, the scientists Peter Ward and Donald Brownlee show us that the time of civilized history has been made possible by a natural aberration, a warming trend in an Ice Age that began 2.5 million years ago. The Earth is 4.5 billion years old, orbiting a sun with a life expectancy (as a star) of eleven billion years. For the first half-billion years of Earth's history, there was no life on Earth; then began the first microbial age, which lasted for 3.5 billion years. Then came the age of animals, of which we are a part. Ward and Brownlee predict that barring human-caused extinction or a catastrophe brought about by some sort of collision with another object, the Earth will die as a result of a slow process, a process that will see for a short time a gradual warming trend, then a period of glaciation, followed by rising temperatures that will first destroy all plant life and then all animal life, returning the Earth to a second microbial age before even this form of life is eliminated by temperatures that will dissipate the oceans. As the sun expands, it will suck what is left of the Earth into its own death throes, vaporizing the remains of our planet before the sun itself is transformed by its own chemical processes into a white dwarf.

Although they purposely avoid speculating about when human life will end on the planet, Ward and Brownlee predict that if animal life ends because of the process just described, the age of animals, including the most primitive and adaptive to high temperatures, is likely not to extend another billion years. During most of that time biological conditions are going to deteriorate significantly regardless of what humans do, creating problems for human values, for what we care about, that we have never faced before. Whether we can expect to extend civilized history as long as it has lasted thus far is anything but clear. In the meantime, we should consider just how fortunate we are.

Most of our history as a biological species has been literally uncivilized and brutally demanding in terms of sheer survival. But somewhere between six and nine thousand years ago – a very brief period of our own species history and not even a blink in Earth's history – civilization began. During that time, human values have enlarged considerably, in no small part due to the fact that we were freed from the simple calculations necessary to meet the demands of a primitive environment to care about other things. Contrary to Rousseau, the appearance of culture was an enormous relief. We were freed to care in more elaborate ways about a wider variety of things. Thus began the history of human culture, the history of our attempts at coming to grips with the conflicts among our values and the losses we have incurred along with the goods we have gained. For most of that history, religion has been our guide. Indeed, much of the age of humanity can be characterized as the age of superstition. However, within Western civilization, something started to change in a significant way about five hundred years ago. Secularism began to emerge as an alternative culture itself. The growth in knowledge and lives liberated from otherworldly constraints has given rise to secularized forms of religion and ways of life that are freed of the more calloused forms of fear and prejudice. That, at its best, is the culture of the West and its promise. It began with hopes of utopia as a replacement for hopes of heaven. But utopian experiments have put that part of our history behind us. Utopia is not to be. For reasons already given, all attempts to fit our values into a utopian formula are bound to distort those values. We are left, then, with either giving up our secularism or constructing a nonutopian conception of the future in which we know that there will be a decline in what we can expect. That is why the issue for us should be about how to construct a life that is on balance good, a life that, however far from utopian, contains more good than bad. Moreover, we should see our point in history as one in which that is still possible.

So how fortunate are we?

We are living within a marvelous biological and cultural window of opportunity for the possibility of good human lives, lives that can be on balance good, though riddled with much pain and sorrow. That itself is a remarkable, highly improbable fact. It should be good news and greeted as such. Indeed, it should be celebrated. That the universe or the planet produced even one opportunity for a meaningful life should itself be viewed as amazing. But we are living within a period in which much more than that is possible. We should not say no to our one and only lives and our one and only history because of an inability to face the tragedy that goes with those lives and that history, even in the full realization that those lives and that history are not going to be good forever. In all probability the future will at some point bring with it a return to more primitive cultural expressions of fear and prejudice as conditions worsen. Very primitive religious attitudes and practices might well reappear to worsen our lives. But for now and for the foreseeable future, we still have the opportunity to live lives that are enriched by all the human joys and sorrows and to appreciate them for what they are while they last. To do this, we must understand, along with the joy, the regret and grief our values involve. There are families, and friendships, and communities yet to nurture. Excellences to be achieved, knowledge to be gained, and beauty to be perceived and produced. This will not always be so. How long depends in part on us, in part on the blind forces of nature. Some day a more tragic era will begin, and after that the era beyond tragedy, the era of nothing. Understanding this and the conditions under which we balance the good against the bad within the window of opportunity uniquely before us is the greatest progress we can make. It is progress toward understanding the crucial insight into what is true in what Yeats said: "We begin to live when we have conceived life as tragedy."

Bibliography

Anderson, Elizabeth. *Value in Ethics and Economics*. Cambridge, Massachusetts: Harvard University Press, 1993.

Annas, Julia. *The Morality of Happiness*. New York: Oxford University Press, 1993.

Anscombe, G. E. M. "Modern Moral Philosophy." In his *Collected Philosophical Papers*, 26–42. Minneapolis: University of Minnesota Press, 1981.

Anton, John P., and Anthony Preus, eds. *Essays in Ancient Greek Philosophy*. Albany: State University of New York Press, 1983.

Aristotle. *Nicomachean Ethics*. Translated by Martin Ostwald. Indianapolis: Bobbs-Merrill, 1962.

Aristotle. *The Poetics*. Vol. II of *The Complete Works of Aristotle*, translated by Ingram Bywater, edited by Jonathan Barnes, 2317–40. Princeton, New Jersey: Princeton University Press, 1984.

Aristotle. *The Politics*. Translated by Benjamin Jowett, edited by Stephen Everson. Cambridge: Cambridge University Press, 1988.

Associated Press. "Gene Links Deep Depression and Traumatic Stress." *Daily Press* (Newport News, Virginia), July 18, 2003, A:4.

Baier, Annette C. *Moral Prejudices*. Cambridge, Massachusetts: Harvard University Press, 1995.

Baron, Marcia. *Kantian Ethics Almost without Apology*. Ithaca, New York: Cornell University Press, 1995.

Becker, Lawrence C. *A New Stoicism*. Princeton, New Jersey: Princeton University Press, 1998.

Bentham, Jeremy. *An Introduction to the Principles of Morals and Legislation*. New York: Hafner, 1948.

Berlin, Isaiah. *The Crooked Timber of Humanity*. Princeton, New Jersey: Princeton University Press, 1990.

Berlin, Isaiah. "The Pursuit of the Ideal." In *The Proper Study of Mankind*, edited by Henry Hardy and Roger Hausheer, 1–16. New York: Farrar, Straus and Giroux, 1998.

Berlin, Isaiah. *The Roots of Romanticism*. Edited by Henry Hardy. Princeton, New Jersey: Princeton University Press, 1999.

Berlin, Isaiah. "Two Concepts of Liberty." In his *Four Essays on Liberty*, 118–72. London: Oxford University Press, 1969.

Berman, Paul. *Terror and Liberalism*. New York: Norton, 2003.

Blotner, Joseph. *Faulkner: A Biography*. New York: Vintage, 1991.

Bradley, A. C. *Oxford Lectures on Poetry*. New York: MacMillan, 1926.

Bradley, A. C. *Shakespearean Tragedy: Lectures on Hamlet, Othello, King Lear and Macbeth*. New York: Penguin, 1991.

Brandon, Robert N. *Adaptation and Environment*. Princeton, New Jersey: Princeton University Press, 1995.

Broad, C. D. *Five Types of Ethical Theory*. New York: Routledge and Kegan Paul, 1962.

Broad, C. D. "Remarks on Psychological Hedonism." In *Readings in Ethical Theory*, edited by Wilfred Sellers and John Hospers, 686–9. New York: Appleton-Century-Crofts, 1970.

Broome, John. "Is Incommensurability Vagueness?" In *Incommensurability, Incomparability, and Practical Reason*, edited by Ruth Chang, 67–89. Cambridge, Massachusetts: Harvard University Press, 1997.

Browning, Robert. "Songs from Pippa Passes." In *The Literature of England*, edited by George B. Woods et al., fourth edition, 657–8. Chicago: Scott, Foreman, 1958.

Burke, Edmund. "From Philosophical Inquiry into the Origin of Our Ideas of the Sublime and Beautiful." In *What is Art? Aesthetic Theory from Plato to Tolstoy*, edited by Alexander Sesonske, 138–53. New York: Oxford University Press, 1965.

Bury, J. B. *The Idea of Progress*. New York: Dover, 1932.

Butler, Joseph. *Five Sermons*. Indianapolis: Hackett, 1983.

Calabresi, Guido, and Philip Bobbitt. *Tragic Choices*. New York: Norton, 1978.

Camus, Albert. *The Myth of Sisyphus and Other Essays*. Translated by Justin O'Brien. New York: Vintage, 1991.

Chang, Iris. *The Rape of Nanking: The Forgotten Holocaust of World War II*. New York: Basic Books, 1997.

Chang, Ruth. "Introduction." In *Incommensurability, Incomparability, and Practical Reason*, edited by Ruth Chang, 1–34. Cambridge, Massachusetts: Harvard University Press, 1997.

Cummiskey, David. *Kantian Consequentialism*. New York: Oxford University Press, 1996.

Dante. *The Inferno*. Translated by John Ciardi. New York: New American Library, 1954.

Dean, Eric. *Shook over Hell: Post-Traumatic Stress, Vietnam, and the Civil War*. Cambridge, Massachusetts: Harvard University Press, 1999.

Diener, Ed, and Eunkook M. Suh, eds. *Culture and Subjective Well Being.* Cambridge, Massachusetts: MIT Press, 2003.

Dinwiddy, John. *Bentham.* Oxford: Oxford University Press, 1989.

Dworkin, Ronald. *Sovereign Virtue: The Theory and Practice of Equality.* Cambridge, Massachusetts: Harvard University Press, 2002.

Dworkin, Ronald. *Taking Rights Seriously.* Cambridge, Massachusetts: Harvard University Press, 1977.

Elster, John, ed. *The Multiple Self.* Cambridge: Cambridge University Press, 1985.

Epicurus. *The Epicurus Reader.* Edited and translated by Brad Inwood. Indianapolis: Hackett, 1994.

Euripides. *Hecuba,* translated by William Arrowsmith. In *Euripides.* Vol. III of *The Complete Greek Tragedies,* edited by David Greene and Richmond Lattimore, 499–559. Chicago: University of Chicago Press, 1992.

Euripides. *Medea,* translated by William Arrowsmith. In *Euripides.* Vol. III of *The Complete Greek Tragedies,* edited by David Greene and Richmond Lattimore, 63–112. Chicago: University of Chicago Press, 1992.

Fichte, J. Gottlieb. *Addresses to the German Nation.* Edited by R. F. Jones and G. H. Turnbull. New York: Greenwood Publishing Group, 1979.

Foot, Philippa. *Natural Goodness.* Oxford: Oxford University Press, 2001.

Frankfurt, Harry G. *The Importance of What We Care About.* Cambridge: Cambridge University Press, 1988.

Fukuyama, Francis. *The End of History and the Last Man.* New York: The Free Press, 1992.

Gilligan, Carol. *In a Different Voice: Psychological Theory and Women's Development.* Cambridge, Massachusetts: Harvard University Press, 1993.

Glover, Jonathan. *Humanity: A Moral History of the Twentieth Century.* New Haven, Connecticut: Yale University Press, 1999.

Goethe, Johann Wolfgang von. *The Sorrows of Young Werther: And Selected Writings.* Translated by Chatherine Hutter. New York: Signet Classics, 1962.

Goldhagen, Daniel Jonah. *Hitler's Willing Executioners.* New York: Knopf, 1996.

Gray, John. *False Dawn.* New York: The New Press, 1998.

Griffin, James. "Incommensurability: What's the Problem?" In *Incommensurability, Incomparability, and Practical Reason,* edited by Ruth Chang, 35–51. Cambridge, Massachusetts: Harvard University Press, 1997.

Hallie, Philip. *Lest Innocent Blood Be Shed.* New York: Harper and Row, 1979.

Harris, George W. "The Significance of Suffering." Unpublished manuscript, Department of Philosophy, College of William and Mary, Williamsburg, Virginia, 2002.

Harris, George W. *Agent Centered Morality: An Aristotelian Alternative to Kantian Internalism.* Berkeley: University of California Press, 1999.

Harris, George W. *Dignity and Vulnerability: Strength and Quality of Character.* Berkeley: University of California Press, 1997.

Harris, George W. "Frankena and the Unity of Practical Reason." *Monist* 64 (July 1981): 406–17.

Harris, George W. "Mill's Qualitative Hedonism." *The Southern Journal of Philosophy* (Winter 1984): 503–12.

Harris, George W. "A Paradoxical Departure from Consequentialism." *The Journal of Philosophy* (February 1989): 90–102.

Harris, George W. "The Virtues, Perfectionist Goods, and Pessimism." In *Virtue Ethics: Old and New,* edited by Stephen M. Gardiner, 193–210. Ithaca, New York: Cornell University Press, 2005.

Harrison, Ross. *Bentham.* London: Routledge & Kegan Paul, 1983.

Hegel, G. W. F. *Aesthetics: Lectures on Fine Art.* New York: Oxford University Press, 1998.

Hegel, G. W. F. *The Philosophy of History.* New York: Dover, 1956.

Herder, Johann Gottfried. *Herder: Philosophical Writings.* Edited by Michael Forster. Cambridge: Cambridge University Press, 2002.

Herman, Barbara. "Making Room for Character." In *Aristotle, Kant, and the Stoics,* edited by Stephen Engstrom and Jennifer Whiting, 33–62. New York: Cambridge University Press, 1996.

Herman, Barbara. *The Practice of Moral Judgment.* Cambridge, Massachusetts: Harvard University Press, 1993.

Hill, Thomas. *Dignity and Practical Reason in Kant's Moral Theory.* Ithaca, New York: Cornell University Press, 1992.

Hill, Thomas. "Servility and Self-Respect." *Monist* 57, no. 1 (1973): 87–104.

Huntington, Samuel P. *The Clash of Civilizations and the Remaking of the World Order.* New York: Touchstone, 1996.

Hurka, Thomas. "Monism, Pluralism, and Rational Regret." *Ethics* 106 (1996): 555–75.

Hurka, Thomas. *Perfectionism.* New York: Oxford University Press, 1993.

Hurka, Thomas. *Virtue, Vice, and Value.* New York: Oxford University Press, 2001.

Hursthouse, Rosalind. *On Virtue Ethics.* Oxford: Oxford University Press, 2002.

James, William. *Essays in Pragmatism.* Edited by Alburey Castell. New York: Hafner Publishing Company, 1968.

Jones, Ernest. *The Life and Work of Sigmund Freud.* New York: Basic Books, 1957.

Kagan, Robert. *Of Paradise and Power: America and Europe in the New World Order.* New York: Knopf, 2003.

Kandel, Eric R., James H. Schwartz, and Thomas M. Jessell, eds. *Principles of Neuroscience,* Fourth edition. New York: McGraw Hill, 2000.

Kant, Immanuel. *The Critique of Judgment.* Edited by J. H. Bernard. New York: Prometheus Books, 2000.

Kant, Immanuel. *Critique of Practical Reason.* Translated by Lewis White Beck. Indianapolis: Bobbs-Merrill, 1956.

Kant, Immanuel. "From The Critique of Aesthetic Judgement." In *What Is Art? Aesthetic Theory from Plato to Tolstoy,* edited by Alexander Sesonske, 196–244. New York: Oxford University Press, 1965.

Kant, Immanuel. *Groundwork of the Metaphysics of Morals.* Translated by H. J. Paton. New York: Harper Torchbooks, 1964.

Kant, Immanuel. *Lectures on Ethics.* Translated by Louis Infield. Indianapolis: Hackett, 1963.

Kant, Immanuel. *The Metaphysics of Morals.* Edited and translated by Mary Gregor. Cambridge: Cambridge University Press, 1996.

Kant, Immanuel. "Perpetual Peace." In *Perpetual Peace, and Other Essays on Politics, History, and Morals.* New York: Hackett, 1983.

Kasser, Tim. *The High Price of Materialism.* Cambridge, Massachusetts: MIT Press, 2003.

Kavka, Gregory S. "Was the Gulf War a Just War?" *Journal of Social Philosophy* 22, no. 1 (Spring 1991): 20–9.

Keats, John. "Ode on a Grecian Urn." In *The Literature of England,* edited by George B. Woods et al., fourth edition, 281. Chicago: Scott, Foresman, 1958.

Keats, John. "Proem from Edymion." In *The Literature of England,* edited by George B. Woods et al., fourth edition, 278. Chicago: Scott, Foresman, 1958.

Kekes, John. *The Art of Life.* Ithaca, New York: Cornell University Press, 2002.

Kierkegaard, Søren. *Fear and Trembling.* Translated by Walter Lowrie. New York: Anchor Books, 1954.

Kojeve, Alexander. "Introduction," translated by James H. Nichols, Jr. In *Introduction to the Reading of Hegel,* edited by Alan Bloom. Ithaca, New York: Cornell University Press, 1980.

Korsgaard, Christine M. *Creating the Kingdom of Ends.* Cambridge: Cambridge University Press, 1996.

Korsgaard, Christine M. *The Sources of Normativity.* Cambridge: Cambridge University Press, 1996.

Ledoux, Joseph. *The Emotional Brain.* New York: Touchstone. 1996.

Leibniz, G. W. *Theodicy: Essays on the Goodness of God, the Freedom of Man, and the Origin of Evil.* New York: Open Court, 1985.

Levi, Primo. *Collected Poems.* Translated by Ruth Feldman and Swann Brian. London: Faber and Faber, 1988.

Levi, Primo. *The Drowned and the Saved.* Translated by Raymond Rosenthal. New York: Summit Books, 1988.

Levi, Primo. *Survival in Auschwitz: The Nazi Assault on Humanity.* Translated by Stuart Woolf. New York: Simon & Schuster, 1958.

Levy, Stuart B. "The Challenge of Antibiotic Resistance." *Scientific American,* March 1998, 46–53.

Locke, John. *A Letter Concerning Toleration.* New York: Prometheus Books, 1990.

Lovejoy, Arthur O. *The Great Chain of Being.* Cambridge, Massachusetts: Harvard University Press, 1936 and 1964.

MacIntyre, Alasdair. "After Virtue." In his *After Virtue: A Study in Moral Theory,* second edition, pp. 256–63. Notre Dame, Indiana: University of Notre Dame Press, 1997.

Marx, Karl. *The Portable Marx.* Edited by Eugene Kamenka. New York: Viking Penguin, 1983.

Mayerfeld, Jamie. *Suffering and Moral Responsibility.* New York: Oxford University Press, 1999.

Mill, John Stuart. *Utilitarianism.* Indianapolis: Bobbs Merrill, 1957.

Moravcsik, J. M. E., ed. *Aristotle: A Collection of Critical Essays*. Garden City, New Jersey: Anchor Books, 1967.

Nagel, Thomas. *The View from Nowhere*. New York: Oxford University Press, 1986.

Neiman, Susan. *Evil: An Alternative History of Philosophy*. Princeton, New Jersey: Princeton University Press, 2002.

Nicholas, Lynn H. *The Rape of Europa: The Fate of Europe's Treasures in the Third Reich and the Second World War*. New York: Vintage Books, 1995.

Nietzsche, Friedrich. *The Birth of Tragedy*. In *The Birth of Tragedy and Other Writings*, edited by Ramond Geuss, Spiers Ronald, and Karl Ameriks. Cambridge: Cambridge University Press, 1999.

Nietzsche, Friedrich. *On the Genealogy of Morals and Ecce Homo*. Edited and translated by Walter Kaufman. New York: Vintage, 1989.

Nisbet, Robert. *History of the Idea of Progress*. New Brunswick, New Jersey: Transaction, 1994.

Nozick, Robert. *Anarchy, State, and Utopia*. New York: Basic Books, 1974.

Nussbaum, Martha. *The Fragility of Goodness*. Cambridge: Cambridge University Press, 1986.

Nussbaum, Martha. *The Therapy of Desire: Theory and Practice in Hellenistic Ethics*. Princeton, New Jersey: Princeton University Press, 1994.

Nussbaum, Martha. *Upheavals of Thought*. Cambridge: Cambridge University Press, 2001.

Nussbaum, Martha. "Virtue Ethics: A Misleading Category?" *The Journal of Ethics* 3 (1999): 163–201.

Panksepp, Jaak. *Affective Neuroscience*. New York: Oxford University Press, 1998.

Parfit, Derek. *Reasons and Persons*. Oxford: Clarendon Press, 1984.

Pasternak, Boris Leonidovich. *Doctor Zhivago*. New York: Pantheon, 1997.

Peirce, Charles Sanders. "The Fixation of Belief." *In Philosophical Writings of Peirce*, edited by Justus Buchler, 5–22. New York: Dover, 1955.

Pert, Candace B. *Molecules of Emotion: The Science behind Mind-Body Medicine*. New York: Touchstone, 1997.

Porter, Roy. *The Creation of the Modern World*. New York: Norton, 2000.

Power, Samantha. *A Problem from Hell*. New York: Basic Books, 2002.

Rawls, John. "A Kantian Conception of Equality." In *Readings in Social and Political Philosophy*, edited by Robert M. Stewart, 187–95. New York: Oxford University Press, 1986.

Rawls, John. *Political Liberalism*. New York: Columbia University Press, 1993.

Rawls, John. *A Theory of Justice*. Cambridge, Massachusetts: Harvard University Press, 1971.

Raz, Joseph. "Incommensurability and Agency." In *Incommensurability, Incomparability, and Practical Reason*, edited by Ruth Chang, 110–28. Cambridge, Massachusetts: Harvard University Press, 1997.

Raz, Joseph. *The Morality of Freedom*. Oxford: Clarendon Press, 1986.

Regan, Donald. "Value, Comparability, and Choice." In *Incommensurability, Incomparability, and Practical Reason*, edited by Ruth Chang, 129–50. Cambridge, Massachusetts: Harvard University Press, 1997.

Rorty, Amelie Oksenberg, ed. *Essays on Aristotle's Ethics.* Berkeley: University of California Press, 1980.

Sartre, Jean-Paul. *Nausea.* Translated by Lloyd Alexander. New York: Norton, 1975.

Sartre, Jean-Paul. *No Exit and Three Other Plays.* New York: Vintage Books, 1989.

Schiller, Friedrich. *The Robbers and Wolstein.* Translated by F. J. Lamport. New York: Penguin, 1979.

Schopenhauer, Arthur. *The Will to Live: Selected Writings.* Edited by Richard Taylor. New York: Ungar, 1967.

Schopenhauer, Arthur. *The World as Will and Representation.* Translated by E. F. G. Payne. Indian Hills, Colorado: Falcon's Wing Press, 1958.

Selby-Bigge, L. A., ed. *British Moralists, Being Selections from Writers Principally of the eighteenth Century.* Oxford: Clarendon Press, 1897.

Sesonske, Alexander, ed. *What Is Art? Aesthetic Theory from Plato to Tolstoy.* New York: Oxford University Press, 1965.

Seyle, Hans. *The Physiology and Pathology of Stress.* Montreal: ACTA, 1950.

Seyle, Hans. *The Stress of Life.* New York: McGraw Hill, 1956.

Shay, Jonathan. *Achilles in Vietnam: Combat Trauma and the Undoing of Character.* New York: Scribners, 1995.

Sherman, Nancy. *Making a Necessity of Virtue: Aristotle and Kant on Virtue.* Cambridge: Cambridge University Press, 1997.

Sichrovsky, Peter. *Born Guilty.* New York: Basic Books, 1988.

Sidgwick, Henry. *The Methods of Ethics.* London: Macmillan, 1907.

Singer, Peter. *Animal Liberation.* New York: HarperCollins, 2002.

Singer, Peter. "Famine, Affluence, and Morality." *Philosophy and Public Affairs* 1, no. 3 (Spring 1972): 229–43.

Singer, Peter. *Unsanctifying Human Life.* Edited by Helga Kuhse. Oxford: Blackwell, 2002.

Sobel, Dava. *Galileo's Daughter.* New York: Walker & Company, 1999.

Statman, Daniel. "Humiliation, Dignity, and Self-Respect." *Philosophical Psychology* 13, no. 4 (2000): 523–40.

Sternberg, Esther. *The Balance Within.* New York: W. H. Freeman, 2000.

Stocker, Michael. "Abstract and Concrete Value: Plurality, Conflict, and Maximization." In *Incommensurability, Incomparability, and Practical Reason,* edited by Ruth Chang, 196–214. Cambridge, Massachusetts: Harvard University Press, 1999.

Stocker, Michael. *Plural and Conflicting Values.* Oxford: Clarendon Press, 1990.

Strassburg, Gottfried von. *Tristan.* Translated by A. T. Hatto. New York: Penguin, 1967.

Styron, William. *Sophie's Choice.* New York: Ramdom House, 1976.

Swanton, Christine. *Virtue Ethics: A Pluralistic View.* Oxford: Oxford University Press, 2003.

Symons, Donald. *The Evolution of Human Sexuality.* New York: Oxford University Press, 1979.

Taylor, Gabriele. *Pride, Shame, and Guilt: Emotions of Self-Assessment.* Oxford: Clarendon Press, 1985.

Thomas, Hugh. *The Slave Trade.* New York: Simon & Schuster, 1997.

Tucker, Robert C., ed. The Marx-Engels Reader. New York: Norton, 1972.

Wagner, Gottfried. *Twilight of the Wagners.* Translated by Della Couling. New York: St. Martin's Press, 2000.

Williams, Bernard. *Ethics and the Limits of Philosophy.* Cambridge, Massachusetts: Harvard University Press, 1985.

Williams, Bernard. *Moral Luck.* Cambridge: Cambridge University Press, 1981.

Williams, Bernard. *Problems of the Self.* Cambridge: Cambridge University Press, 1973.

Williams, Bernard. *Shame and Necessity.* Berkeley: University of California Press, 1994.

Wood, Gordon S. *The Radicalism of the American Revolution.* New York: Knopf, 1992.

Wordsworth, William. "Observations Prefixed to 'Lyrical Ballads'." In *What Is Art? Aesthetic Theory from Plato to Tolstoy,* edited by Alexander Sesonske, 261–74. New York: Oxford University Press, 1965.

Index